# Shakespeare and Company, Paris:

## A History of the Rag & Bone Shop of the Heart

# Shakespeare and Company, Paris:

## A History of the Rag & Bone Shop of the Heart

Edited by
KRISTA HALVERSON

SHAKESPEARE AND COMPANY PARIS

Shakespeare
and Company Paris

37 rue de la Bûcherie
75005 Paris, France
www.shakespeareandcompany.com

First edition

Edited by Krista Halverson
Foreword by Jeanette Winterson
Epilogue by Sylvia Whitman

Designed and typeset
by Loran Stosskopf (Mucho)
assisted by Camille Bardes

Image scanning and retouching
by Samuel Rouge

Copyediting by Justine Cook
Proofreading by Ben Brown
and Tara Mulholland

The composite photograph on the
front cover is copyright Shakespeare
and Company. The various
photographers are unknown;
the images come from the
Shakespeare and Company archive.

Imprimé en juin 2016 par Snel Grafics
à Vottem en Belgique

ISBN: 979-10-96101-00-9
Dépôt légal: Juin 2016

We're deeply grateful to all of you who helped make this book possible: the poets, writers, diarists, storytellers, interviewers, interviewees, illustrators, photographers, models, musicians, archive-sorters, transcribers, translators, Tumbleweeds, Tumbleweed-trackers, readers, proofers, advisors, and beyond. There've been so many generous people that we'd need another four hundred pages to name you all! To each of you who gave your time and care, we say here: thank you!

Sylvia Whitman
& David Delannet, publishers

Camerado!
This is no book;
Who touches this,
touches a man;
(Is it night?
Are we here alone?)
It is I you hold,
and who holds you;
I spring from the
pages into your arms...

WALT WHITMAN
"So Long," *Leaves of Grass*

The bookshop façade captured today and in a photograph from the late 1960s. *Photo:* KITSUNÉ JOURNAL.

"Opening bookshop in Paris. Please send money."

Every story starts somewhere — this one begins in 1919 when Sylvia Beach, from Princeton, New Jersey, U.S.A., opened her shop, Shakespeare and Company — the most famous bookstore in the world.

There's Hemingway, flexing his fists from the boxing ring, stopping by to pick up a book. James Joyce never arrives before noon and usually needs to borrow money. The big woman with the white poodle is Gertrude Stein. By the stove, beautiful and tired, Djuna Barnes is talking about her novel *Nightwood* to T. S. Eliot.

Scott Fitzgerald likes to sit and read on the stoop in the sun, and Sylvia Beach has made up her mind to publish *Ulysses*, because no one else will.

This is 3-D history. The past alive and well and time-traveled into the future. If you read somewhere that the book is dead, come to Paris. One hundred years later, Shakespeare and Company is busy like the book has just been invented and everyone wants one.

Young and old, rich and poor, writers and readers from around the world meet friends and make friends, come to browse the stock, buy the books, read all day in the library, get good coffee from the café, organize pop-up poetry slams, find a home from home.

"Be not inhospitable to strangers," says the sign, "lest they be angels in disguise."

Go inside Shakespeare and Company today and you will see that sign written up as George Whitman left it.

George attributed it to Yeats. In fact it's the Bible, Hebrews 13:2. But George believed that all good books are bibles, in the sense of how to live, and in the sense of something transcendent, bigger than, or beyond, the here and now.

When George Whitman arrived in Paris soon after World War II, he knew all about Sylvia Beach and Shakespeare and Company — anyone interested in books knew all about it — but the shop had been forced to close in 1941. The Germans had occupied Paris and Sylvia Beach had been interned.

George fell in love with Paris, living in cheap hotels and collecting so many books that in 1951 he had to open a bookstore to find somewhere to put them.

That store, where it is now, 37 rue de la Bûcherie, kept up the spirit of the Shakespeare mother ship, inviting writers to eat, sleep, and work there.

George was really operating as Son of Sylvia, as banker, sponsor, hotel keeper, publicist, evangelist for the new, defender of the known. So much so that when Sylvia Beach went along to a reading at the store in 1958, she gave a short speech and the famous name went up again. Shakespeare and Company was back in business.

The shop is like a Tardis — modest enough on the outside, a labyrinth on the inside. Every vertical space is shelved with books of every kind. A rickety staircase carries you like a fairy-tale hero to a warren of rooms on the first floor where you will find treasure. There's a piano, a typewriter in a booth, a few armchairs, a couple of cats, a big reading room looking out onto Notre-Dame. The bustle is the energetic kind of the life of the mind. It is uplifting to be here. It is an antidote to commercialism. Yes, this is a great business doing a good trade, but Shakespeare and Company is a reminder that business and pleasure can go together. As George put it, "the business of books is the business of life."

George loved writers as much as Sylvia Beach did. He took in the Beat poets Allen Ginsberg and Gregory Corso. Henry Miller in Paris ate from the communal stewpot but was too grand by then to need to sleep in the writers' room. Anaïs Nin left her will under George's bed. There are signed photos on the walls from Rudolf Nureyev and Jackie Kennedy, signed copies of Jack Kerouac and William Burroughs.

And the spirit of Sylvia Beach traveled over the ocean back to her homeland, too, as George's great friend, the poet Lawrence Ferlinghetti, opened his own bookstore, City Lights, in San Francisco, on the same principles of sharing, reading, writing, and a lot of fun.

I first met George Whitman in 2007 when he hit me over the head with a book. George was ninety-three by then, and the book was a missile lobbed from the third-floor window and aimed at his daughter, Sylvia — named after Sylvia Beach. Sylvia was twenty-something and had come back from England to live in Paris and gradually take over the running of the shop.

But George, even in silk pajamas, was still in charge.

Another volume whizzed past us. Sylvia said, "Do you want to meet Dad?"

Perched upstairs like an old eagle was the man himself. "Who's she?" he said, as Sylvia took me in. When he found out that "she" was a writer, and a writer whose books he knew, he was at once ordering Sylvia to fetch tea and cake and inviting me to move into the writers' room for as long as I wanted.

George was a Paris legend on a red moped. The maverick on YouTube trimming his hair with a lighted candle. The democratic despot who let anyone sleep the night in the store, provided they agreed to work for him for two hours a day (like something magic in a fairy tale) and to read a book a day. No exceptions. No excuses.

If the authorities came round to inspect, George would forget he spoke French, or start sticking down the loose carpets with pancake batter, or reprise his routine of setting fire to his hair. No one in a suit or a uniform stayed long. Others — writers, readers, students, hoboes and hippies, adventurers, and the lost and found — stayed for weeks or months. You washed in the public showers and you slept between the stacks of books.

When Sylvia took out one of the makeshift beds and installed a computer, George was furious. But father and daughter adored each other, too, and Sylvia is exactly whom Shakespeare and Company needs to carry it forward into the next hundred years.

After George's death in 2011, Sylvia and her partner, David Delannet, expanded the bookstore on the ground and in cyberspace. Adjoining buildings have become a café, event spaces, and an extended children's section. There is a wonderful website where you can order books embossed with the Shakespeare and Company stamp. This isn't the Amazon-warehouse model with depressed underpaid employees and books as merchandise. This is books as batteries, recharge moments, envelopes of energy sent across the world with love.

Shakespeare and Company is an English-language bookstore but the fact that it is in Paris changes things. The French have always welcomed and respected artists and writers. I am reading Philip Glass, *Words Without Music*, and he says exactly this — he feels at home in Paris — by which he means a spiritual home, a shared seriousness about art and culture and their centrality to civilization.

That is not true of Britain and I don't think it is true of America, outside some of the great cities like New York or San Francisco. This purposeful, practical view of art and culture assumes they are essentials you can't measure by totting up their net worth to the economy. It is the opposite of the propaganda war against art and culture where creativity is misrepresented as a luxury item to be crossed off the list in hard times.

As the world becomes ever more obsessed with wealth, as all of the people and all of the planet must be turned into one vast money-making machine, I wonder what will happen to the creative drive deep in all of us? We aren't all artists or writers, but we are all on the creative continuum, seeking and needing an outlet for what money can't buy—especially if you don't have any money. The gap between rich and poor has never been wider. The world has never been as unequal as it is now.

Shakespeare and Company is like a pocket of air in an upturned boat. Breathe slowly. Relax. Read. If you can't afford a book, go and sit in the library. You can stay all day, and you don't have to believe in God to find the view of Notre-Dame uplifting.

No, you don't have to believe in God, but you do have to believe in something. Sylvia Beach and George Whitman believed in books and writers, and made their vision visible to all, though the strange fact is that visions depend on what is invisible. It's whatever it is that we can't see and touch that drives us so hard to create something we can see and touch.

You don't have to believe in God but you do have to believe in your own soul.

I come to Shakespeare and Company as often as I can. I sleep upstairs, read books, sit on the street, and walk Colette, the bookshop's black dog, who loves me as much as I love her.

I come here and sit in a hundred years of time with a hundred years more waiting their turn. Books don't date; the language changes, the problems shift, but the wrestle with what is human stays the same.

That's why we can read Shakespeare or Balzac in the morning and A. M. Homes or Dave Eggers in the afternoon.

Shakespeare and Company is part of that inheritance. Shakespeare and Company—its books, its readers, and its writers—is part of that creative continuum.

What you're holding here in your hands is a memoir by Shakespeare and Company, the English-language bookstore in Paris situated on the left bank of the Seine, in the shadow of Notre-Dame. I call it a "memoir" because it's the shop's own story, the one it told to me after I'd arrived at this wonderland of books, myself just another literary wanderer who'd "drifted into the bookstore on the winds of chance," as George Whitman described visitors.

George, an American, founded the bookshop in 1951. As many of you readers may know, there was a previous Shakespeare and Company, located, for most of its run, on rue de l'Odéon. It was opened and operated by Sylvia Beach, another American, from 1919 to 1941. George named his bookstore after Beach's, and Beach is said to have considered George's a spiritual successor to her own.

While the story of Sylvia Beach and her shop has been told before, the tale of George's bookstore has never been fully documented. There have been magazine and newspaper articles, television and radio stories, cameos in movies, novels, and poems — but, until now, there hasn't been a book devoted to the history of George Whitman and his shop.

It should be said before we go further: it's impossible to talk about today's Shakespeare and Company without talking about George Whitman. The bookstore is the physical embodiment of the man's ideals. George was a socialist entrepreneur, an ardent bibliophile who built an ever-expanding institution in order to share riches of books, beds, and Irish stew with strangers from around the world. George dedicated most of his life to the bookshop, and he was resolved that it should live past him, that it should be, as he said, "more than just a project of one man's personality, which has been the case with most literary bookstores, almost none of which have outlived their owners." Today, the bookstore continues on with George's daughter. It is in its mid-sixties and still flourishing in the digital age.

Over the years, millions of people have happened into Shakespeare and Company, finding new and antiquarian titles for purchase on the ground floor, and on the first floor discovering thousands of books in George's personal library. There visitors can read all day while reclining on cushioned benches, a cat curled up nearby, the opening notes of "La valse d'Amélie" or Satie's "Gymnopédies" drifting from the piano. At night, the benches transform into beds, where writers and artists are invited to sleep for free in exchange for helping out a few hours in the shop, writing a one-page autobiography, and promising to read a book a day. George named these guests "Tumbleweeds" after the dry, rootless plants that roll across the American plains. Since the bookstore opened, it's sheltered more than thirty thousand Tumbleweeds, almost the same number as the population of George's hometown of Salem, Massachusetts.

Perhaps you were once among these bookish vagabonds, or maybe you will be in the future. I wasn't a Tumbleweed myself, though I did first arrive at the shop as a volunteer. I had recently left my job at a literary magazine in San Francisco, a position I'd held for close to ten years, and come to Paris to enjoy a couple of months abroad and to improve my schoolgirl French. After three weeks had passed, knowing no one and having discovered my limit on museums and *croissants aux amandes*, I got in touch with George's daughter, Sylvia Whitman. She'd been managing Shakespeare and Company since 2005, when she was twenty-four years old and George handed her the reins to the bookstore.

At our first meeting, I was — like so many others before me and since — dazzled by Sylvia's warmth and enthusiasm, her sharp mind and keen ambitions for the shop. It happened that she was looking for someone to help work on a book about Shakespeare and Company's history, which the shop itself would →

Opposite: The bookshop's motto painted above the entrance to the first-floor library. *Photo:* BONNIE ELLIOTT

BE NOT INHOSPITABLE TO STRANGERS
LEST THEY BE ANGELS IN DISGUISE

publish. The bookstore's comanager (and Sylvia's fiancé), David Delannet, along with the events director at the time, Jemma Birrell, had each started on the book only to be distracted by more pressing projects — such as finding lodgings for the dozens of writers participating in the shop's literary festival or replacing the building's prewar electrical wiring, which was threatening to go kaput. Would I be able to help out while I was in Paris? Of course, gladly and gratefully. I extended my stay in France six weeks… and then another six weeks, and then another, to what eventually turned into more than four years.

What I didn't know at that first meeting was that George's apartment, located two floors above the bookshop, housed a century's worth of archives. George didn't throw anything away, and he was absolutely opposed to his papers being taken out of his room and properly read and cataloged.

Several people over the decades had asked George if they could be the shop's biographer. George always declined, sometimes vehemently. Despite welcoming tens of thousands to sleep in his bookstore and demanding that each of them leave behind an autobiography, and despite his often fiery manner, George was — as I came to learn — a private man and, in many ways, even a shy man. His nature wouldn't have permitted an academic to scour through the apartment above his bookshop, to dig under his bed and through the wardrobe, to root around above the stovetop, refrigerator, and bathroom shower — all of these among the various places George had stored his papers and the shop's memorabilia.

George may also have hoped that he himself might yet write the shop's history. Several times in the 1970s and 1980s, he had taken sabbaticals from the bookstore with the intention of penning his memoirs — yet he never got further than a few pages and the title: "The Rag & Bone Shop of the Heart."

The phrase comes from Yeats's "The Circus Animals' Desertion": "I must lie down where all the ladders start / in the foul rag and bone shop of the heart." The lines are equally exquisite and curious. A rag-and-bone man was a nineteenth-century junk man who scavenged refuse, carting it from house to house, trying to sell one person's castoffs to someone else down the line. George related his bookshop to the "shop" in Yeats's poem — though apparently not in all aspects; he did drop the word "foul" from the phrase. I think, for George, the lines represented Shakespeare and Company in its bohemian ideal — not precious or sophisticated, but instead a trove of humankind's primal desires, emotions, and ambitions, all manifested together and at once by the books on the shelves and the souls walking through the door — a place where things unexpressed start seeking expression, a place where art begins, the shop like a heart unfettered. Something else I didn't know back when Sylvia and I first met: George had experienced a serious stroke shortly before I arrived. He would pass away a couple months later, in December 2011 — ninety-eight years old, a literary legend, mourned by a multitude of readers and wanderers the world over and by a daughter in Paris who was determined to continue her father's vision. Shakespeare and Company, George had said, "is not simply an emporium for selling books; it is an empire of the spirit."

The following summer, I found myself nestled in George's old bedroom, forging through his papers. My companion each day was his cat, Kitty, who would sprawl across the musty, yellow letters I was reading and eat from a bowl of peanuts that had been left in the room.

Among the archives were thousands of Tumbleweed autobiographies, along with thousands more thank-you notes and updates from former guests, announcements of books published and children born, requests to stay at the bookshop. There were poems, novels, memoirs, artwork, pressed flowers, and woven bracelets — all gifts to George. There were innumerable newspaper clippings, some about the shop, most about book debuts and writers, expats in Paris, the hazards of smoking, the CIA. There were résumés dating back to 1973, one adhered to a letter from Anaïs Nin by a dead cockroach. There were more dead cockroaches and more letters from Nin, along with a copy of her will, reportedly left with George for "safekeeping." There was correspondence from Allen Ginsberg, Lawrence Ferlinghetti, Carolyn Cassady, Paul Bowles, Graham Greene, Lawrence Durrell, Noam Chomsky, and even Upton Sinclair, who'd written in 1934 when George was in college and attempting to launch a literary magazine. There were documents about shipping books from the U.S. and U.K., taxes, banks, cellars, burst water pipes, all manner of French business bureaucracy. There were audio-cassettes and floppy discs and VHS tapes and CDs and DVDs. There were thousands of random business cards, along with one from a now-famous and seemingly unlikely visitor, Dick Cheney, then CEO of Halliburton. There was a near endless accumulation of photographs; plus, George's diaries, travel journals, and personal correspondence, including missives from his mother, who never stopped insisting her son would soon weary of Paris and return to the States. And then there were George's love letters — some carbon copies, others drafts—not meager in number and, judged by my sighs, quite affecting. →

LIVE FOR HUMANITY

All of this was mixed together, stashed into various old wine crates and large plastic tubs, hidden in nooks and books, stuffed under George's bed and bureau and sink, piled atop the toilet's water tank — that's where Sylvia and David discovered Gregory Corso's notebook, with handwritten drafts of poems and sketches, from 1961. Had it really been moldering up there all this time?

For almost two years, I sorted and read and filed the archives and, as I did, current and former Tumbleweeds, employees, and George's "comrades" (as he called those he liked) stopped by to share their favorite bookstore lore. Did William Shakespeare really establish the shop while on vacation from playwriting in London? Was James Joyce buried in the building's cellar? Was George the "illegitimate" son of Walt Whitman? There's a definite mythology to Shakespeare and Company. For me, I don't find that the tall tales are meant to make something of the shop that it isn't. Instead, I think many result from visitors wanting to understand why it is that they feel so strongly for a bookstore. Of course, George himself was the originator of a few stories. "I created this bookstore like a man would write a novel," he said, "building each room like a chapter, and I like people to open the door the way they open a book, a book that leads into a magic world in their imaginations."

For those who've entered into the magic of the book-shop, the story of Shakespeare and Company is not simply a set of facts and dates; it's also a feeling, an emotion. As I neared completion of the archives, I started envisioning how this history project would take shape. I wanted to construct a book like a box of treasures that would be valuable both to those who know the shop well and to those who've only just learned of it. A book that would, as much as possible, recreate my experiences sitting in George's bedroom, unearthing amazing photographs — such as the one of Langston Hughes reciting poetry to jazz accompaniment or George in his pajamas posing next to President Bill Clinton—and precious ephemera, like a 1956 flyer advertising events with both James Baldwin and Richard Wright. I wanted to share the stories I had heard—like those about Henry Miller's midnight rendezvous at the bookstore, Maria Callas arriving in dark sunglasses hoping not to be recognized, and Italo Calvino and Pablo Neruda drinking wine from old tuna tins. I wanted readers to encounter some of the same newspaper articles I had, to get a perspective of the bookstore within the span of Paris history, including the arrival of the Beat writers in the 1950s, the May '68 student protests, and the feminist movement of the 1970s. And, of course, I wanted to present all of this alongside an actual set of dates and facts.

This book isn't intended as an academic endeavor. While the dates have been checked and the quotations noted, this is the shop's own story, with all the benefits and faults of a memoir. Similarly, it isn't intended as a biography of George Whitman or his daughter, Sylvia. Throughout, I've included only aspects of their private lives that are relevant to the shop's history.

Shakespeare and Company is a place where oral storytelling still thrives, where tales are passed from one generation of staff to the next, from one week's Tumbleweeds to the following week's. I hope you'll find that these pages capture the same quality.

As much as possible, I've quoted George directly—the text taken from letters, diaries, and news articles, among other sources—and I've presented other people's stories in their own words. Some of the first-person tales in this book were abridged from letters in the archives; one was transcribed from an audio-cassette, another two from videotapes. Some stories and poems were found in previously published books; others came from Tumbleweeds' old diary entries. Several pieces were written in response to our open call for submissions announced via social media, and further stories came from interviews conducted while researching this project. →

George's chapter was assembled from letters and journals he wrote between 1935 and 1951, the years between graduating college and opening his Paris bookshop. In them, he described his "hobo adventures," including train-hopping during the Great Depression, army service during World War II, and studying on the G.I. Bill in postwar Paris. Wherever he went, George was met by the hospitality and generosity of strangers. These experiences sharpened his socialist ideals and shaped the founding ethos of his bookstore: "Give what you can. Take what you need."

While George's shop and Sylvia Beach's are not one and the same, they are related in spirit, both through the kinship of their founders and in the minds of writers and readers. Because of this, it would have seemed remiss not to include a chapter about Beach and her bookshop. Sylvia Beach told her story in the memoir *Shakespeare and Company*. I was thrilled when her estate agreed to our adapting portions of the text into a graphic chapter, to present to readers Beach's own words alongside original illustrations. After receiving the proof, Beach's heir said he felt certain Sylvia Beach would have liked what we'd created in her memory. I couldn't have imagined more welcome words.

This book wouldn't have been possible without the invaluable contributions of so many others, including

Shakespeare and Company staff, volunteers, and Tumbleweeds. Countless people pitched in, from transcribing hours of crumbling audiotaped interviews to collating dusty press clippings to tracking down a Swedish New Wave film director. Milly Unwin, DD Porush, and David Grove served as dedicated project assistants, and Laura Keeling read hundreds of pages of George's journals and letters for her moving selection of his travel writing.

The Shakespeare and Company history book wouldn't be what it is without the brilliant designer Loran Stosskopf and his assistant, Camille Bardes, the *photograveur* Samuel Rouge, who's responsible for the excellent reproductions of materials from the archives, and the eagle-eyed copyeditor Justine Cook. (Justine set off the alarms when she realized I intended to refer to George Whitman as "George" rather than "Whitman"—but how else, I countered, to refer to a man whom thirty-thousand people knew on a first-name basis, who invited the same number to sleep in his house?)

Most importantly, this book wouldn't be here in your hands if it weren't for all of you who've participated in George and Sylvia Whitman's "socialist utopia masquerading as a bookstore." This includes the generations of Tumbleweeds who've contributed to the shop—from washing its floors to assisting with the weekly events to making it a welcoming place for others — and it includes bookshop friends spanning more than sixty years, such as the Danish carpenter who constructed the shop's staircase, the Canadian artist who built the poetry corner, and the Chinese caretaker who assisted George in his final years. This includes patrons who've been coming to the shop for decades and those who may have only visited once. Sylvia likes to quote John Cheever: "'I can't write without a reader. It's precisely like a kiss — you can't do it alone.' For independent booksellers like us, it's a similar sentiment. Without all the passionate readers out there, we simply wouldn't exist."

I hope that Shakespeare and Company casts its magic on you, that it inspires you to everyday kindnesses, to give what you can, take what you need, to read, to write, to carry with you—wherever you may go—this home for literary wanderers, this place where a ladder starts, this rag and bone shop of the heart.

Opposite: George's cat, Kitty, in the library.
*Photo:* RACHAEL HALE MCKENNA

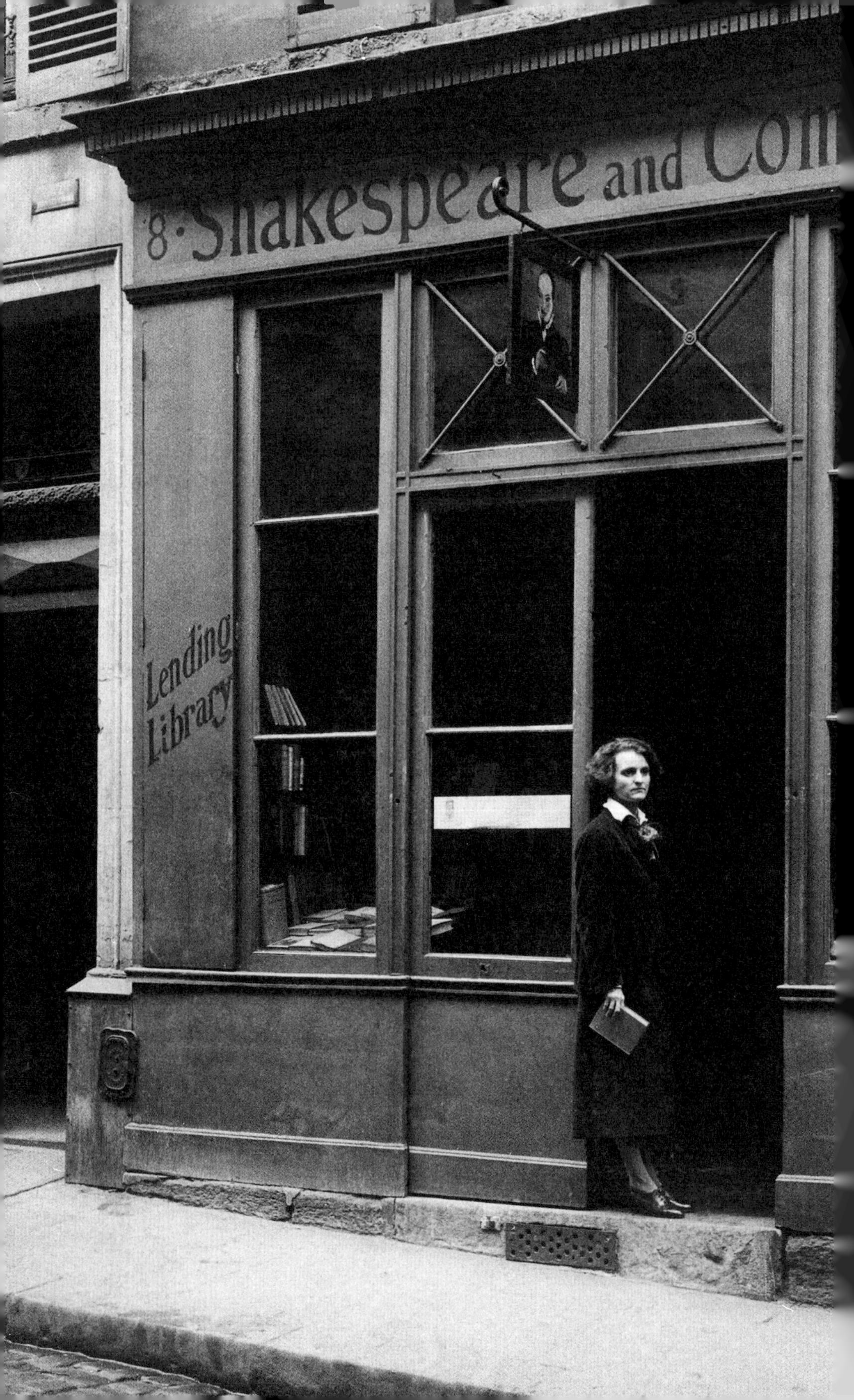

8 · Shakespeare and Com
Lending Library

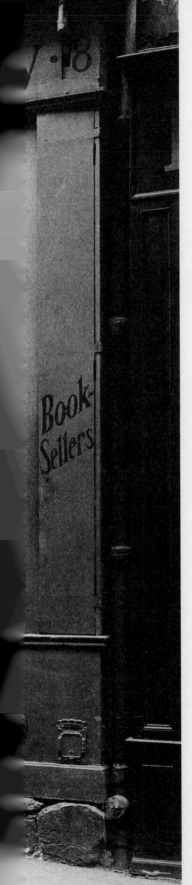

Sylvia Beach

# Shakespeare and Company, 1919–1941

Beach in front of Shakespeare and Company at its first location, 8 rue Dupuytren, Paris, in 1920 or 1921. *Photo:* PRINCETON UNIVERSITY LIBRARY

DWIGHT GARNER
*book critic,* The New York Times

Sylvia Beach was the soulful and fearless owner of the first Shakespeare and Company, which she founded in Paris in 1919 at age thirty-two. Her bookstore, packed with fresh journals, good sunlight, and plump armchairs, was a sanctuary for the era's best writers, expat and otherwise. The shop's literary clientele wasn't wealthy, and Beach lent books, for a small fee, in addition to selling them. Her friends — she introduced many of them to one another — included James Joyce, Gertrude Stein, Ezra Pound, Ernest Hemingway, F. Scott Fitzgerald, Janet Flanner, and the poet H. D. For her favorites, she operated as banker, post office, clipping service, and cheering section. Beach was a prizewinning translator of Paul Valéry and Henri Michaux. And she was the first publisher of Joyce's *Ulysses.*

The child of a Presbyterian minister, Beach grew up in Bridgeton and Princeton, New Jersey. She was the second of three daughters. She didn't attend college but saw the world, working during World War I as a volunteer agricultural laborer in France and then as a Red Cross volunteer in Serbia. She was plucky. One letter home from Belgrade describes a spring-like day ruined by the "bomby" air. A bibliophile from an early age, Beach had debated opening a bookstore in New York or London. But in Paris she met Adrienne Monnier, owner of the prestigious La Maison des Amis des Livres, one of France's first bookshops to be founded by a woman.

Despite her lack of experience as a publisher, Beach brought out *Ulysses* in 1922. Portions had previously appeared in literary journals in the United States and England, where the work had been declared obscene and banned; no one had yet dared to publish the book in its entirety. Beach borrowed money to keep her store afloat while printing *Ulysses*; fought with the printers to give Joyce more time to revise; and organized protests of pirate editions of the novel in the States. And it was she who coined the term *Bloomsday* to describe the day on which the novel is set. Beach was scalding about the censorship of *Ulysses*. "What a dark age we are living in and what a privilege to behold the spectacle of ignorant men solemnly deciding whether the work of some great writer is suitable for the public to read or not!" she wrote a friend.

By the 1930s, Beach's bookstore was so famous that the docents on American Express tour buses pointed it out to vacationing passengers. The store also struggled during that decade, however. The Great Depression was upon America; fewer expats were living in Paris. "The situation," Beach later

wrote, "was quite alarming." Beach got by with a little help from her friends. André Gide helped organize Friends of Shakespeare and Company, a subscription club. Its membership was limited to two hundred ("the largest number of people who could be stuffed into the little shop," Beach wrote) and thus especially prized. Members were invited to readings by Stephen Spender, T. S. Eliot, Paul Valéry, Ernest Hemingway, André Maurois, and others.

Shakespeare and Company closed in December 1941, during the Occupation and under threat from German soldiers. Although the bookshop never reopened, Sylvia Beach continued to be an influential literary figure in Paris and beyond. She died in 1962 in her apartment above her former bookstore.

Recommended books about Beach include *Sylvia Beach and the Lost Generation* by Noël Riley Fitch and *The Letters of Sylvia Beach* edited by Keri Walsh.

The text on the following illustrated pages was adapted from Sylvia Beach's memoir, *Shakespeare and Company*.

Illustrations by JOANNA WALSH
Lettering by MELANIE AMARAL

Opposite: Photographs that once hung on the walls of Beach's bookshop include friends and visitors such as Ernest Hemingway, D. H. Lawrence, Katherine Anne Porter, and George Gershwin. *Photo:* PRINCETON UNIVERSITY LIBRARY

Page 57: Beach in her apartment, located above her former bookstore, photographed in the mid-1940s. *Photo:* PRINCETON UNIVERSITY LIBRARY

MY FATHER WAS PASTOR OF THE FIRST PRESBYTERIAN CHURCH IN PRINCETON, NEW JERSEY.

THE WHOLE FAMILY OFTEN WENT TO FRANCE FOR VISITS—FATHER, MOTHER, MY TWO YOUNGER SISTERS, HOLLY AND CYPRIAN, AND MYSELF.

PARIS WAS PARADISE TO MOTHER—AN IMPRESSIONIST PAINTING.

IN 1917 I MOVED THERE TO PURSUE MY STUDIES OF FRENCH WRITING AT THE SOURCE.

CYPRIAN WAS ALSO IN FRANCE. WE LIVED TOGETHER IN THE PALAIS ROYAL. DURING THE NIGHTLY AIR RAIDS, WE HAD THE CHOICE OF CATCHING THE FLU IN THE CELLAR OR ENJOYING THE VIEW FROM THE BALCONY...WE USUALLY CHOSE THE LATTER.

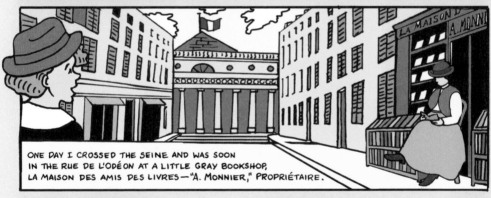

ONE DAY I CROSSED THE SEINE AND WAS SOON IN THE RUE DE L'ODÉON AT A LITTLE GRAY BOOKSHOP, LA MAISON DES AMIS DES LIVRES—"A. MONNIER," PROPRIÉTAIRE.

A HIGH WIND SUDDENLY BLEW MY HAT OFF MY HEAD AND INTO THE STREET...

...AND AWAY IT WENT BOWLING. A. MONNIER HERSELF RUSHED AFTER IT.

WE BOTH BURST OUT LAUGHING.

DURING THE LAST MONTHS OF THE WAR, I SPENT MANY HOURS IN THE LITTLE GRAY BOOKSHOP OF ADRIENNE MONNIER.

I HAD LONG WANTED A BOOKSHOP, AND IT SEEMED TO ME THAT A LITTLE AMERICAN BOOKSHOP ON THE LEFT BANK WOULD BE WELCOME. ADRIENNE NOTICED A PLACE FOR RENT IN THE RUE DUPUYTREN, JUST AROUND THE CORNER.

MY MOTHER IN PRINCETON GOT A CABLE FROM ME.

WESTERN UNION

OPENING BOOKSHOP IN PARIS. PLEASE SEND MONEY. S.B.

SHE SENT ME ALL HER SAVINGS.

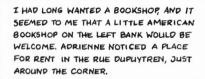

SHAKESPEARE AND COMPANY OPENED ITS DOORS NOVEMBER 19, 1919. THE SHUTTERS WERE HARDLY REMOVED WHEN THE FIRST FRIENDS BEGAN TO TURN UP.

ONE DAY JAMES JOYCE CAME WALKING UP MY STEEP LITTLE STREET. HIS CHIEF CONCERN WAS THE FATE OF ULYSSES.*

* Portions of Ulysses had appeared in literary journals in the U.S. and England; the work was deemed obscene, and no one dared publish the novel. —Ed.

ALL HOPE OF PUBLICATION IN THE ENGLISH-SPEAKING COUNTRIES WAS GONE. IT WAS A HEAVY BLOW FOR HIM, AND HIS PRIDE.

My book will never come out now.

Would you let Shakespeare and Company have the honor of bringing out your Ulysses?

HE ACCEPTED IMMEDIATELY AND SEEMED DELIGHTED. SO WAS I.

JOHN QUINN * CAME TO INSPECT CONDITIONS AT SHAKESPEARE AND COMPANY. OUR LITTLE PREMISES DIDN'T MAKE A GOOD IMPRESSION ON HIM, I FEAR. THERE WAS A DEPLORABLE LACK OF OFFICE FURNITURE AND FITTINGS, AND THIS, COUPLED WITH THE FACT THAT I WAS A WOMAN, AROUSED HIS SUSPICIONS.

* patron of Joyce, Yeats, and T. S. Eliot, among others —Ed.

THE PRINTER FOLLOWED MY ORDERS TO SUPPLY JOYCE WITH ALL THE PROOFS HE WANTED. HE WAS INSATIABLE. HE WROTE A THIRD OF ULYSSES ON THE PROOFS.

SHAKESPEARE AND COMPANY

IN THE MIDST OF THIS, SHAKESPEARE AND COMPANY MOVED AROUND THE CORNER TO 12 RUE DE L'ODÉON, OPPOSITE ADRIENNE'S.

JOYCE'S BIRTHDAY WAS APPROACHING. HE HAD SET HIS HEART ON CELEBRATING ULYSSES THE SAME DAY.

I RECEIVED A TELEGRAM ON FEBRUARY 1, ASKING ME TO MEET THE EXPRESS FROM DIJON AT 7 A.M. THE CONDUCTOR WOULD HAVE TWO COPIES.

MY HEART WAS GOING LIKE THE LOCOMOTIVE. I SAW THE CONDUCTOR GETTING OFF, LOOKING AROUND FOR SOMEONE—ME.

HERE AT LAST WAS ULYSSES, IN A GREEK BLUE JACKET, SEVEN HUNDRED AND THIRTY-TWO PAGES, "COMPLETE AS WRITTEN."

ULYSSES

BY JAMES JOYCE

IN A FEW MINUTES, I WAS AT THE JOYCES' AND HANDING THEM COPY NO. 1. IT WAS FEBRUARY 2, 1922— JOYCE'S BIRTHDAY.

THE PERIOD IMMEDIATELY FOLLOWING WAS SO EXCITING THAT JOYCE COULDN'T KEEP AWAY. HE APPLIED HIMSELF TO HELPING US WITH THE PARCELS, LAVISHING GLUE ON THE LABELS, THE FLOOR, AND HIS HAIR.

WE MANAGED TO GET SOME OF THE GLUE OUT OF JOYCE'S HAIR AND ALL THE COPIES SAFELY IN THE HANDS OF SUBSCRIBERS IN ENGLAND AND IRELAND BEFORE THE AUTHORITIES REALIZED IT.

IN THE UNITED STATES, EVERY COPY WAS CONFISCATED.

HEMINGWAY HAD A PLAN. I WAS TO SEND BOOKS TO A FRIEND OF HIS IN CANADA, WHERE THERE WAS NO BAN. DAILY, THE OBLIGING FRIEND WOULD...

...BOARD A FERRY TO THE UNITED STATES, A COPY STUFFED INSIDE HIS PANTS.

WHAT A WEIGHT OFF WHEN HE GOT THE LAST OF THE GREAT TOMES TO THE OTHER SIDE!

ERNEST HEMINGWAY. MY "BEST CUSTOMER," HE CALLED HIMSELF, A TITLE NO ONE DISPUTED.*

* Here's Hemingway's description of Beach in A Moveable Feast: "Sylvia had a lively, sharply sculptured face, brown eyes that were as alive as a small animal's and as gay as a young girl's . . . She was kind, cheerful and interested, and loved to make jokes and gossip. No one that I ever knew was nicer to me." —Ed.

HIS JOB AS SPORTS CORRESPONDENT TOOK HIM TO EVENTS THAT ADRIENNE AND I HAD NEVER PENETRATED. WE WERE READY TO BE ENLIGHTENED.

WE WERE AFRAID THEY WERE GOING TO BLEED TO DEATH. HEMINGWAY REASSURED US; IT WAS ONLY SLUGGING AND NOSEBLEED.

53

A LOVELY JUNE DAY IN 1940. ONLY ABOUT 25,000 PEOPLE WERE LEFT IN PARIS.

ADRIENNE AND I, THROUGH TEARS, WATCHED THE REFUGEES MOVING THROUGH THE CITY.

CLOSE ON THEIR HEELS CAME THE GERMANS.

SHAKESPEARE AND COMPANY

ONE DAY A HIGH-RANKING OFFICER STOPPED TO LOOK AT A COPY OF FINNEGANS WAKE. HE SAID HE WOULD BUY IT.

It's not for sale.

Why not?

My last copy. I was keeping it.

For whom?

For myself.

A FORTNIGHT LATER THE SAME OFFICER STRODE INTO THE BOOKSHOP.

Where's Finnegans Wake?

I put it away.

We're coming to confiscate all your goods today.

MY FRIENDS AND I CARRIED ALL THE BOOKS, PHOTOGRAPHS, AND FURNITURE TO AN APARTMENT UPSTAIRS. WITHIN TWO HOURS A HOUSE PAINTER HAD PAINTED OUT THE NAME SHAKESPEARE AND COMPANY. THE DATE WAS 1941.

55

I FLEW DOWNSTAIRS; WE MET WITH A CRASH; HE PICKED ME UP AND SWUNG ME AROUND AND KISSED ME.

ADRIENNE AND I ASKED IF HE COULD DO SOMETHING ABOUT THE NAZI SNIPERS ON THE ROOFTOPS IN OUR STREET.

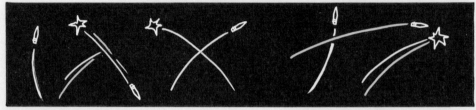

WE HEARD FIRING FOR THE LAST TIME. HEMINGWAY AND HIS MEN RODE OFF IN THEIR JEEPS—"TO LIBERATE THE CELLAR AT THE RITZ." *

* Paris was also liberated and the war ended. Sylvia Beach never reopened her Shakespeare and Company. —Ed.

GEORGE WHITMAN

# Writings from a Young Literary Vagabond, 1935–1950

Before George Whitman founded the second incarnation of Shakespeare and Company, in 1951, he was an enterprising young man with a lust for adventure and a love of learning and books.

George was born on December 12, 1913, and grew up in Salem, Massachusetts. In 1923, his father, Walter, accepted a two-year teaching post in China at Nanjing University (then known as Nanking University), and brought along his wife and children. George revered his time in Nanjing, and this early experience abroad established his lifelong affection for far-flung places, China in particular.

In the spring of 1935, in the midst of the Great Depression, George graduated from Boston University with a degree in journalism. It was a difficult time for finding work, so his mother, Grace, was especially pleased when he was offered an assistant reporter's job in Washington, D.C. George, however, had other ambitions. In July of that year, at age twenty-one, he set out on a "hobo adventure," as he called it, hitchhiking, walking, and train-hopping across Mexico, Central America, and the United States. His journey continued with a brief stint at Harvard, four years in the U.S. Army during World War II, and, eventually, with a move to Paris. These travels inspired his ethos, "Give what you can; take what you need," and later the motto of Shakespeare and

Company, "Be not inhospitable to strangers lest they be angels in disguise." What follows are excerpts from George's journals and letters from 1935 to 1950.

### July 1935
Boston

On July 1, 1935, I set out to investigate the condition of the human race in all of the six continents and the seven seas of the planet earth. My object is to take a Bohemian Holiday spent in pursuit of seductive mysteries and extravagant adventures.

For four years at Boston University, I lived in the dark and fantastic universe of ideas and aesthetic speculation. Upon graduation, I felt the invincible desire to depart into the unknown, the unseen, and the unexpected. For many nights, I pored over maps — maps of Asia, maps of Africa — showing regions of romance where mysterious rivers flowed past mysterious cities. I saw a world whose skies were filled with many flags, whose seas were covered with many ships, whose continents were covered with monstrous cities. And each flag, each ship, each city was a symbol of human power and human weakness, a symbol of glory — the glory that shines like a meteor, dazzling, enchanting, but revealing nothing of the inscrutable darkness of life.

My journey is undertaken to penetrate, wherever possible, the secret meanings of existence, to observe in all regions of earth the influence of those supreme forces — love, destiny, and death — and to enjoy in meditation and solitude the soft illumination that the true, the beautiful, the adventurous, and the heroic shed like the stars of another universe on meadow and metropolis.

This is a record of the different customs observed and the different scenery explored by the author, who set out in good health and good humor to live, to breathe, to sing, to laugh, and to love in the shadow of Siberia and the sunlight of the tropics.

My wish to the people of all nations is that they may rise out of their common misery into a common joy, in which they embrace the creed: "My country is the world. My religion is humanity."

### August 1935
Monterrey to Mexico City

Monterrey, which means king of the mountains, is a city situated in a valley in northeast Mexico. One morning I set out to climb Mount Chipinque, which is not tall but extremely steep and precipitous. I reached the top just past sunset after the most laborious exertion that I can remember. I could have slept with pleasure there on the jagged rocks but, because of hunger and thirst, I turned my footsteps toward a light about halfway down the mountain. In the darkness, I lost my way several times but at about ten o'clock, thoroughly exhausted, I knocked at the door of the general who owned the mountain. The general's daughter, a beautiful girl of nineteen who spoke perfect English, welcomed me hospitably. She brought out a platter of six cold chickens and other delicacies to which I helped myself. I slept that night at the general's home and, early the next morning, I began my trek back to Monterrey.

Later in the week, I set out for Mexico City. In the afternoon of the first day, I reached Montemorelos, a farming community with a population of twenty-five thousand. The second day, I hiked twenty-one miles to Linares, a town smaller than Montemorelos but more lively. In the evening, the streets were full of cowboys from the surrounding ranches with revolvers at their waists. From each of the four or five cantinas, music and laughter drifted over to the few solitary figures sitting in the plaza beneath my hotel window. The proprietor of the hotel had offered me room and board and fifty centavos a day for waiting on the American tourists but then took back his offer after talking with his wife.

The third day, I got a lift with a Mexican farmer who had studied mechanical engineering. I ate lunch and took a siesta at his home in a small village of thatched houses, where I found an excellent opportunity to observe the rural life of the Mexican campesinos. Late in the afternoon, after a hot and weary tramp, a new Buick with California license plates stopped in front of me. For an interminable distance the road was visible — a thin ribbon of black between dreary patches of sagebrush. In the car was a three-gallon water jug, an extra tank of gasoline, and other equipment sufficient for an advance upon the Sahara desert. The driver expressed astonishment to see anyone walking in the solitude. Late that evening, we reached Tasquillo, situated in a fertile valley surrounded by mountains. And the next day, we reached Mexico City, with snow-capped Popocatépetl towering in the distance and the streets lined with peddlers selling fruit, candy, flowers, clothing, and articles of every description. I'd traversed six hundred and six miles in four days.

October–November 1935
Mexico City and Back Again

The road from Mexico City to Vera Cruz winds a tortuous path over rugged cordilleras, precipitous barrancas, and rain-swept savannas. I followed roughly the trail of Cortez when he made his perilous march of four centuries ago. In Ayapango, I stood on the desolate ruins of the convent of El Calvario and watched the sun set and the fingers of night creep out of the foothills and rush over the soft valley. The moon shed pale radiation over the lava slopes of the encircling mountains, and the thousand lights of the town were reflected by a thousand cold, glittering stars in the sky.

After a week in Tampico, I started out along the railroad track for San Luis Potosí. The hot tropical sun drenched my shirt with perspiration, leaving rings of salt crystals when it evaporated. I soon formed the habit of soaking my shirt in every pond that was passed, but this gave relief for only a moment. I began to appreciate the advice of friends in Mexico City that it might be necessary to walk in the cool of nighttime through humid and tropical regions. After twenty miles, I was glad to stop at the Hacienda de Chila, where one of the campesinos invited me to share his supper of meat, chili, beans, and tortillas. Later, at ten o'clock, the stationmaster arranged for me to ride in the caboose of a freight train to San Luis Potosí, which I reached at midnight. Daybreak disclosed a row of unpainted wooden shacks parallel to the railroad track with a few cantinas and *tiendas* that made up the commercial center of the town.

That night, when the express pulled out of the station, I leaped between the locomotive and baggage car in the position called "riding blind" by the hoboes of Louisiana. As the train entered the open country, the faces of two Mexican tramps stared suspiciously at me over the top of the coal car directly behind the engine. We were soon on good terms, and I shared their position lying flat on the back, facing the stars or watching the red shadows flash from the boiler fire into the tall grass. At one of the stations, the Mexicans were put off by the fireman; as all my clothes were dark, I remained undiscovered in the shadows of the baggage-car entrance. At the next stop for water, I concealed myself on top of the locomotive in an empty tool chest about the size of a coffin. It was just possible to squeeze into it by doubling the feet and spraining the neck.

The following day, in mid-afternoon, I entered the town of San Juan de los Lagos. The stone road sloped down to a plaza sparkling with greenery; church steeples gleamed in the sunlight. A smiling Mexican took my arm and insisted I have dinner with him. He had lived in the States for six years and was glad to welcome me as a brother. Because of his hospitality, I was delayed until six o'clock in San Juan but was still determined to reach the destination I had picked for that night — Jalostotitlán, fifteen miles over the mountains. At seven o'clock, a heavy shower began. Soon afterward, a farmer came by and offered me one of his donkeys to ride, marking the first time I ever hitchhiked a donkey and, if Providence is kindly disposed, the last. The burro idled along, slipping in the clay underneath the rivulets of rain, leaving pieces of my clothes on the thorny bushes we passed. To make matters worse, he was continually frightened by the farmer's spirited pony, which attempted to kick him but only succeeded in kicking me.

When the farmer and his animals turned off the path, the sun had already set and the purple mountains stood naked in the fierce blasts of lightning. Not a star was visible. No sound interrupted the profound silence except my footsteps and the steady patter of raindrops. It seemed strange to think that, while I was stumbling through mud and water, in thousands of cities people were drifting past the bright lights of Broadways and Scollay Squares, and in thousands of towns families were sitting down to savory suppers of meat and vegetables.

I was in a little town about fifty miles from Guadalajara. There was a flood in that region and, after hiking all day in a feverish condition, I had to wade through deep waters in order to reach the station.

A mixed-blood Mexican lounging on a bench smiled at me. "¿Adónde vas?"

"Mexico City," I answered. "When's the next freight train go through?"

"The only train tonight is the passenger express from St. Louis," he answered. "You can ride the rods with me. That's the safest place, underneath the cars where the soldiers can't see you."

Just then, the stationmaster's wife passed by and joined us in the conversation. "You had better not do that," she said. "Only a few days ago, a hobo fell under the train a little way down the track. His body was sliced into two pieces that were thrown thirty feet apart."

In spite of her warning, when the train roared into the station, we slipped underneath a car. Within ten seconds, the train was moving again — but before it could gain momentum, my companion discovered the car was not of the right construction for riding underneath. He hollered at me and dashed out between the moving wheels. I was still hanging precariously

From top: George's hand-drawn map of his route through Mexico and Central America; the "Bohemian Holiday" letter written at the outset of George's travels; George with his sister, mother, and father in Nanjing in the mid-1920s; George's visa to travel in Guatemala.

## BOHEMIAN HOLIDAY

★ ON JULY ONE nineteen-thirty-five I set out to investigate the condition of the human race in all of the six continents + the seven seas of the planet EARTH • My object was to take a *Bohemian Holiday* in life to spend in pursuit of seductive mysteries + extravagant adventures.

FOR FOUR YEARS at Boston University I lived in the dark + fantastic universe of ideas + aesthetic speculation. Upon graduation I felt the invincible desire to depart into the unknown, the unseen + the unexpected. For many nights I pored over maps — maps of ASIA, maps of AFRICA showing regions of romance where mysterious rivers flowed past mysterious cities. I saw a world whose skies were filled with many flags, whose seas were covered with many ships, whose continents were covered with monstrous cities. And each flag, each ship, each city was a symbol of human power + human weakness, a symbol of glory — the glory that shines like a meteor, dazzling, enchanting but revealing nothing of the inscrutable darkness of life.

MY JOURNEY was undertaken to penetrate, wherever possible the secret meanings of existence, to observe the influence in all regions of the earth of those supreme forces — love, destiny + death.

from two iron rods when the engine suddenly gathered speed, giving me no chance to escape with the Mexican.

Desperately, I tried to raise my body up and squeeze it between the two rods so that I could rest on top of them — but the space was too narrow. I could only cling there by my hands and feet. My body sagged dangerously near the ground, which had become an indistinct blur. The click of the wheels over the rails had a sinister intonation, like the crunching jaws of a tiger. My energy was slowly draining away. I clung to the rods, not knowing when the express train would stop again.

No sound was ever more welcome, more gratefully heard, than that wild whistle as, thirty minutes later, the train approached a suburban town and slowed to a stop. I exchanged the bottom of the passenger car for its top. As I rode on, the night's cold mists enveloped me and shrouded the mountains that encircle the plateau. The following day, I came to my journey's end as the train pulled into the freight yards of Mexico City.

## Spring 1936
## Nicaragua

I arrived in Nicaragua in company with a doctor from Tegucigalpa, a leader in the abortive uprising against Honduran president Tiburcio Carías Andino. With one horse between us, we'd alternately walked and ridden along the Gulf of Fonseca, through the mangrove swamps until, to my mystification, we arrived at the lair of revolutionists — the large Casa de Huespedes, where the General Staff plotted amid the ruins of Chinandega (bombed out during the affair of Augusto César Sandino). After visiting the sunburned plazas of León, the liberal stronghold, and Granada — that madly beautiful and sprawling city of the ultra-conservative faction — I was ready to say good-bye to those Nicaraguan nights of intrigue and subterfuge. But the day before I embarked on the ferry across Lake Nicaragua, General Anastasio Somoza, director of the National Guard, made a palace revolution against President Sacasa, and the motherland of Rubén Darío was once again under martial law. The port authorities in San Juan del Sur — always ready to make sinister deductions about an equivocal-looking vagrant — were shaking their heads over my papers. Opportunely, an alert American sea-wolf who captained a freighter materialized and suggested that I stowaway, not in a cask the way Balboa had arrived at Castilla del Oro, but in a first-class cabin.

## June 1936–June 1938
## Panama Canal Zone

For the past fifteen days, I have not set foot outside the Canal Zone, partly because of my absorption with my studies, partly because of the police drive against vagrants. What did I read at the library today? Fragments from anthropology, Greek literature, and humanist philosophy. I was also pleased to discover a copy of my father's book *Household Physics*, which is often referred to by soldiers in the forts and pupils in the high schools. At closing time, I was in the back room of the library reading some of the newly issued books, especially Rabindranath Tagore's *Collected Poems and Plays*.

My mother's suggestion to "drop communism" is an interesting idea, or so I said to her out of filial duty, but it doesn't seem to me in harmony with the modern age. Communism is making more converts among students than any other political philosophy or religious creed. Those radical students of my parents' generation whom my mother says "wasted their time and all to no avail" at least perceived that the capitalist mode of production was incompatible with the greatest moral and economic advancements of the human race. For my part, I would rather fail in attempting something great than succeed in achieving something petty. I will bet every cent I have and every stitch of clothing I possess that socialism in some form will triumph everywhere in the world before the end of this century! Just wait until after the next war when the soldiers revolt from the futile slaughter and turn their bayonets against the Hitlers and Mussolinis who insanely lead them to the empty victories of militarism and imperialism.

My article "Reaction Rides the American Balkans" was returned by *Current History* with a note saying despite its "valuable facts" they were unable to publish it due to the pressure on their limited space by the cataclysmic events in Europe.

Astropo, an acquaintance of mine, informed me that the badly disorganized Communist Party of Panama is holding an important meeting tonight in order to work out plans for going underground and combating the fascism of the isthmus. They intend to establish new cells in the Santa Ana ward and one in the Canal Zone.

The skies were overcast when I went to bed under the stars but, around midnight, the clouds opened sufficiently for me to read the charts in Olcott's *Field Book of the Skies* by moonlight and trace out several groups in the heavens. I found that the constellation that for so many nights had attracted my attention due to the brilliance of its stars is none other than Orion.

I've had several sleepless nights recently due to mosquitos and cold east winds sweeping across the isthmus — also snakes rustling in the grass. Yesterday an inquisitive lizard crawled up my trouser leg!

Friday I read *A Thousand-Mile Walk to the Gulf* by the vagabond-botanist John Muir, skimmed through *Philine* by Amiel, and delved into herpetology (*Snakes and Their Ways* by Curran and Kauffeld); as the library closed, I was immersed in *Roan Stallion* by Robinson Jeffers. Yesterday I read a very marvelous tale, *The Golden Ass* by Apuleius, a Roman epic of an ancient vagabond's adventures, and studied Marxism — *Capital* and the Encyclopedia Britannica article by G.D.H. Cole. Today I was reading Beals's *America South* very attentively, but in the afternoon I became sidetracked by Langston Hughes's *The Ways of White Folks*.

There are so many great books in the world, all of them islands in the infinity of man's ignorance.

July–August 1938
Hawaiian Islands

There are strange systems of life, strange orbits in which our ideas revolve, strange focal points from which to wave back at the past and move on to the future — to wave back with a sadness at heart for the pleasures that have died away and to march on, unweaving our destinies with a heroic will to make the best of life.

This summer marked a turning point in my career as a vagabond for it was in June that I said *adiós* to Panama and in July that I said *aloha* to Honolulu. An ordinary seaman on board the Matson freighter *Lihue*, a merchant marine ship, was taken off at the Canal Zone sick with yellow jaundice, and I took his place,

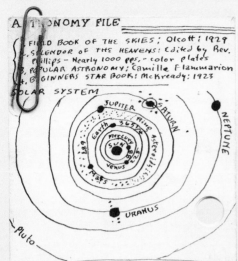

## ASTRONOMY FILE

1. FIELD BOOK OF THE SKIES; Olcott: 1929
2. SPLENDOR OF THE HEAVENS: Edited by Rev. Phillips — Nearly 1000 pgs, — color plates
3. POPULAR ASTRONOMY; Camille Flammarion
4. BEGINNERS STAR BOOK! McKready: 1923

SOLAR SYSTEM

*(diagram of solar system with orbits labeled: JUPITER, SATURN, Ring, Asteroids, NEPTUNE, Earth 365¼, Mercury 89, SUN, VENUS, Mars, URANUS, Pluto)*

SUN: over M x's mass Earth, 1,000 M. such suns been photographed. (Entire earths orbit easily contained inside Betelgeuse) 1. Group 4 terrestrial planets resemble earth the largest Mercury (1/22 earth's mass, 3 x's moon, 3,000 mi diameter) Mercury, moon, probably all small worlds devoid atmosphere, gases always trying to escape require strong attraction to hold fast (large planets, other obstacle to life, begin career hotter state, cool slower, Venus + Mars only plausible abodes of life) 2. Asteroids or planetoids, thousands of tiny worlds, orbits mostly between Mars + Jupiter. 3. Outer group planets: Jupiter weighs 2½ times all other planets, 318 x's earth, Saturn 95 x's, Uranus 15, Neptune 17, heated state probably molten surfaces, surrounded thick vapours.

### Gallant Rescue At Haulover

A very gallant rescue was made at the Haulover on Friday when one of the men employed on the construction of the bridge fell into the river. The man, Richard Usher, was handling concrete when the plank on which he was standing slipped and he fell into the water, George Whitmann another workman immediately dived in and brought the drowning man to the surface and safety. Usher cannot swim.

Whitmann lost three dollars in his efforts, and Mr. H. C. Carter the Director of Public Works, very sportingly replaced the money when told of the incident. Whitmann is an American citizen.

## HONOLULU: SUNDAY: AUGUST 13, 1938

I hitch-hiked the 85 miles around Oahu today. 10 miles from Honolulu I reached the PALI (gap in Koolau mountains, largest of the island ranges). It was here Kamehameha's army forced 13,000 of the enemy over the jagged cliffs. The scene has a barbaric majesty — naked pinnacles covered on the slopes by an emerald veil of grass, each blade waving like a green flag in the shivering wind. Mist. Far below roads + houses + cane-fields ending in the sea. To the right: Kailua Bay, week-end resort with one of best beaches in the world. As I was walking along Kaneohe Bay it started to rain + I was picked up by 2 men going fishing. One was from New Zealand called the Maori champion, had run all kinds of marathons, ran 85 miles around the island in something like 11 hours. We stopped at a well-to-do hapa-haole's house where they had a shot of gin + they left me at Kahuku. Next ride was with a mechanic of the air corps who took me to Schofield Barracks where I stayed 5 hours reading Fred Beal's PROLETARIAN JOURNEY, a purported exposé of the Stalinist regime. Returned to Honolulu about 6, read Dana's: 2 YEARS BEFORE THE MAST at the Y.M.C.A. Library until 10 P.M.

exchanging for a time the hiker's knapsack for the sailor's oilskin and chipping hammer. On the ship, the crew spends its leisure talking of past adventures in a humorous vein and reading dime novels and detective stories. Ashore, the time goes to a large extent to drinking and fighting.

Meanwhile, I stand lookout on the prow as falling stars drop into the blue ocean. All human voices are stilled, and the cosmic voice of the Universe speaks to the lonely seaman on his watch.

After having left the island of Oahu, we called for sugar at Hilo, on the island of Hawaii, and at Kahului, on Maui. Now, five weeks later, the ship has returned to Honolulu. This morning I arranged with Mr. Rolph at Castle & Cooke for a non-passenger ticket to California, studied up on surrealism at the Academy of Arts Library, and said good-bye to a friend in the Hawaiiana room at the public library. At six P.M., the ten-thousand-ton *Manuai*, on which I am sailing, left Pier 19 for California. The Punchbowl crater, Aloha Tower, and freights at twenty docks faded into the distance.

September 1938
Los Angeles

A vagabond lives and dies many times and is reincarnated into new worlds. Here in Los Angeles, degenerate burlesque shows paste the walls with female breasts, silk-stockinged legs, and painted eyelashes for the dull-eyed gaze of the aimlessly passing bums, dead pans, and drunks. This is what financiers have made of America. Idiotic voices, lips that never laugh, hearts that never hope. Joyless cities where ragged shadows wander like ghosts in a cemetery. The land of the almighty dollar where

banks are filled with gold, skies are filled with smoke, and men are choked with despair.

This morning Henry Kearney, who works in the sociological department of the library, presented me with a new suit and so many articles of clothing that I'll have to give most of them away. Later Mrs. Edward Hall, whose husband published a story in *New Masses*, signed me up for the Communist Party and drove me out to a meeting of new members. Now I am in a park reading Faulkner's *The Sound and the Fury*. In front of me, a refined woman is sitting behind the blue covers of a book — immaculate white gloves, thin black coat open at the throat to reveal a necklace of pearls like a lot of fish eyes strung together.

The highest quality of an individual is to be human. The phrase "to be human" means to follow life wherever it may lead, up and down, down and up, from the bottom of the world to the top, from darkness into light, through each degree of good and evil. As the circle of knowledge widens, life grows more beautiful and heroic. We are a part of everything — men, women, books, cities, railroads — all made from the same atoms and molecules, all living together and dying together, joined into one imperishable unity that can never be divided. In Tennyson, Ulysses, the greatest vagabond in history, says:
… I am a part of all that I have met;
   Yet all experience is an arch wherethro'
   Gleams that untravel'd world, whose margin fades
For ever and forever when I move.
How dull it is to pause, to make an end,
To rust unburnish'd, not to shine in use!
As tho' to breathe were life! Life piled on life
Were all too little …

November 1938
San Diego to Mexicali to Yuma to Phoenix
to Las Vegas to Carmel-by-the-Sea

Following Highway 101 down the coast,
I reached San Diego, where I slept and shivered
in an obsolete car in a junkyard. From San Diego
it was a matter of half-a-day's journey to cross
the hot Imperial Valley to the melancholy town
of Mexicali — capital of Baja in the great republic
south of the Rio Grande. After a few more
hours hitchhiking beneath the stars, I came
at midnight to the down-at-heel city of Yuma,
Arizona, which lies beside the muddy Colorado
River. The next morning at daybreak, I jumped
from the empty boxcar that had given me partial
refuge from the cold wind and stood with
half-a-dozen other road kids, all of us lined up
at intervals along the highway with our thumbs
pointing north. It was in vain that we signaled
every passing car. One of the hitchhikers had
been trying for three days to get out of Yuma,
but the small traffic and a recent case of hijacking
militated against success.

That night we filed down to the hobo jungles
in time to swing onto the eight o'clock freight
as it rolled out of the yards. There were no
empty boxcars but about thirty or forty of us
rode in the dirty cattle cars — a ragged crew
varying racially and ranging in occupation from
petty criminal to plodding cotton picker. There
were six in the car with me, including a leather-
faced tramp drinking wine from a quart bottle,
a Negro man rolling cigarette after cigarette,
and a Mexican talking Spanish to himself.

A nacreous dawn poured its light upon
Phoenix as we were coming into the freight
yards and revealed an unlovely city with a spot
of amber in the foreground, which proved
to be a fire made of railroad ties. As we headed
for it, we saw a piece of dust lift off the ground

and resolve itself into the figure of a human
being. It was a southern boy of seventeen,
and he met us with the question with which he
met all incoming trains from the south. He was
looking for his brother from whom he'd been
separated. The boy had been living for several
days in the freight yards, begging a little raw
meat and potatoes from the wholesale district
across the tracks and sleeping as dogs often do,
a few hours at day and a few hours at night,
in the yellow dust of which he seemed to have
become an organic part.

After tramping through the white snows around
the Grand Canyon and the monochromatic
desert at Boulder Dam, I came at last to the
portals of Las Vegas, Nevada. Three days passed
of which all I can remember is an hallucinatory
vision of the gilded roulette wheels spinning
in the cabarets and the mixed sound of church
bells, their liquid notes expanding on the air
until suddenly broken apart by the fierce whistle
of locomotives coming and going.

Las Vegas is, in hobo parlance, a "hungry
town," but I had no trouble eating at least
one good meal a day. Every noon I would look
around for a house that needed a little work
done, either cleaning up the yard or chopping
kindling wood, and then I would go to the back
door and ask if I could work for something
to eat.

It was the day before Thanksgiving when
I arrived at Carmel-by-the-Sea. The following
morning, even though it was a holiday,
I ventured up the steps of the Harrison
Memorial Library. Printed in black letters
on white cardboard was the dreadful
word CLOSED. I wasn't entirely dismayed,
however; the previous evening while browsing

among the books, I'd noticed that the librarian, Miss Elizabeth Niles, was precisely the type of person who might leave the door unlocked for vagabonds to enter at will. I tried the handle. The door opened.

While Carmel was eating turkey, I was feasting on the great literature of all ages, dipping into one precious volume after another. At about two o'clock, Miss Niles walked into the library like a fisherman come to see what he'd caught in his net. She assured me that it had been an oversight that the door had been left unlocked; nevertheless, she belittled my crime as a mere humorous episode. Its sequel occurred the next afternoon: Miss Niles came over to where I was reading and asked, "Did you notice a tall, rather thin man in the library just now? If I had known you were here, I would have introduced you. It was Robinson Jeffers. I told him how you had slipped into the library yesterday and were reading from a Greek dictionary, a Russian grammar, and his poetry. He thought the combination was quite amusing."

January–April 1939
Denver to Kansas City

For several hours this morning, I walked slowly through the Denver sunshine memorizing "A Los Niños" by Gabriela Mistral. Beyond question she is one of the purest and highest geniuses of South America. I followed one of the big viaducts over the freight yards, and it seemed that even the most commonplace objects revivified, took on a more lyric form, due to the enchantment cast upon my spirit by the poem I was learning. Truly the poorest man is the richest if he but knows how to extract the treasures from books, from nature, and from humanity.

In the course of my ramblings, a squad car bore down upon me, and the policeman asked what I was doing in this part of town. He ordered me to leave the city and then got out of the car to frisk me. Quite a crowd gathered to see if I had any deadly weapons, but all he found in one pocket was a turnip and, in the other, articles of an equally prosaic nature. My travel notes were of chief interest to him, and he studied them for so long I hope he derived some value.

I long to bury myself in a really exciting city, a city where culture is vibrant, a city where music is passionately loved, and where love is something holy and beautiful — a city like Paris or Moscow — where poetry is part of life, where men are poets and life is a poem.

*In October 1941, while in San Francisco, George was inducted into the army. Two months later, on December 7, the Japanese bombed Pearl Harbor in Hawaii, bringing the United States into the Second World War. While waiting for the order to report to basic training, George enrolled in Latin American studies at Harvard University. He received his order to report in the summer of 1942.*

Fall 1942–Summer 1944
Greenland

In September, our outfit, the 73rd Infantry Battalion, was at the staging area in Camp Curtis Guild, Wakefield, Massachusetts, awaiting shipment overseas. We'd been issued so much heavy clothing that a few of us anticipated the coming journey into the northland and spent evenings in the library reading up on Greenland. Happily, though, I believe the majority of men were having a last fling with the Victory Girls.

Picture us steaming up the largest fjord in the world to a journey's end that would have made us laugh in the face of any fortune-teller who'd predicted it. From Greenland to Madagascar, from China Seas to "Araby the blest," America's fingerprints are to be stamped across the map. Our outfit's part in all this is to operate an airport and weather station sixty miles north of the Arctic Circle, a hundred miles from the sea, and a few miles below the Greenland ice cap. Our base has several code names, but it's best known as Bluie West-8.

Due to a glacial anticyclone — where high currents of warm air from the equator become chilled and move out in cold fronts over a large part of Europe — Greenland is strategically important militarily for forecasting the weather on the front. The only German activity here aside from reconnaissance is in operating weather stations. One by one, these German stations are put out of commission through attacks by our ice-breakers, airplanes, or patrols, but inevitably new ones appear to replace the old.

The days pass on their own even course, and each one exacts its toll on our exuberant youth. Multiplied by millions, this is the story of lonely outposts the world over, where men separated from both home and battlefronts wait for the war to end and life to begin anew.

I've worked on the ships, in the warehouse, on the dog team, and as a base censor. But I've now found a more permanent vocation as a medical technician, and I was recently assigned to replace a man on Cruncher Island. This is a weather and radio station with a complement of twenty-four men located on the mouth of Sondrestromfjord. Hardly a day passes that several boatloads of Eskimos don't stop at the island to talk with us and exchange ivory statues and other souvenirs for clothes and cigarettes.

We barter corned-beef hash for their fresh caribou meat, ducks, and trout, to our mutual satisfaction. When the Eskimos put on shows, such as turning over in their kayaks, I reciprocate by diving off the icebergs into water six degrees above freezing. After dusk has fallen, they enter the dispensary and talk and smoke their pipes or play their concertinas while I serve cough medicine as a cordial.

I've fallen in love with Enoch's daughter, Little Bird. She is a golden-skinned acolyte of Venus with black hair tied in red ribbons. Usually she bubbles over with the wonderful comradeship of the Eskimos but, when she feels shy among all these pale strangers, she buries her face in my arms and whispers *asavakkit*, which in English takes three words to say.

July 1944–July 1946
Taunton

After twenty-one months above the Arctic Circle, I flew back to Presque Isle and was placed in the station hospital in Taunton, Massachusetts. All through the noiseless nights, I watch over the sick in Ward 113. Outside our windows, snowflakes silently drift to the earth, while farther away men are killing and being killed in flaming cities, icy marshes, and tropical atolls. I believe in the value of every human being, whatever his accidents of birth and conviction. Even in disunity, all men are interdependent, and every city on earth is a part of the whole. We are all links in the chain of simultaneous events whose dimming echoes will one day be called "history" after we and our prejudices and our follies have disappeared.

Today the talk in the barracks was about goats. I left the conversation, went to the Red Cross, and sat down at the piano. As I was playing

From top: George with a customer in his bookstore in Taunton, Massachusetts; a World War II bookplate found among George's papers; a photo-booth picture of George.

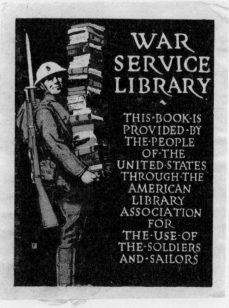

WAR SERVICE LIBRARY

THIS·BOOK·IS PROVIDED·BY THE·PEOPLE OF·THE UNITED·STATES THROUGH·THE AMERICAN LIBRARY ASSOCIATION FOR THE·USE·OF THE·SOLDIERS AND·SAILORS

"Bandiera Rossa," the anti-fascist Italian song, two new patients back from overseas came and sang with me. Both had been volunteers in the International Brigades during the Spanish Civil War, so we began quite a conversation in Spanish. Before long, some Mexicans joined us and kept me playing "Pajarillo Barranqueño" and other favorites.

Tonight in the ward, I made ice cream for the patients. After lights out, I put my books on the table and studied: *Sunday After the War* by Henry Miller, *Advanced Russian Reader*, *Anatomy of the Nervous System*, *La Vie littéraire* by Anatole France, and *Verdun* by Jules Romains.

I recently opened a bookstore, the Taunton Book Lounge, modeled on the Paris salons that are the rendezvous of writers and book-lovers. It has roses in a Chinese porcelain vase, ivy vines hanging over the shelves, and leather-covered chairs in which to read or talk or watch the passing show. It is on the main street next to Taunton Green, and there are always crowds walking in front of the window from early morning until late at night. I stay open whenever possible until eleven P.M., when the two theaters down the street close their doors. I look over the pages of a book and watch the faces that move under the yellow street lamps, hoping that someone interesting will come through the door.

*On August 5, 1946, George set sail from New York City to Paris. He'd intended to work at the MacJannet Camps, a holding site for French war orphans, but on arrival he discovered that the camps had been disbanded. Instead, he enrolled at the Sorbonne on the G.I. Bill and was given housing at Cité Universitaire, a foundation for students and visiting academics. George soon began exchanging his G.I. food allowances for other G.I.s' book allowances.*

December 1946
Paris

As I've now accumulated a fine stock of books, I've begun running a lending library, the University City Book Counselors, from my room, number 117, in the United States House. Here there is a weekly Saturday night dance, a piano I can play, a typewriter I can borrow, and, if other resources fail, a window that looks out over Paris.

I found that a good way to become oriented geographically with the city is to climb Montmartre to the church of the Sacré-Cœur. From its steps, the contours of greater Paris, with its three million inhabitants, are plainly marked, and one can follow the windings of the Seine, which allegedly makes so many turns because it hates to leave the city.

Paris is still Paris even though its name, "The City of Light," is only figurative in this period of dim-out, when electricity is periodically shut off to save fuel. The famous pastry shops have unappetizing displays compared to pre-War days, or so I hear, but the bookstores seemingly defy every law of economics with a clientele that is faithful despite astronomical prices. Paris probably has more bookstores and art galleries than any other city, not to mention the miles of *bouquinistes* on the Left Bank and the outdoor art exhibits on the Boulevard St.-Michel.

January 1947
Paris

I am currently taking ten courses at the Sorbonne of which I will have to pass an oral and written examination in five in order to receive the *diplôme d'études de la civilisation française*. The student body is a hodgepodge, ranging from a large representation of English

From top: George and a woman, perhaps Gisèle, at the lending library on Boulevard de Courcelles; George and a friend in a Paris café; a poem George wrote for Gisèle, whom he nicknamed "Mistral"; a 1948 postcard from Lawrence Ferlinghetti, then called Lawrence Ferling.

3 May 48
Letellier
2 Place Voltaire
8 A.M.

Citizen —
If you still have that bookstore perhaps you will sell me the *Limit* of books allowed for one term under the G.I. Bill — including a couple of big dictionaries + the new Proust

?

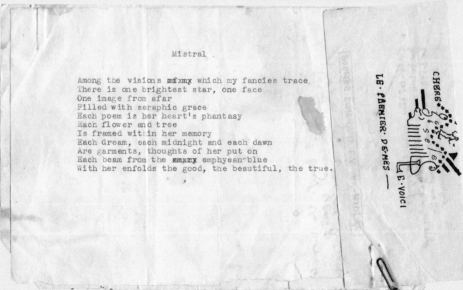

```
                    Mistral

       Among the visions which my fancies trace
       There is one brightest star, one face
       One image from afar
       Filled with seraphic grace
       Each poem is her heart's phantasy
       Each flower and tree
       Is framed within her memory
       Each dream, each midnight and each dawn
       Are garments, thoughts of her put on
       Each beam from the emphyean blue
       With her enfolds the good, the beautiful, the true.
```

girls, both charming and erudite, to the American veterans who show variable proficiency in French, as well as variable susceptibility to what the Methodists call "the finer things in life."

There are innumerable small hotels with rooms for one hundred francs a day. As a student, I'm allowed my room in University City for only fourteen hundred francs a month. Vegetables, cornmeal, and certain meats such as hamburger are plentiful, and I cook most of my own meals. Occasionally, I buy a pound of duck or some eggs to make an *omelette flambée*. At restaurants, one can dine economically on fifty francs or one can have anything from oysters to ice cream on one hundred francs.

### May–June 1947
### Paris
On May Day, I organized the progressive students at the United States House in the march to the place de la Concorde. When we reached the reviewing stand shouting *"Échec à Truman"* (Down with Truman) and carrying banners against atomic-bomb diplomacy, Thorez, Cachin, Marty, and other government ministers stood up. Our slogans won bravos all along the march, and the cinemas of France included us in their newsreels: the first group of American students to participate in a French May Day.

Although I have lived in Nanking, Mexico City, Constantinople, and many other exotic cities, I have never been so infatuated with any place as with Paris. For the first time since the War, life has regained its colors of romance. I am working on a series of verses in French called *Poèmes écrits dans l'après-midi*, which I shall probably set up and print myself since Raymond, the eccentric brother of Isadora Duncan, has offered me the use of his print shop.

My girlfriend, Gisèle, and I opened a lending library in June after I had accumulated a large enough stock of books. It is called the Librairie Franco-Américaine and is on the Boulevard de Courcelles.

### Winter 1948
### Paris
I have moved into the Hôtel de Suez at 31 Boulevard St.-Michel. Richard Wright lives next door to me on rue Monsieur-le-Prince, and I often see him driving his Cabriolet down the Boul' Mich'. Out of my room, I've started up another little lending library consisting mostly of old American and English books. The other day, a tall, well-dressed young man walked in, saying he knew my sister at Columbia. His name is Lawrence Ferling. We got on well from the first, talking about writers and Paris. He comes by all the time now. If I'm not here, he just sits and reads.

I dread the Paris winters, but this November has been warm and marked by long spells of fog that drift between the plane trees and the mansard roofs like stagehands who shift the scene for another act in a play that never ends. Here in room seven of the Hôtel de Suez with my nose in a book, with brandy in my coffee, with the Seine flowing a few yards to the north, with friends from Indo-China, Africa, England, Venezuela, Brazil, the States, and all the latitudes of the world, I feel that I am in the heart of civilization. There is no other country except France, no other city except Paris, no other street in Paris except the Boul' Mich', no other hotel on the Boul' Mich' except the Suez, no other room in the Suez except number seven.

Spring 1949
Paris

For the past week, I have done nothing but make money — lots of it. My friends have just published a little magazine called *Janus*, and I earn five or six hundred francs an hour selling it in the cafés around St.-Germain-des-Prés. So, at the moment, I am an extrovert, but it is a necessary stage on the road of life.

After studying the book trade for a number of years, I have concluded that the main field where a person can use his limited capital and specialist knowledge to greatest advantage is in the international exchange of books. I'd need two thousand titles for a proper lending library. The basic installation would be books in conformity to what one might find in the home of a dilettante polyglot, well-traveled, and with a knowledge and interest in the arts and sciences, the novel, and the people who inhabit the imagination. As a public service, I'd maintain a free reading room, as well as a system of filing cards hanging from the facade where anyone can advertise for exchange of conversation, an out-of-print book, a puppy, or a ride to Rome.

Spring 1950
Paris

I live for the day when I'll have a bookstore to embellish this workaday world. I now own one of the best private libraries in the Latin Quarter and, living as I do on less than a dollar a day, I have accumulated a small capital augmented by English lessons and occasional book sales. I've talked with Sylvia Beach, the daughter of a minister from Princeton, New Jersey, who started a bookstore in Paris that became the rendezvous of André Gide, James Joyce, and the most famous writers of Europe. There is a possibility that she would consent to go into business with me — although I've been avoiding offers of partnership, it would be an honor and a privilege to work with Sylvia Beach, should she decide to re-open Shakespeare and Company. Either way, I hope finally to have a niche where I can safely look upon the world's horror and beauty.

Opposite: Rue de la Bûcherie, future home to George's bookstore, photographed in the early 1920s.

# the
# 1950s

"In the year 1600, this building was a monastery, La Maison du Mustier. In the Middle Ages, each monastery had a monk called the *frère lampier*, whose duty it was to light the lamps at nightfall. I'm the *frère lampier* here now. It's the modest role I play."

GEORGE

George Whitman opened his bookshop at 37 rue de la Bûcherie on August 14, 1951. It was a humble space, with no electricity and just three narrow, ground-floor rooms, set one after the other like railroad cars, each no more than fifteen feet wide. The shop's sole window faced onto the river Seine and Notre-Dame Cathedral. Behind the store were the cobblestone streets and medieval monuments of the Latin Quarter.

"I'd long wanted a bookstore of my own in Paris," said George. "After the Second World War, there were innumerable shops for sale — France was in a bad situation economically — but I held off until I finally found the exact one of my dreams, the ideal location in the whole world."

A month prior, in July, George had met an Algerian grocer while reading in a park near his residence, the Hôtel de Suez on Boulevard St.-Michel. The grocer was hoping to move his family to the countryside and was offering to sell his shop space for five hundred dollars. "I almost didn't take it when I learned that the building had been condemned," said George. "But then I found out it had been condemned in 1870, so I decided to take a chance on its holding up for a few more decades."

The war was barely over. France and its people were hard-hit and poor; Paris, gray and rundown. The Latin Quarter was especially grim, "a slum, with street theater, mountebanks, junkyards, grimy hotels, wine shops, little laundries, and tiny thread-and-needle-shops," as George described it. The *quartier* got its name from the medieval universities that filled it, Latin being the language of international scholarship in the Middle Ages. The Sorbonne has its origins on nearby rue du Fouarre, next to St.-Julien-le-Pauvre, one of the oldest churches in Paris, built in the 13th century. In front of the church stands the oldest tree in Paris, planted in 1601, around the same year the bookshop's building was constructed.

In the 1950s, the Latin Quarter was still populated by students, who lived in small, dingy, no-star hotels, alongside the *quartier*'s working class residents. They were joined by American G.I.s and the new bohemians — writers, artists, homosexuals, musicians, drug users — who were flooding into Paris to take advantage of the weak franc and the culture's relative permissiveness.

George opened his shop with a stock of one thousand books from his personal collection, which he'd acquired using his G.I. benefits. The U.S. Army had been relatively generous, giving its veterans enough to live on in Paris, including rations for food and vouchers for books. George had traded his rations for other vets' book allowances, thereby amassing an impressive number of titles given how expensive →

Opposite: George and a friend preparing a meal in the shop's Blue Oyster Tea Room.

## DOLORES
*student/George's girlfriend*

November 28, 1951

Dearest Mother and Daddy, Yesterday I walked out in the park and just got struck dumb with the sight of it. To my left was Notre-Dame Cathedral, the color of mother of pearl, and the trees in the park were black silhouettes against a vivid coral pink sky. I stood in the middle of all of it and gaped.

Didn't know we're becoming famous, did you? One of our regular visitors is Richard Wright, author of *Native Son* and *Black Boy*. He has a pretty white wife, and they've been living in Paris for several years. Yesterday we bought eighty books from his library, and he says he has stacks of review copies from publishers, which he will bring us later. Then who should happen in here but journalist George Seldes and his wife. After getting the habit of coming in the store, they gave us some books before going on a trip through Spain.

We meet so many different kinds of people. Last night an English boy from Liverpool and an Australian girl from New South Wales kept on staying and talking, so we split the potato soup and the rest of the lemon meringue pie, which George had baked in Mrs. Eme's kitchen. Fun but not as nice as the night before last when Sonia (a Polish girl married to an American named Mike — two of George's best friends) brought over a whole baked chicken, which we ate in the lamplight with some *patates douces* we'd managed to find at 100 francs the kilo, rather than 150 francs for Irish potatoes.

Late this afternoon while Kris the Hindu, a German boy, and Mrs. Frances Cox from Capetown were sitting in the reading room, a stooped old man looking like Nathaniel Alden

in Santayana's novel *The Last Puritan* came into the shop and began talking to George. When George said he'd originally come to France to work in the MacJannet Camps for war orphans, the man answered, "I'm Donald MacJannet." George asked him if he remembered when his brother, Carlton, had come to dinner at Dr. MacJannet's house in Arlington, and soon Dr. MacJannet was showing the group in the bookstore his color slides in three-dimensions of the camp at Lake Annecy.

George is one of those persons like you, Mother, who hums and whistles all the time almost without knowing it, which is very nice because it puts me in the mood for music, too, and as soon as I take up a melody he puts in the alto. A few weeks ago, we had nothing but the Brahms *Variations*, and then it changed to "Eine Kleine Nachtmusik." Now it's Schubert's "Impromptu."

So much energy abounding around this place. In the last week, George has built new shelves in the tearoom and dismantled a counter to make a divan, which runs along one entire wall in the lounge. The bookstore and reading room face the Seine, and Notre-Dame Cathedral is about like our dining room. The room is painted a light emerald green. The lounge or tearoom, up two steps through a gothic arch, is longer and narrower and painted gold. The back room is reached through another picturesque arch between huge cement walls, and George plans to paint it a rose color.

Wrote the grape people, Pa — should hear soon. TONS OF LOVE TO ALL!

— D

books were in France. He wrote home to his parents: "American books are very popular. Prices range from forty dollars for a not especially attractive edition of *Tobacco Road* bound in vellum to thirty cents for a second-hand copy of *The Constant Sinner* by Mae West, which was published to sell for half that."

George called the bookshop Librairie le Mistral after an ex-girlfriend or a Mediterranean wind or the Chilean poet Gabriela Mistral — he was mysterious about its provenance with guests and journalists. (The name lasted more than ten years before being changed in 1964 to Shakespeare and Company.) →

The front room in the mid-1950s, after George had greatly expanded on the shop's original stock of one thousand books.

Looking out from the shop onto
Notre-Dame and Kilometer Zero,
the point at which all French roads begin.

"We spend our life,
it's ours, trying to bring
together in the same
instant a ray of sunshine
and a free bench." SAMUEL BECKETT

Two months after opening the shop, George wrote to his sister, Mary: "In the morning I wake up with the sun in my face and a vision of chimney pots floating above the treetops in the garden of St.-Julien-le-Pauvre. At night I look out the window at the illuminated spires of Notre-Dame. This is the bookstore I have always dreamed of."

Of the shop's three rooms, the farthest one back was converted into a reading space. George dubbed it the Old Smoky Reading Room, the same name he'd given to his room at the Hôtel de Suez, presumably because there were no windows and many smokers.

# Roving Yank Settles Down in Paris Book Shop

By RICHARD C. MILLER.

ARIS.—The Left Bank Art Center, a book store which faces Notre Dame on the Rue la Boucherie, is one of the w businesses in town which longs to an American and its ne:. George Whitman, is a an whose story is striking even a quarter where many people's es are interesting and different.

The first time I went in his op there were several Americns, Australians, English and ench drinking coffee and disssing the paintings and books at George displays around the lls. Roy Dalgarno, a bearded stralian painter, asked George w he could possibly make a ing when all his customers er seem to do is talk, read oks and drink free coffee.

George answered quietly, say- g that he only has to sell ne book a day to get cigaret money, the lending library aying his expenses. Some ays he sells fifteen or twenty ooks and others none, but he store brings him plenty of telligent and stimulating iends and that's all he needs o be happy.

## THE DENVER POST

Founded Oct. 28, 1895, by K. H. Tammen and F. G. Bonfils.

_edicated in perpetuity to the rvice of the people, that no od cause shall lack a cham- on and that evil shall not rive unopposed._

PALMER HOYT,
Editor and Publisher.

E. RAY CAMPBELL,
President.

HELEN G. BONFILS,
Secretary-Treasurer.

December 2, 1951.

"There are no public libraries in Paris," he went on. "I don't have to worry because no matter how hard times get people here will always need books."

A FEW evenings later I was passing by the book store and, noticing that George was sitting alone at his table eating mussels and reading by candle light, I decided to drop in and find out more about him. People had told me that this would be well worth while, because George is a cousin of Walt Whitman and is probably the only book store owner around who has read everything in the shop.

George shared his mussels with me and explained that the candles make up for the lack of electricity in the place, then began to talk about himself.

His father, Walt Whitman II, used to be an editor of Mark Twain's book company. As employes of this firm weren't allowed to write, he quit and turned out several books, finding time to be a professor at Columbia, the University of Pittsburgh, and the University of Nanking in China. As a child, George read proofs for his father. Later he went to Harvard, wrote a weekly column for a small town paper and, now, is working on his Ph.D. at the Sorbonne.

All this suggests a stuffy, academic background, but by the time he was 20 he had hitchhiked through every state in the union. Then he decided to look at some foreign countries and, with $40 in his pocket, he caught a ride to Mexico City, the start of a trip which was to last two years and wind 3,000 miles through Mexico and Central America, then through Hawaii and back to the west coast.

He was near death many times, but the closest call was in the Yucatan when sick with dysentery he walked for three days through swampy jungles with no food and water. He found a coconut tree, then was nursed to health by a tribe of Maya Indians.

"The jungle," he says, "is a basic part of human experience. Today, for the first time in history, people are able to live in artificial surroundings where they can ignore nature. But there, in the jungle, I rediscovered the mean-

ing of nature, saw its immense, indifferent forces and realized how small man is in time and space and how much of history is a record of our desperate fight against these forces."

He was also impressed by the fact that the Indians, who make up about 90 per cent of the population of Guatemala, are worse off than before Columbus and that despite their poverty everyone he met was extremely friendly.

After this trip George spent four years in the army, five months of it as the only white man in an isolated post in Greenland. He lived with the Eskimos; took a long trip with them on a schooner.

AFTER the war he came to Paris, then worked his way home and started a bookstore in a small town in the east. "The employes," he says, "soon had the largest private libraries in town. I enjoyed it there, but came back to Europe in '48 because I couldn't renew my lease."

Since then he has visited most of the countries here and spent part of a summer in a chateau with the French aristocracy. "I didn't like them very much," he said. "They never speak with sincerity and have no thoughts of or affection for anybody but themselves.

"The world is big and beautiful and, although I don't have anything material to show for my life, I went out and saw it; used my youth as best I could. I've always been compelled to find out what makes the world go, both by using my own eyes and the eyes of others through the books they wrote.

"I've always wanted a book store because the book business is the business of life. It took years of planning and months of red tape and messing around with lawyers to get one, but now that I have it, I want to use it right. As soon as I can, I'm going to make a community center of it—put a tea shop and a reading room in the back where artists and writers and the people who live around here can come and read or talk over their problems."

(George himself was known to light one cigarette after the next.) It was at the Suez that George had first encountered a young Sorbonne Ph.D. student named Lawrence Ferling, who would later be known as Lawrence Ferlinghetti, cofounder of City Lights bookstore in San Francisco, the publisher of *Howl* and other works, and one of America's most celebrated poets. Ferlinghetti recalled meeting George:

A reading nook on the first floor, which was added to the shop in the mid-1950s.

"When I was in Columbia University graduate school, I used to see his sister, Mary, who was in the philosophy department and, while she was not exactly my girlfriend, I remember sitting with her in her front window as she told me about her brother George who had recently arrived in Paris after wandering the Orient and South America. I imagined this romantic wanderer, a kind of wayward Walt Whitman carrying Coleridge's albatross. When I took off for Paris in late 1946 to go to the Sorbonne and get a *doctorat*, Mary gave me George's address. It turned out that his albatross was books, and they had a passionate relationship. I found him in an airless window-less hole-in-the-wall in the Hôtel de Suez, with books up to the ceiling on all walls, and himself the ghost of Stephen Dedalus cooking supper over a can of Sterno (or some other eternal flame of his own making). He was selling books out of his hotel room to American students on the G.I. Bill. He was already in the thrall of a kind of mistral bibliomania."

The middle room of the bookshop was called the Blue Oyster Tearoom, despite its gold-colored walls. It had a makeshift sofa that doubled as a bed at night. George slept there, though he was quick to give up the space for writers and artists in need. →

Brendan Behan with George and a friend.

HELEN MARTIN
*Tumbleweed* °

My husband, Philip, and I made our first visit to the bookshop in the fall of 1951, soon after it opened. We were walking by and looked in the window. There was a tall, thin man — George — sitting on the floor with a suitcase full of books, with more books on a narrow stand, and next to that a little stove. Seeing us peering in, he asked, "Would you like a cup of tea?" We said yes. It was nice to find a bookshop there, beside the Seine. We looked around, very modestly, to see whether we could find anything that wasn't too expensive for us.

Philip and I came back a few months later, after having briefly lived in Austria, and that's when our friendship with George really began. By this time, in March 1952, the bookshop was furnished a bit more, and George had some lovely books. He knew we weren't very well off, I think. He kindly asked, "Would you like an Irish stew?" We said yes, and George got the meat, and I brought the potatoes. We cut and trimmed and made the stew right over the books. There was only one tiny table.

In the back room was an old divan. When we needed to, Philip and I stayed there, in that back room, sleeping on the divan, in George's little place, with all the Henry Millers piled to the ceiling.

Soon this was more nights than not as word got around of a free place to stay in Paris. "The philosophy of the bookstore is to reciprocate the hospitality I received in the past, when I hoboed through the U.S., Mexico, and Central America," George would say. "I believe we're all homeless wanderers in a way."

George called his guests "Tumbleweeds" after the dry, rootless plants that "drift in and out on the winds of chance." In exchange for a bed or floor space, Tumbleweeds were asked to help out occasionally at the shop. By early 1952, there were so many guests that George rented a studio apartment around the corner on rue Galande for himself and his dog.

° Story contributors are identified as "Tumbleweeds" if they were residing at the bookshop when the events they describe occurred; otherwise, they are identified by the occupations they had at the time of their visits. —ED.

The shop's front room, looking onto Notre-Dame, held a tiny alcohol stove on which George would fix meals for himself and his guests. There being no electricity, dinners were eaten by candlelight, surrounded by the small stock of books. Some of the titles were for sale; others could only be borrowed by a subscription to George's library. There was a fee of a few francs, although George often waived it for writers, artists, and students.

George was rather reluctant to part permanently with his books. He'd often refuse to sell a title to a customer, saying he'd changed his mind and would prefer to keep the book for himself. These whims likely had only a limited effect on revenue. Most of the

Beckett translator Patrick Bowles; *Paris Review* editor George Plimpton (in hat); *Merlin* publisher Jane Lougee; and *Merlin* editor Christopher Logue. *Photo:* OTTO VAN NOPPEN

shop's visitors had no money to spend on anything but essentials — food, rent, cigarettes. They came instead to meet one another, to read the books for free, or to work on their own writing. Some days George didn't make any money from the shop at all. "When I'd not sold my daily quota of books," he said, "I'd close the store and go to tourist cafés with a bunch of Henry Miller's books, which were banned in the U.S."

In the spring of 1952, the avant-garde literary journal *Merlin* was founded out of the bookshop by a band of bohemians: publisher Jane Lougee and editors Alexander Trocchi, Christopher Logue, and Richard Seaver, among others. "They were a group of hoboes, a really creative group of young writers," said George. "Jane was getting a little money from her father, who was a banker in Maine. With that money, she financed *Merlin* because she was in love with Trocchi. Jane was scrubbing floors to pay for food and lodging. Trocchi was very persuaded of his genius." George gave the editors space to work, and they would sometimes stage readings in the bookshop. *Merlin* published Jean Genet, Eugène Ionesco, Jean-Paul Sartre, and a then little-known Samuel Beckett, whom the journal is credited for having "discovered." It was one of the first to publish him in English. →

CHRISTOPHER LOGUE
*founding editor of* Merlin/*poet*

George resembled one of Daumier's Don Quixotes. Tall, skinny, with a faraway look in his bright blue eyes, he wore a plaid waistcoat and had a liking for richly embroidered ties.

It was his habit to break off a conversation in mid-sentence, take up a book, dust it, begin to read it, and forget you, wandering away, book in hand, to disappear through the curtains at the back of his shop. Not that George neglected those in his company. Likely enough, a few moments after leaving you, he'd reappear carrying a trayful of steaming yogurt jars. "Tea, tea, tea for all who like it," he would announce — which most people did, for the Mistral was more than a bookshop. "My philosophy is sharing, my love is literature, my home, like-minded company," George said.

Librairie le Mistral became *Merlin*'s first editorial address. One of the copies George lent out was returned with "Drivel" written in a neat hand on the bottom right-hand corner of each page. Another had: "See you in the Royal at 15.30 — Jennifer," scrawled across the title page in lipstick.

Robert Silvers
*early managing editor of* The Paris Review

It was only a few years after the war. Paris was still quite a broken-up and poor place. There were many streets where the gutters, and even the sewers, would be erupting. This poverty conferred an advantage on people who had dollars. You could live cheaply, and you could put out a magazine cheaply.

When I first went to work for *The Paris Review* in 1954, one of my tasks was simply to carry around the magazines to the various bookshops. I walked into Le Mistral on a cold night. There was George Whitman, sitting at the front of the shop, which was *his* space, as if he were receiving visitors. I said, "Here's the new number. I hope it's OK." And he said, "*Oui, mais tout d'abord prenez un verre de vin.*" It was sweet of him to offer me a glass of wine, and then — with a definite gesture — he displayed the *Review* right in front. That made me feel I was getting somewhere in my new career.

At Le Mistral, you'd bump into all sorts of people, writers who were living in Paris or passing through: Terry Southern or Peter Matthiessen or Donald Windham. There was our *Paris Review* group, and there were the editors of *Merlin* magazine, which was an important, radical literary journal edited by Alex Trocchi. *The Paris Review* published some work by Beckett — *Merlin* published more; they published *Molloy* first. Both journals published Genet.

Apart from publishing talented American writers who were then hardly known — Philip Roth and Terry Southern among them — we were particularly concerned with portfolios by artists then in Paris, including Giacometti, Tal-Coat, Henri Michaux, and Zao Wou-Ki. Most were accompanied by remarkable commentaries by Pierre Schneider.

Trocchi was one of the few people I've known who was an ardent drug addict; that is, he thought it was a marvelous thing to be a heroin addict and to enter what he called "castle keep." But he was a brilliant editor and writer, and he had some very talented people on his staff. One was Christopher Logue, a kind of Brechtian poet at the time, who went on to do his own astonishing new version of the *Iliad*. Logue and Trocchi were two people from *Merlin*, and we were friends — we were all friends.

George hosted free seminars out of the shop. "The writers' and artists' workshops, in addition to informal discussions, now function as an evening school for those who regard education as a permanent life process," George wrote his sister, Mary. "We have a Russian class on Wednesday evenings at nine and Italian conversation on Fridays, and we have an ambitious project for a seminar in socio-psychological research." He added: "We put in a fourteen-hour day, seven days a week, buying and selling books and serving coffee to surprised English girls, Viennese doctors and architects, South African émigrés, and Latin American poets."

By the mid-1950s, George had greatly increased his stock of books and bought the first-floor apartment above the shop. (By French counting convention, the first floor is the one above the ground floor, what in some other countries is referred to as the second floor.) In addition to allowing George access to the building's electricity, the first floor also gave →

George's Bookstore has a collection of books
as inviting as your own private library
**DAVID ARMSTRONG** - Lecturer in Philosophy, University of Melbourne

**RICHARD WRIGHT**
One of the Institutions of Paris

**MAX ERNST**
Continues the Tradition of the Paris book-salon

**CLAUDE ROY**
A Cultural Center of the Left Bank with Notre Dame in its Front Yard

**MRS**
**BERTHOLDT BRECHT**
Poetic and stimulating atmosphere

**PRESTON STURGES**
A Very Friendly & hospitable bookshop

What is unique about George's Bookstore is the range
of books and magazines that may be read, purchased or
borrowed – M. ARRHE, Literary Section, UNESCO

**MISTRAL BOOKSHOP** - George Whitman - 37 Rue de la Bucherie - PARIS V

A flyer with praise from some of the shop's early visitors.

In the back room: Richard Wright and his wife, Ellen; George; and *Paris Review* editors Max Steele and Peter Matthiessen. *Photo:* JACQUES ROUCHON

VLADIMIR POZNER
*writer*

I took Brecht and his family to a brasserie on the banks of the Seine. In Paris, *The Caucasian Chalk Circle* had recently exploded like a bolt of lightning. The restaurant served, on a wooden board, numerous rare cheeses—one was steeped in brandy and eau-de-vie, wrapped in vine leaves, rolled in spices, and dusted with ash. It was enough to make us forget the towers of Notre-Dame on the other side of the river.

Earlier in the evening, we'd discovered a nearby bookshop, Le Mistral, open in the evenings and selling second-hand books.

We perused one shelf after the other. Brecht even got down and went through the boxes languishing on the floor, picking out several detective novels. He'd read everything, was familiar with most of the authors. Our wives grew impatient.

Brecht eventually bought about thirty dog-eared titles. Now, seated on the terrace of the restaurant, he sampled the cheeses, as numerous as the books piled up next to him on a chair, so keen was he to keep the volumes close at hand.

him a large space to devote solely to his lending library. "With these new premises, it should be possible to have one of the finest stocks of English books anywhere in the world outside of England and the United States," he wrote a friend.

Established writers and artists frequented the bookshop: Julio Cortázar, Anaïs Nin, James Baldwin, Max Ernst, Richard Wright, William Saroyan, Terry Southern, and William Styron, along with editors from *The Paris Review* — Peter Matthiessen, Robert Silvers, and George Plimpton.

George was honored by the association of these celebrated writers and artists, particularly the African-American authors who'd come to Paris seeking refuge from the racism they'd encountered in the States. Richard Wright wrote, "There is such an absence of race hate that it seems a little unreal. Above all, Paris strikes me as a truly gentle city, with gentle manners." →

A customer browsing through the bulletin-board messages.

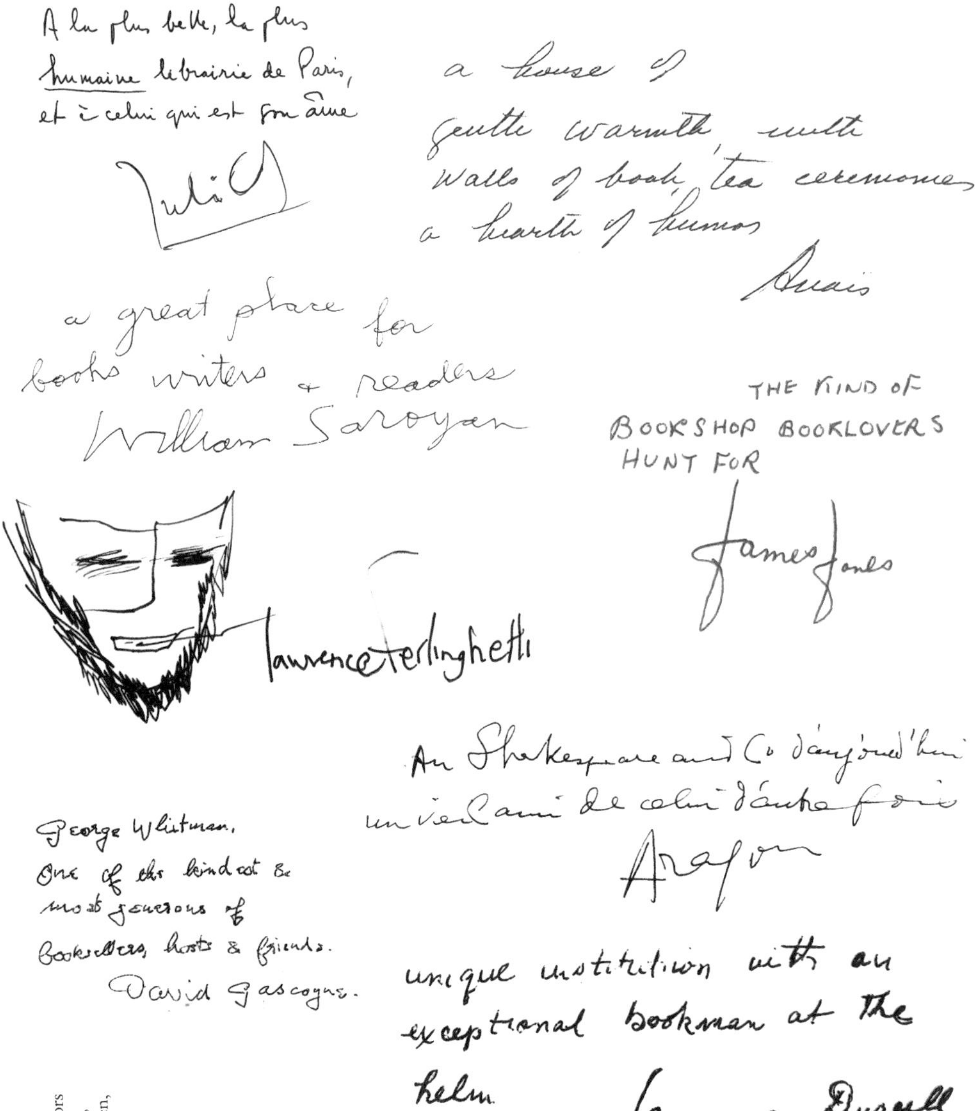

A la plus belle, la plus _humaine_ librairie de Paris, et à celui qui est son âme

Julio C

a house of gentle warmth, with walls of book, tea ceremonies a hearth of humor

Anaïs

a great place for books writers + readers

William Saroyan

THE KIND OF BOOKSHOP BOOKLOVERS HUNT FOR

James Jones

Lawrence Ferlinghetti

An Shakespeare and Co d'aujourd'hui un vieil ami de celui d'autrefois

Aragon

George Whitman, One of the kindest & most generous of Booksellers, hosts & friends.

David Gascoyne.

unique institution with an exceptional bookman at the helm

Lawrence Durrell

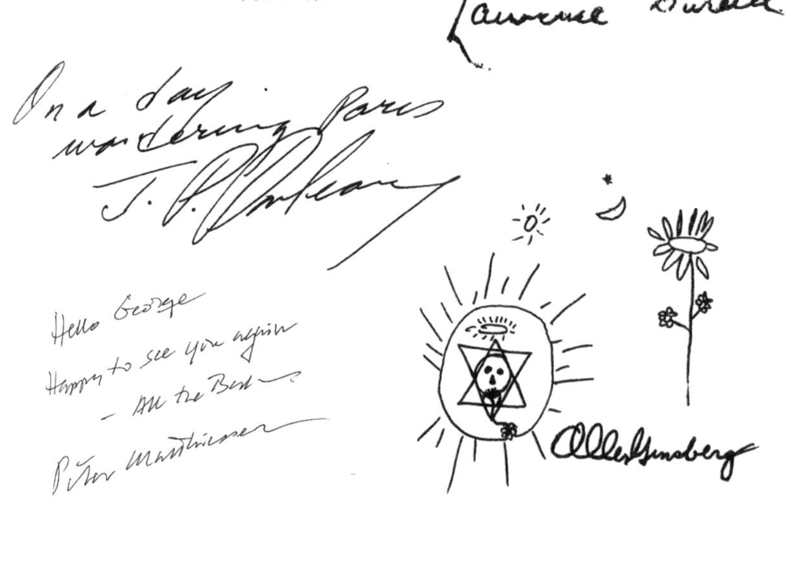

On a day wandering Paris

J. P. Donleavy

Hello George Happy to see you again — All the Best —

Peter Matthiessen

Allen Ginsberg

Inscriptions in the shop's guest books include ones from early visitors such as (clockwise from top) Julio Cortázar, Anaïs Nin, James Jones, Louis Aragon, Lawrence Durrell, David Gascoyne, Peter Matthiessen, J. P. Donleavy, Allen Ginsberg, Lawrence Ferlinghetti, and William Saroyan, as well as one from James Baldwin (opposite).

Nice to be back in
The old Curiosity Shop—
Beautiful

Jimmy Baldwin

# PARIS BOOK NEWS

Winter 1956. Published By

## THE MISTRAL BOOKSHOP

THE AMERICAN BOOKSTORE ON THE LEFT BANK
FACING NOTRE DAME. OPEN NOON TO MIDNIGHT
37 Rue de la Bucherie. Paris 5

---

A BOOKSTORE FOR BROW-
SING ON WINDY AUTUMN
EVENINGS

■ ■ ■

## BOOKS
ALWAYS IN STOBK

■ ■ ■

## ULYSSES
Old Fags & Cabbage Stumps
D. H. LAWRENCE
(Shakespeare & Co. edition bound in
leather 3 to 6,000 frs. Modern Library
edition 1100 frs)

■ ■ ■

LEAVES OF GRASS
The Author Should Be Kicked
From All Decent Society As
Below The Level Of A Brute -
BOSTON INTELLIGENCER

■ ■ ■

REMEMBRANCE OF
THINGS PAST
Ploughing A Field With Knit-
ting Needles - GEORGE MOORE

---

**WINTER BOOK SALE**
FIRST WEEK IN FEBRUARY

Tropic of Capricorn by
Henry Miller reduced from
600 to 300 frs. Dozens of similar bargains. Minimum
discount of 20 % on new
American paperbacks &
all used books

---

LENDING LIBRARY
READING ROOM
ART REPRODUCTIONS

---

| | |
|---|---|
| SAT.<br>NOV.<br>17<br>4 P.M. | Reception For **RICHARD WRIGHT**<br>BLACK PHOWER, COLOUR CURTAIN, NATIVE SON,<br>12 MILLION BLAÇK VOICES & UNCLE TOM'S<br>CHILDREN AVAILABLE FOR AUTOGRAPHING<br>EXHIBIT OF BOOKS ON AFRICA |
| SAT.<br>DEC.<br>8<br>4 P.M. | **JAMES BALDWIN** will autograph<br>Go Tell It On The Mountain & Notes Of A Native Son<br>The Mistral Girls Will Serve Light Refreshments |
| DEC.<br>24 & 25 | OPEN HOUSE CHRISTMAS EVE & CHRISTMAS DAY<br>**CAROL SINGING** |
| SUN.<br>JAN.<br>6<br>4 P.M. | MODERN FRENCH POETRY : Dialogue entre Un<br>Poete et Un Critique (Jean Breton et Henri Rode) |
| SON.<br>JAN.<br>13<br>4 P.M. | CYBERNETICS & THE ARTS<br>CHARLES HATCHER<br>Poet & Statistician |
| SUN.<br>JAN.<br>20<br>4 P.M. | THIS SEASON IN THE FRENCH THEATRE<br>GORDON KINGHAM<br>Paris Theatre Correspondant Of The London Times |
| SUN.<br>JAN.<br>27<br>4 P.M. | CONTEMPORARY BRITISH DRAMA<br>ISAAC MATALON<br>Impresario |
| EACH<br>SUN.<br>IN<br>FEB. | CYCLE OF FOLKSONGS<br>Shetland, Islands, U.S., France & Latin America |

---

## WE BUY USED ENGLISH BOOKS - LARGEST STOCK IN PARIS
### 25 % Discount On Christmas Cards - Name Printed Free

Wright was welcomed by the French literary establishment, with Jean-Paul Sartre among his champions.

Wright's supporters also included Sylvia Beach, founder of the original Shakespeare and Company on rue de l'Odéon. She would come to George's shop for Wright's book signings, as well as for those of Lawrence Durrell, another friend she and George shared. "Sylvia Beach was a very hospitable woman and, with others, I was invited to tea in her apartment," said George. "She was a unique customer. →

ANAÏS NIN
*writer*

And there by the Seine was the bookshop, not the same, but similar to others I had known. An Utrillo house, not too steady on its foundations, small windows, wrinkled shutters. And there was George Whitman, undernourished, bearded, a saint among his books, lending them, housing penniless friends upstairs, not eager to sell, in the back of the store, in a small overcrowded room, with a desk, a small gas stove. All those who come for books remain to talk, while George tries to write letters, to open his mail, order books. A tiny, unbelievable staircase, circular, leads to his bedroom, or the communal bedroom, where he expected Henry Miller and other visitors to stay. There is a toilet three floors below, and in the hall, a small stove on which he cooks for everyone.

On Sundays he made ice cream, which he felt homesick Americans needed. He had fixed the guest room, the front room, expecting all of us would stay there, books and authors offered communally to those passing by, printed words and their voices in unison. He forgot that these writers from old Paris now had wives, children, mistresses, homes in America, fame, and hotel reservations. He forgot they could not always give themselves as freely or there would be no books to give, no books written.

George could not understand why they did not stay there, by a fireplace often without wood to burn, in a room without a door. In the hallway, there is a hole in the floor with an iron grille through which one could see what was happening in the bookshop below. A spy window on the floor, and those from below, if they had looked up, could have seen George as he stood by his dusty stove baking American pies for his expatriates, who were looking for a drink.

She would buy all the books she could carry home at one time." Beach attended Wright's autographing party on November 17, 1956, where George overheard Wright telling her, "You are one of the mothers of American literature."

Lawrence Durrell's first autographing party at the bookshop was in 1957 for *Justine*, the debut volume of *The Alexandria Quartet*. It would soon become one of the most famous books of its time. "Larry liked to meet his admirers," said George, "and afterward I'd make dinner for him and a few guests. At one dinner party, a young woman recited whole poems by Durrell. He was naturally delighted. Most people think of him as a novelist, but he was proud of his poems, and he was impressed that this girl knew his poetry. He actually invited her to marry him!"

The Beats arrived in Paris in the fall of 1957. First came Gregory Corso, followed by Allen Ginsberg, Peter Orlovsky, and William Burroughs. They lived a few streets away, at 9 rue Gît-le-Cœur, in a ratty, no-name hotel renowned in bohemian circles for its cheap accommodations and sympathetic proprietor. Madame Rachou rented rooms to writers and artists, often letting them pay with artwork when they were low on cash. Anything went at the hotel, which would later be referred to as the Beat Hotel. Guests could openly have interracial or homosexual →

## Saturday Night

# BAKED BEAN SUPPER

salt pork - corn bread
pickles & rhubarb
iced tea & strawberry shortcake

We also offer a
touch of spring cleaning
to help the digestion

*Mistral*

I forgot to mention the lemon
ice cream & chocolate pudding
with whipped cream

Top: George offered dinner to his guests, often in exchange for help around the shop. Bottom: Jazz musicians perform in the bookstore. Among George's customers were Eric Dolphy, Kenny Clarke, and Archie Shepp, who played on nearby rue de la Huchette, then home to several iconic jazz clubs.

Above: Reading in the upstairs library.
Right: Richard Wright (center, in glasses) gathers with others in front of the shop.
*Photo:* RUSS MELCHER

Before the S&Co stamp,
George glued a Mistral label
onto books' front flyleaves.

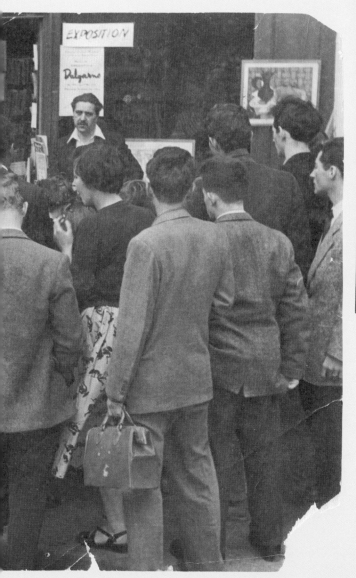

George photographed
in the bookstore.

Desmond O'Grady
*Tumbleweed*

It was August 1955. In a few days I would turn twenty years of age. Like James Joyce had, I'd left Ireland to come to live in Paris and write. A painter in Montmartre, sensing fellow artistic aspirations, directed me to the Latin Quarter on the Left Bank of the Seine.

Just after midday, reconnoitering off place St.-Michel, I chanced on an eccentric corner of the question-mark shape that is rue de la Bûcherie. To my surprise, the street right-angled an English-language bookshop. It faced on the Seine and the Île de la Cité, site of the Parisii tribe of Celts, who founded the city there in 250–200 B.C.

Inside, a rainbow of books from ceiling to floor encircled me and shimmered in the light that shone through the high, wide window. It was an all-embracing light that warmed a solitary heart becoming aware of its exile. To my right, sitting at a narrow, upright, boxlike, tiny table, a lanky man sat reading. The *propriétaire*, I presumed. He glanced up, and I asked politely if he had James Joyce's *Ulysses*. His face returned to his reading, and his right arm pointed to the shelves on my left. There before me, with gold letters on its dark green spine, stood the book that was forbidden reading in Ireland. Taking it down, I sat on the bench, which ran along the bookshelves.

"Are you Irish?" Looking up, I replied, "Yes." The *propriétaire*'s eyes were slender, his look direct as was his nose, mustached mouth, and slightly bearded chin. His accent was American: "You write?" Hesitation. "Poems," I replied. Pause. Then he said, "The store is open from midday to midnight, seven days a week. It's all poetry, with some prose like Joyce, Beckett —"

He gave me this name, one that I'd heard mentioned in Dublin but that I knew absolutely nothing about, much less had read. He said we were not sitting in a bookshop but in an open library for people who read and write. He did not sell books to penniless poets. "You can sit and read here whenever you like. My name is George Whitman."

He offered me one of his Lucky Strike cigarettes, as he sipped from a bottle of Coca-Cola. For me, these were names in American films. When I told him one couldn't get *Ulysses* in the bookshops of Ireland because it was disapproved of, he said, "Now you have it. Read it."

After that afternoon, the bookstore became the anchorage of my new life in Paris. I sat and read there every day; I met my wife there. After I had gotten to know George a little, I asked him about his name. He told me he was a descendant of Walt Whitman. I believed him.

relationships, then taboo, and they could freely engage in drugs, drinking, and late-night parties.

Corso spent a lot of time at George's bookshop. On Christmas Day, 1957, for example, he passed the afternoon reading, writing, and enjoying the holiday fare on offer: ice cream, donuts, and Scotch. Burroughs regularly attended the Sunday afternoon tea parties, though he'd complain that he had no luck meeting available young men there. Occasionally, he'd consult the library's medical section as he refined

The front window display with copies of Gregory Corso's "Bomb," 1958, a satirical love poem about the atomic bomb. *Photo:* HAROLD CHAPMAN

# "Who were all these strange ghosts rooted to the silly little adventure of earth with me?" Jack Kerouac

his work-in-progress *Naked Lunch*, which would be published in 1959 by Maurice Girodias's Paris-based Olympia Press. Ginsberg's collection *Howl and Other Poems* had been published in 1956 by Lawrence Ferlinghetti's City Lights. After the book's debut, Ferlinghetti was arrested and charged with obscenity. While a judge eventually ruled that the poems were not obscene, the well-publicized trial brought fame to Ginsberg, who'd chosen to hide out abroad rather than endure the attention back in America.

During this time, Ginsberg described Beat poetry to Art Buchwald, the *New York Herald Tribune*'s popular Paris columnist: "We're experimenting; we have a new basis of measure. We measure our lines by breath, not by beat. Give us time, and we'll take over from the priests. We have a message. People have to understand. Our mission is to make them." →

ALLEN GINSBERG
*poet*

The first impression I had was that the store was somewhat of a jumble, that there were books all over, and I couldn't figure out how to find stuff. But there was a poetry section, somewhere, and a lot of interesting old books.

On the first floor, George would cook soup in rather grimy pots. The soup smelled a little funny, but it was edible. And George gave it out freely. It was very comforting to have a point of reference where you could get books and, if you were starving, you knew you could get a place to sleep and a bowl of soup. It was really like a kind of maternal cow somehow. Even if you had enough money, there was always that place in the background where you could take refuge just in case. There were a lot of just-in-cases who did take refuge there.

George and I had a nice arrangement. If I knew any young poet who was going to pass through Paris, I would give the poet a note and send him to George. And if he was a penurious, penniless poet like Corso and I were, George would provide a place to stay.

# Gargoyles

GREGORY CORSO

    The gargoyles trumpet Paris to me
when it rains out of their mouths
    For centuries the same tremulous
petrified sepulchre cries
all into the Seine's narrow ear
    It's the way they're placed
    Outstretched gargy necks
screammouthed    haunched pensivity
blasting golden era echoes from cathedral nests
as though avenging    I imagine    speechless Quasimodos
    My ear is unlike the ear of the Seine
    In my ear more resounded unsepulchre birds
loom the sphere    the pinioned dome that is mine
this dream frontier    the brief flight    the zoomed utterance
that is mine to hear

O I don't know what to think when they sit
like spies with no clothes     with no real eyes
watching me in the rain     gushing storms like a defiance
     They too would like raincoats
or something     I don't know     yet enough to know
their image false     their purpose contagious     counterfeit
I cannot feel that demondrains benefit the houses of God
on a rainy day     forbidding or decreeing nourishment for
     the river's diet

He continued: "We've changed the course of poetry in the United States. Do you realize what that means? There's been a revolution in poetry, and we've done it. There's no equivalent to it in France. England is dead. They're in the cellar with iambic." Corso jumped in to add: "Dame Edith Sitwell told us the hope of English poetry is in America. She also gave us tea and watercress sandwiches."

Ginsberg agreed to do a public reading of "Howl" at the bookshop, accompanied by Gregory Corso and a few other poets, the afternoon of April 13, 1958. To promote the event, he and Orlovsky made flyers and pasted them all over the Latin Quarter, drawing a sizable crowd to the Sunday reading. People packed into the bookshop's ground floor and spilled out onto its esplanade. The first reader was not an unequivocal success. The "poet was reciting some uncommunicative junk, and we didn't like it," Ginsberg explained to Buchwald, who described the bookshop reading in one of his *Herald Tribune* columns. Corso continued: "I protested it wasn't real poetry. Someone asked me what I meant by real poetry. So I took off all my clothes and read my poems naked…I had two big, bearded friends of mine as bodyguards, and they

threatened they'd beat up anybody who left while I was reciting. I was a big success."

Ginsberg, who by then had also taken off his clothes, read next. While he was a bit drunk (he blamed his nerves), his "Howl" caused a sensation. Musician Ramblin' Jack Elliott then played songs and read from Jack Kerouac's *On the Road*, which had recently been released. Burroughs had initially refused to participate but, once at the event, he was lured up front by a young man, a bookshop regular, and gave what was said to be the first-ever reading from his yet-unpublished *Naked Lunch*. "Nobody was sure what to make of it, whether to laugh or be sick. It was something quite remarkable," said George. →

CLAIRE KAHANE
*resident of the Beat Hotel*

This morning Corso knocked on my door to borrow a cup of sugar. I think he was just checking me out as a potential sweetener. He's good-looking, impish, but clearly a hustler; he leers and has a rather thuggish demeanor. He did tell me that he and Ginsberg were giving a reading soon at Le Mistral, an English-language bookstore just a few blocks away. I intend to go.

Went to the poetry reading today at Le Mistral. What a scene! Many people crowded into the store. By the time I got there, I had to stand far from the center of the action, but I could see Ginsberg and Corso cavorting nude on a table at the far end of the room. After each had finished declaiming in the buff, George served fruit punch and cookies to the crowd — as if this were a church social! A bizarre conjunction.

Last night we had dinner at Le Mistral upstairs in George's private rooms. He cooked a huge stew for about ten people, and we all sat around on the floor eating and talking and listening to George's stories. The best one: George has trained his dog to go around to the various butcher shops begging for bones, which it brings back for George to cook up into his regular evening stews. The dog really brought home the bacon tonight! A delicious meal.

I entered the bookshop and was accosted by
a fierce thin man who grabbed me with strong
hands and pushed me behind the till, saying,
"Look after the shop, I'll be back in half an hour,
if anybody buys anything, write it in the book,
put the money in the till, good-bye." I sat there,
rather confused, waiting for a customer. There
was a crowd of silent readers, who stood or
sat on chairs or on the floor, but none bought
a book. About an hour or so later, the man
returned with what looked like a collection
of vegetables and said, "OK, thanks, you can
go now." That's how I met George.

The bookshop had a first floor where poetry
readings were held. I went to one by Piero
Heliczer, who had also done the cooking. Free
food for the occasion. He'd been out collecting
stinging nettles and made a soup of them that
he had, unfortunately, burned. He told me
the first person in was a tramp who was attracted
by the idea of free food, but as he was unable to
eat the badly cooked nettles, he left. The poetry
reading was chaotic, packed out by young
ladies who were squashed together. Piero was
extremely handsome.

One day while I was in the shop, George —
for no reason that I could imagine — started
to lecture me on the economics of the French
book trade and how they could do much better
if they took a much smaller markup. This
was interrupted by half-a-dozen English people
who came into the shop and rather aggressively
started reading their lists of obscure books to
George, trying to find out if he had any for sale.
A rather animated and angry sort of discussion
started up, with George accusing them of being
book dealers. He suddenly rushed to the door

and removed the handle so that nobody could
walk out, saying, "Admission is free, but you
have to pay to leave!" The crowd donated a few
centimes and departed.

Corso, Ginsberg, and Burroughs were
having a poetry reading on April 13. I lent
Ginsberg a fifteen-by-twelve-inch enlargement
of him and Orlovsky on the double-sided bench
in place St.-Germain-des-Prés to help promote
the poetry reading at the shop. A couple
of days after, I went round to collect the
photograph, which was an early favorite of mine.
As I was leaving the shop, George appeared
like a whirlwind. Rushing at me, he snatched
the photograph away and said, "I'll have that,"
and disappeared into the bowels of the
bookshop, leaving me quite bewildered. George
must have had a flash of foresight because
since then the photograph has been published
many times and has become iconic. I was
quite irritated at the time, but all is forgiven
if not forgotten.

In August of that same year, author James Jones and his wife, Gloria, moved to Paris, taking an apartment on Île de la Cité, across the Seine from the bookshop. Jones was then a literary superstar; his novel *From Here to Eternity* had won the National Book Award and been adapted into a film starring Burt Lancaster, Montgomery Clift, and Deborah Kerr. George welcomed the couple to Paris with a dinner party at the bookshop, preparing what he called *"un menu très Américain"*: oyster cocktail, army bean soup, chicken with dumplings, pumpkin, rice and curry sauce, and lemon ice cream. "Jones was the most American American, a real army sergeant," said George. "He was given to grand gestures, potent drink, and strong cursing. He was affable, absolutely, but always underneath one felt that he wanted to be back fighting in the Pacific."

Sylvia Beach attended the dinner, as did the young Joyce scholar Clive Hart (who in later years would become a founder-trustee of the James Joyce Foundation). Hart recalled: "At the party, Sylvia made a brief announcement saying that she would like to offer to George the old name of Shakespeare and Company. George was, of course, delighted." Although George didn't change the shop's name for another six years, he did display a brass plaque reading "Shakespeare and Company—Writers Guest

House," which Beach had given him, in the bookshop's front window. Next to it was placed a Shakespeare and Company original edition of *Ulysses*. Beach, George said, gave him the impression that she considered his bookstore a "spiritual successor" to her own.

The following year, in 1959, William Burroughs met a young man who would become his long-term companion, Ian Sommerville. A twenty-something mathematics student at Cambridge and a summer-term Tumbleweed, Sommerville was reading in the shop's upstairs library when a book fell from a shelf, landing on his head. It was *Naked Lunch*. A few days →

Jean Fanchette (right) edited his literary magazine, *Two Cities*, out of the shop, with support from Lawrence Durrell (left) and Anaïs Nin. The journal, which ran from 1959 to 1964, included contributions from Ted Hughes, Octavio Paz, and Henry Miller.

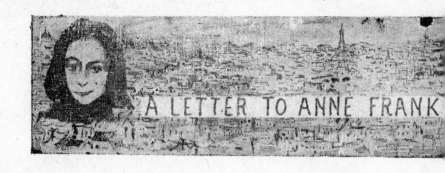

# A LETTER TO ANNE FRANK

If I sent this letter to the postoffice it would no longer reach you because you have been blotted out from the universe. So I am writting an open letter to those who have read your diary and found a little sister they have never seen who will never entirely disappear from earth as long as we who are living remember her.

You wanted to come to Paris for a year to study the history of art and if you had, perhaps you might have wandered down the quai Notre-Dame and discovered a little bookstore beside the garden of Saint-Julien-le-Pauvre. You know enough French to read the notice on the door — **Chien aimable, Prière d'entrer.** The dog is not really a dog at all but a poet called François Villon who has returned to the city he loved after many years of exile. He is sitting by the fire next to a kitten with a very unusual name. You will be pleased to know she is called Kitty after the imaginary friend to whom you wrote the letters in your journal.

Here in our bookstore it is like a family where your Chinese sisters and your brothers from all lands sit in the reading rooms and meet the Parisians or have tea with the writers from abroad who are invited to live in our Guest House.

Remember how you worried about your inconsistencies, about your two selves — the gay flirtatious superficial Anne that hid the quiet serene Anne who tried to love and understand the world. We all of us have dual natures. We all wish for peace yet in the name of self-defense we are working toward self-obliteration. We have built armaments more powerful than the total of all those used in all the wars of history. And if the militarists who dislike negotiating the minor differences that separate nations are not under wise civilian authority they have the power to write man's testament on a dead planet where radioactive cities are surrounded by jungles of dying plants and poisonous weeds.

Since a nuclear war could destroy half the world's population as well as the material basis of civilization, the Soviet General Nicolai Talensky concludes that war is no longer conceivable for the solution of political differences.

A young girl's dreams recorded in her diary from her thirteenth to her fifteenth birthday means more to us today than the labours of millions of soldiers and thousands of factories striving for a thousand-year Reich that lasted hardly more than ten years. The journal you hid so that no one would read it was left on the floor when the German police took you to the concentration camp and has now been read by millions of people in 32 languages. When most people die they disappear without a trace, their thoughts forgotten, their aspirations unknown but you have simply left your own family and become part of the family of man.

# MISTRAL BOOKSHOP

### GEORGE WHITMAN

*37 rue de la Bûcherie*                                           *Paris 5*

later, the same thing happened again, only in reverse: Sommerville was atop a ladder shelving stock when he dropped a book, which landed on the head of the man standing below him. It was William Burroughs. Within weeks, the two were lovers. Sommerville later wrote in the shop's guest book: "Sitting in the upstairs of 37 [rue de la Bûcherie] in the Summer of '59, I was literally hit on the head by a book which tumbled from on high; this was *Naked Lunch* and my pre-introduction to its author; a couple of days later I gouged my girdle of Venus on the left hand of destiny." →

Ian Sommerville, a Tumbleweed, photographed in Paris around the time he met William Burroughs. *Photo:* HAROLD CHAPMAN

George's dog François Villon, named for the poet-ruffian who lived in the *quartier* in the fifteenth century.

Pages 122–123: *Two Cities* published a piece from George addressed to Anne Frank, whose diary had been released in English in 1952.

KEN TINDALL
*Tumbleweed*

I wonder how many of the people who pass through the bookstore come to Paris to fall in love, or to enjoy an affair here. Finding love in Paris is probably an idea many of them entertain in a cranny of their hearts but, because they suspect what it might entail, they regard it as something that would compromise them. When I came to the bookstore, in 1958, I put a notice in the little cardex file hanging outside the front door. A few days later, I met a French girl at the bookstore, and we began seeing each other. Her name was Christine. For about a week, we "played at love," going places together, strolling by the Seine, and I realized that she was testing me. I'd been living a celibate existence in the west of Ireland for nearly a year, so of course I was very ardent with Christine. One afternoon we were sitting on the quay on la Cité, below the Petit Pont, and she asked me if I loved her. I said, yes, I loved her. So she asked me if I loved her enough to throw my watch into the Seine. Well, I was very poor, to say the least, and had been for a long time, but I was wearing a good watch that I had bought when

I was in the navy. So I said, no, I wouldn't throw my watch in the Seine. So she said I didn't love her enough. We both laughed. Later we went to her place. She and her sister lived in an apartment in the rue de la Harpe. When we got there, her sister was ironing a dress — *on fait le repassage*. I was already learning French. We had something to eat. Then Christine asked if she could cut my hair. It was very long, hadn't been cut in more than a year. Her question was a test. I said yes, and I sat on a kitchen chair while she gave me a haircut, the naked lovers' slow-motion playing in Agnès Varda's *L'Opéra-mouffe*. She put my hair in a little round basket and said she would keep it forever.

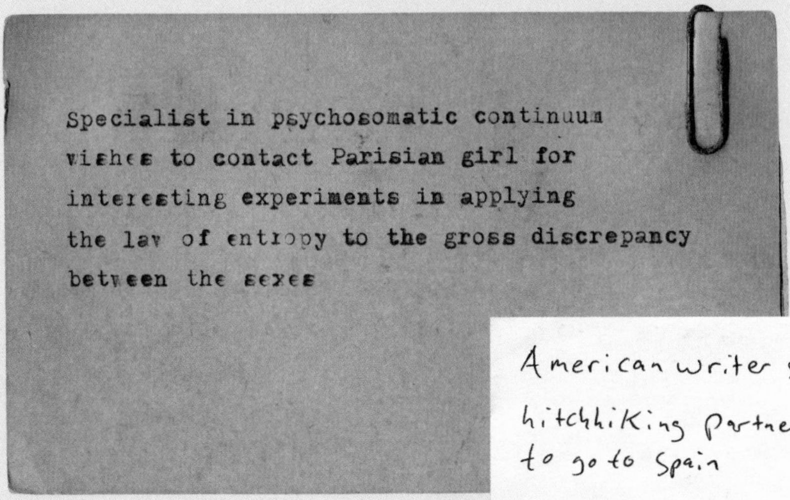

Specialist in psychosomatic continuum
wishes to contact Parisian girl for
interesting experiments in applying
the law of entropy to the gross discrepancy
between the sexes

Messages posted on the shop's bulletin board — according to newspaper accounts — which have been replicated for this book.

American writer seeks girl
hitchhiking partner
to go to Spain

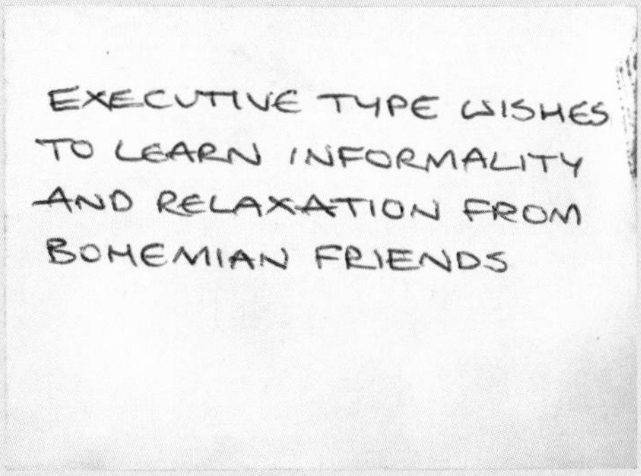

EXECUTIVE TYPE WISHES
TO LEARN INFORMALITY
AND RELAXATION FROM
BOHEMIAN FRIENDS

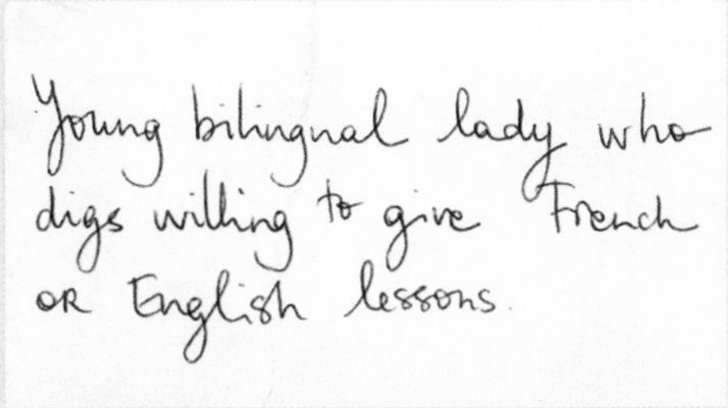

Young bilingual lady who
digs willing to give French
or English lessons.

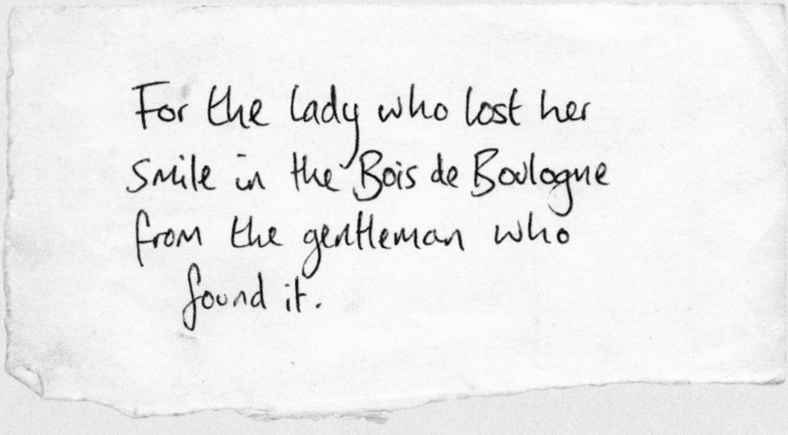

For the lady who lost her
smile in the Bois de Boulogne
from the gentleman who
found it.

127

The decade's final surprise landed in an airplane from the United States. It was Henry Miller come back to visit Paris. His old friend Lawrence Durrell brought him by the bookshop. "It was about two o'clock in the morning. Durrell had been wandering the streets of Paris, celebrating the return of Henry Miller," said George. "He and Miller came to the shop, awakening our guests to listen to their inimitable conversation while sharing a bottle of wine." It was then that Miller called the shop "a wonderland of books," a description that delighted George for the rest of his life.

Below: George drinks tea with a bookstore visitor. Opposite: A photo of Henry Miller once decorated the shop.

I SOMETIMES FEEL SURROUNDED BY INSECTS
MASQUERADING AS MEN FOR SOME DIABOLI-
CAL PURPOSE

*Henry Miller*

The future chairman of Foyles bookshop, Christopher Foyle, was among those who hung out and helped around the bookstore.

# the
# 1960s

The bookstore was bursting. George's once small stock had grown into twenty thousand books, filling every nook and surface of the shop, towering in precarious stacks that threatened to crash down at any moment. There were new titles from Ray Bradbury, Mary McCarthy, Italo Calvino, Iris Murdoch, J. D. Salinger, Vladimir Nabokov, and Jack Kerouac, in company with first editions by Virginia Woolf, Ernest Hemingway, Gertrude Stein, Katherine Anne Porter, Nathanael West, and Willa Cather. There were books in English, French, Russian, Spanish, German, and Italian; along with sections for poetry, fiction, travel, psychology, history, and children's literature.

To accommodate his expanding book collection, in 1960, George purchased the little gallery space next door to the shop. The windowless succession of rooms comprised what is now the left side of the bookstore's ground floor, including the area under the skylight. George wrote to a friend: "I want to open a tearoom with symphonic recordings in the afternoons and guitars in the evening, a fountain of mercury like a cascade of jewels, and, in a small pool, two baby seals. The shop will still be modest and uncommercial, but it will be the most unusual bookstore anywhere on earth."

Alas, George was unable to procure a mercury fountain or the baby seals. He did, however, build a

pyrotechnic wishing well. A young traveler, Daniel Pierre McClenaghan, helped George dig a hole in the floor to access the Renaissance-era water well below. McClenaghan explained: "The wishing well was originally designed to have a perpetual flame burning on the surface of the water. We ran in gas with a Calor cylinder, but the incomplete combustion — caused →

A gathering around a wishing-well fire.

Opposite: George shows off his customized wishing well. The surrounding stone tiles have long been rumored to be pieces of broken gravestones from the Montparnasse Cemetery.

KATHLEEN SPIVACK
*Tumbleweed*

George gave us space to live and to write. He cooked us pancake breakfasts, let us read his precious books, quizzed us on them, and in every way nurtured us strays. On Sunday afternoons, he served tea. Afterward, he'd dry the chipped dishes with pieces of torn newspaper, which later he'd uncrumple to use as toilet paper. Guests had to crawl over a pitted bathtub to get to the so-called toilet, and then the door didn't close. It was really exotic. The Tumbleweeds were "writers," in George's exalted view, and we tried to live the part for him, as well as for ourselves. One condition of staying in the bookshop was to help out in the store. It was chock-full of books, crammed together, filled with treasures. The travel section is still one of the best I've ever seen in any bookstore anywhere. The Tumbleweeds tried to help as much as we could, but we couldn't keep up with George. He worked hard — though he had a rather random way of keeping track of things, whether it was shelving titles or doing the accounting. He hid sums of money in books and then, of course, forgot where he'd put them. Customers were quite astonished when they walked out with some old two-pence book, opened it, and found — surprise — a bundle!

by the bad design of this inherently bad idea — filled the air with huge oily smuts within seconds." The smuts didn't discourage George; he simply tried another technique, placing a basin in the well, filling it with water, and squirting gasoline on top. He then took a flaming torch to the well, igniting a brilliant blaze, in hopes of thrilling customers (which was unfortunate for the fashion model who ended up with her hair burned off).

At the same time, George also renovated the first-floor library. The front room, with its magnificent view of Notre-Dame, was laid with red wall-to-wall carpeting and dubbed the Writers' Guest House. While still a public reading room by day, it was to be a private accommodation for distinguished authors come night. To inaugurate the Guest House and to advertise the expanded ground floor, George hosted a series of literary events. On May 7, 1960, Lawrence Durrell signed his recently released *Clea*. James Jones read on May 14, and, on May 21, Gregory Corso signed his latest poetry collection, *The Happy Birthday of Death*. "I think it is a pleasant tradition in Paris that makes bookstores places where people occasionally meet writers in person, as well as through the medium of the printed page," George wrote Nelson Algren, the American novelist and the former lover of Simone de Beauvoir. In the early 1950s, the then-couple had lived down the street at 11 rue de la Bûcherie.

That September, in 1960, the American military newspaper *Stars and Stripes* published an article about the bookshop. While George was pleased by the flattering profile, he wondered if there might be a larger →

The bookstore's facade set amid several famous Paris landmarks. *Illustration:* D. R. MULLIGAN

Lynn Haney Trowbridge
*Tumbleweed*

I worked as an assistant *vendeuse* for Christian Dior on Avenue Montaigne. It paid paltry wages, but the social life was terrific. While my French employers were inclined to be sympathetic to any kind of sexual indiscretion, they would have been horrified to learn that I'd mismanaged my money. Asking for a raise was out of the question, so — on a bone-chilling winter evening — I made my way to the bookstore and asked George if I could move in.

Though I frequented the place, it was the first time George had seen me in my Dior working outfit. He loved it: the elegant black dress, the shiny white pearls, and polished sling-back shoes. As it happened, he needed someone to step in and motivate guests into actually performing their chores. Showing me to my cubbyhole in the children's section, George proclaimed to anyone in earshot, "Lynn's an organizer. She's going to put this place in shape." I'd been called many things, usually along the lines of "blithe spirit," "adventure prone," and "scatterbrained," but never had anyone before even hinted that I might be an "organizer."

One night a young woman with Goldilocks ringlets and performing ambitions was standing over the stove on the first floor. Stirring a giant pot of clam chowder and fortifying herself with red wine, she sang Edith Piaf's "La Vie en Rose" in fractured French. Lifting the cauldron off the stove, she stumbled, and the steaming clam chowder poured down through a square hole on the floor. (The opening was used to lower a dumbwaiter, often full of tea, to the bookstore below.) The chowder landed on an American socialite wearing an ermine coat. The woman was not amused. Of course,

George handled it with aplomb. Producing a soiled dishrag, he swatted the clams off the fur and offered her one of his famous brownies.

Despite my pep talks, the habitués of the bookstore showed little interest in the art of housekeeping. One morning I got so fed up that I dropped to my knees and scrubbed the floor. Then I scrambled to get ready for work, shimmying into a Playtex Living Girdle and putting on nylons, dress, and coat. At Christian Dior, I was waiting on a countess when — suddenly — my boss let out a loud gasp. She pointed to my knees. They were pitch black from the dirt on George's floor. Without a word of explanation, I washed them off, sprayed myself with Miss Dior Eau de Parfum, and got on with the day.

Walking along the river Seine not far from the bookshop. *Photo:* HAROLD CHAPMAN

significance to it and other recent press attention. In the 1950s, the U.S. had launched a covert campaign to encourage American-style democracy and capitalism in other countries by engaging in a "cultural cold war" with the Soviet Union. The initial target was the hearts and minds of Western European artists and intellectuals who often held Marxist and communist-leaning views. Channeling money from the Central Intelligence Agency (CIA), the U.S. secretly financed artists and arts institutions, promoting American music, film, and literary endeavors abroad.

In Paris, during these paranoid days of Cold War politics, practically every American was suspected of being either a CIA agent or the target of CIA surveillance. *The Paris Review*, for example, was long rumored to have CIA connections, which turned out to be somewhat true. Decades later, cofounder Peter Matthiessen admitted that he'd helped establish the magazine as a personal cover for his own CIA involvement but, he said, the journal itself hadn't engaged in any activity. Some people suspected George of being CIA. In fact, he wasn't connected to the agency, nor did the bookshop receive funding, direct or indirect. What George and the shop did get from the CIA, according to George, was unwanted attention.

In December 1960, George began writing Cyrus S. Eaton about his suspicions. Eaton was a successful businessman-cum-philanthropist, known for championing world peace and for his criticism of the U.S.'s Cold War policy. George wrote to Eaton:

"Since on the one hand, the bookstore maintains a free lending library and promotes the sale of books in English and, on the other hand, is about the only American institution in Paris that opposes the Cold War, we have experienced alternately encouragement and harassment from various official agencies. We've been visited by patrician professional agents at the top of the CIA, posing as the president of a firm of New York underwriters or as an Australian millionaire (going home by the Trans-Siberian), and by lower-ranking spies being transported from Jakarta, Hong Kong, or Singapore to other world capitals…

Opposite: George's friend Colette Pillon (left) founded Mademoiselle de Paris out of the bookstore in 1963. For the next ten years, her business offered tours of the city.

**Mademoiselle de Paris**

invites you to

**LEARN FRENCH**

**SEE PARIS**
the French way with
Parisiennes

COME IN AND CHECK OUR BULLETIN
BOARD FOR OTHER ACTIVITIES

If you like you can sit outside at the round table thumbing through books.

Whitman enjoys a game of chess outside the shop.

S&S Photos by **MERLE HUNTER**

The towers of Notre Dame are reflected at upper left in the window.

Author Jean Fanchette uses Le Mistral as an office.

There are 20,000 volumes the crowded sh

This summer the atmosphere of the bookstore was being poisoned by daily visits by a dozen spies, so I went to the liberal weekly *L'Express* and asked to consult their legal service for subscribers. I never did get to see a lawyer, but the next week *L'Express* published a short article about our 'Refuge for Writers.' The Americans mulled over this development, and the cultural agencies that want to support the bookstore seemed to overrule the repressive influences. They initiated a publicity campaign with pictures of the bookstore in the Sunday papers and a two-page spread in *Stars and Stripes*, and soon I was being interviewed by journalists from all over the world… Though the bookstore has been under surveillance ever since its opening, I never realized how saturated it was with agents until I explored the idea of publishing a magazine here. They began offering copy, posing their candidacy for the editorial board, attempting to gain my confidence and foretell or modify the magazine's editorial policy…As well, there have been very minor but unpleasant incidents to remind me of my isolation as a foreigner, [barely] tolerated by the authorities and subjected to constant pressure to eliminate controversial books."

In the spring of 1964, in the midst of growing tensions — both political and, more generally, between the younger, liberal generation and the

Opposite: A page with photographs by Merle Hunter from the 1960 *Stars and Stripes* article about the shop.

145

older, conservative one — the shop closed briefly for renovations. When it reopened, it was under the name Shakespeare and Company. Sylvia Beach had passed away in 1962, so she wasn't there to witness the event. George had wanted to wait until April 1964, the four hundredth anniversary of William Shakespeare's birth, to rechristen the bookstore. *The New York Times* reported: "New Shakespeare and Company Will Be Doing Business in Paris… Miss Beach was a frequent browser and occasional customer at Mr. Whitman's store situated, as was hers, in the Latin Quarter. Mr. Whitman, a Bostonian with a goatee, believes in Miss Beach's idea of the 'literary bookshop,' a place where writers meet." In her honor, George named the first floor the Sylvia Beach Memorial Library, where, as the *Times* noted, "by informal arrangement almost anyone can take out almost any book for almost any length of time."

Above the bookstore's front door, the words "Librairie le Mistral" were painted out. George had commissioned two young women with making a Shakespeare and Company sign, and they'd told him that he would receive it the same month, April 1964. It didn't arrive until November 1967. Explaining the three-year gap, during which the shop had no outdoor signage, one of the women wrote: "Apologies for the delay — I had to do the banner in between

Opposite: After French *Marie-Claire* published photos of the shop, including this one, George arrived in the morning to find several people waiting to be let in, each holding a copy of the magazine. *Photo:* JEAN-PHILIPPE CHARBONNIER

urgent happenings." The term "happening" was used to describe places where people gathered, particularly for events with performance art at their centers and often with a political element, as well. The counterculture movement was growing worldwide, spurred by protest to the American war in Vietnam, civil rights, →

*Ils sont arrivés de Boston ou de Copenhague, assoiffés d'indépendance et d'horizons nouveaux. Ils repartiront demain sac au dos.*

ROBERT STONE
*Tumbleweed*

In July of '64, along with several thousand other American tourists, my wife, Janice, and I arrived in Paris at the Gare du Nord train station. Our college friend Michael Horowitz was beginning his career as a dealer in rare books and had a job at Shakespeare and Company. George Whitman had recently changed the name of his establishment, quite appropriately as he was carrying on Sylvia Beach's traditions, providing a hangout, sometime hostel, and lending library for anglophone writers and students of literature in English. Through Michael, Janice and I were able to take up George's offer of a bed on the shop's upper floor after its midnight closing time.

The neighborhood was a raw, heavily immigrant part of town where Arab music could be heard far into the night in narrow courts. The appearance and feel of the streets back from the river was still a touch medieval, the rooftops inclining to meet over the cobblestones in a manner to intimidate and beguile the imagination. This I suppose would have been the Paris of Godard's *Breathless*, whose ultra-American ingenue-temptress, played by Jean Seberg, lived at the Hotel Californie and sold *Herald Tribunes* on the street. It was also a quarter that for the denizens of Shakespeare and Company was presided over by the genius of Samuel Beckett, who lived not far away in Montparnasse.

Opposing Algerian factions were still actively planting bombs on their fellow countrymen. Charles de Gaulle had instituted the Fifth Republic, ruling in the name of order, and the gendarmes, their capes weighted with coshes like the flippers of homicidal penguins, turned out regularly to brawl with the students who turned out regularly to protest whatever you had got. One day an American poet friend turned up at the bookstore shaken. He had just rescued his small daughter from in front of a police charge outside the Luxembourg Garden, where she had been licking an ice-cream cone, oblivious of the oncoming juggernaut of law enforcement bearing down on her like the Wrath of God Express.

In the store, we browsed and chatted, waiting for closing time so we could go upstairs and claim our assigned sleeping spaces among the shelves. This could on occasion assume some aspects of a lottery if George, carried away by hospitality, had welcomed one or two more indigent scriveners than there were beds. At least once, Michael found that the *patron* had taken pity on a homeless street dweller and assigned his space to the clochard.

On certain nights, we would buy some kif from the Algerian hustlers in the backstreets and then, in the hours after midnight, tune in Radio Luxembourg. Across the river, visible through the enormous first-story window, was Notre-Dame. The cathedral's towers, spires, and buttresses were deliriously floodlit, and we would feast our eyes on the beauty of the place, sipping wine, tripping on fond absurdities, and generally rejoicing in the good fortune that had placed us so wonderfully at the center of our childhood dreams. Life sometimes can be subsumed in magic, although the supply is not inexhaustible. One time it touched us was during that summer in Paris. A little of that shimmer will always flicker in our hearts.

sexual liberation, and an increasing distrust of Soviet-style communism, which no longer seemed a desirable alternative to capitalism.

In early 1966, the French government began closely examining the bookstore's legal documents. George had never received a foreign businessman's license, which would have been required for him, an American, to be the sole owner of the bookshop. Instead, George had profited from a provision that allowed for foreign ownership provided the business had French shareholders, as well as a French managing director, called a *gérant*. At a court hearing, George presented government officials with paperwork and testimony demonstrating that a French friend of his was the bookstore's *gérant* and that two others were shareholders. The authorities were not persuaded. In spring 1966, the bookshop was closed for business by order of the Préfecture de Police.

It was never known why officials had just then taken an interest in George's bookstore, after its fifteen years in business. Some people assumed it was CIA influence — perhaps the agency was trying to stifle George's anti-Cold War politics, as well as undermine the American draft evaders and war protestors who frequented the bookshop. Others thought the French authorities were taking advantage of an administrative technicality in order to help drive →

Pages 150–151: A 1966 article from the *International Herald Tribune* mockingly describes the French police's attempt to keep beatniks out of the country.

# French Police Push Drive to Purge Beatniks

### By Edward Hotaling

PARIS, June 16.—As hundreds of haircuts testify, the police effort to purge the "beatnik" influence from France has been a brilliant flop.

But what the police themselves have called "Operation Antibeatnik" has helped to dramatize France's version of the worldwide youth boom. The boom, as anyone at Unesco will explain, is a matter of statistics.

Some 18 million of France's 49 million natives now are under 24. Only a fraction have gone beat, but few of the city teen-agers are uninfluenced by the cult.

As guardians of the older, adult order, the police are natural antagonists of the beatniks, and this has now been made remarkably clear in a masterpiece of police literature.

The work consists of two articles in "Liaisons," the weekly public-relations bulletin founded several months ago to improve the public image of the police. The articles explain the antibeatnik campaign launched by the Ministry of Interior and the Paris police in April.

The campaign consists mainly of turning away unheeled and unkempt young foreigners at the frontiers and arresting visiting or resident beats in Paris for identity checks and either expulsion or a

Dalmas.

STRANGE LANDSCAPE—Beatniks, such as these, have been unhappy about the treatment they're getting from Parisian police. The Préfecture has explained that long hair and carrying a guitar does not necessarily make a person offensive, but...

noted in the heart of American youth.

"We do not want to judge this malaise, neither in its origins nor

eign tourists," the article says of Frenchmen running around with "one long hair.

the plans for the roundup, "one long hair.

could not dream of including the 'classic' streets of which la Hu-

In the meantime, some of the questions posed by the later-day

## Policeman's Philosophy

In an off-hand literary and philosophical style that might well please prefect and author Maurice Papon, if he did not write them himself, the articles reveal the tendency of the police to form their own opinions about public behavior and act accordingly.

Although "neither a particular style of hair, nor the act of carrying a guitar are illicit," the first article says, "one has often noted that young people with long hair and carriers of this instrument of music, are, more than music-lovers or heralds of capillary exuberance, stripped of resources. They must therefore be considered as vagabonds, since they do not manifest an intention to work.'

A 15-line history of the West Coast beat movement follows, with reference to Allen Ginsberg, Charles Olson, Jack Kerouac and William Burroughs.

They "expressed the desire to acceed to the supreme beatitude by different means—alcohol, drugs, sex (sic), mysticism, etc."

Possibly untouched by their published poetry and novels, the writer goes on: "They stood up against the idea of all effort, pretended to be poets without writing poems, and they did not dream at all of translating their sentiments or their ideas into novels."

### American Malaise

The movement was "tied to the malaise that several observers have

American society, an 'industrial society'... and we cannot therefore eliminate the hypothesis of a malaise of the same order in our society.'

But then the police scribe remembers the Paris existentialist experience. His reply, without calling it a malaise, might embarrass a few French policemen: "... among those who pretended to be 'existentialists' and haunted a given quarter with literary pretentions, how many had read 'l'Etre et le Néant'...?'

The second article, which appeared this week, was called: "For the Cleanliness of the Streets: Two Operations of Salubrity."

The two operations were the rounding up of 95 prostitutes from the Rue Saint-Denis, which it found picturesque, and of 86 beatniks—47 Frenchmen and 39 foreigners—whom it did not find picturesque.

### Are they Picturesque?

The question of whether beatniks are picturesque has yet to be solved. The country's leading photo magazine, "Paris Match," concedes. "For the tourists who haunt the Latin Quarter, the beatniks are a windfall: they constitute a sought-after attraction."

The police find them "an undesirable spectacle," but either feel that the tourists disagree or that a police roundup is also an undesirable spectacle.

ed at certain banks of the Seine and the Square du Vert-Galant. Moreover, the weather was nice, and if one wants to find lizards, he has to go into the sun.'

The police found 90 "lizards," but four were not beatniks. Among many references to fingernails, "Liaisons" cited an American girl, a 22-year-old student, who had clean ones—fairly sure proof that she was a nonbeatnik.

"Then what are you doing here?" asked the police.

The girl burst into laughter. "I don't know anything about it. I was with three friends. The weather was nice, we were in the sun and we were reading. Look!" "From her handbag," the police report read, "she took out a book, on one of the most obscure poets of today."

### Critical Problem

The problem of telling beatniks from nonbeatniks is critical. But a more difficult one may be that, as the earlier article stated, "this degradation is today much more spectacular, it affects a much more considerable number of individuals, because of the diffusion modern means give to a book, a film, a mode."

The speeds fads now travel at had the police defeated before they started. They have since run into a real problem—drug trafficking and some cases of LSD among youth—and are likely to give more attention to this than to the hundreds of non-drug-taking young

fore them—are now being asked by a great number of students and workers. Most happen to cut their hair, but it is suspected some play guitars.

Concerned, "Paris-Match," is now conducting one of its "great inquiries," based on the question: "Youth from 16 to 20 Years Old: Who Are You?"

Its preliminary polls produced the shocking conclusions that most French youth today enjoy having money but not as an end in life; they are increasingly interested in an educationally rewarding job rather than a better-paying one; they find patriotism old-hat but are deeply concerned with international problems; they are generally for premarital sex but marital fidelity; and they believe —being French—happiness is love.

Considering the population boom, the influence of the young on commerce and their potential influence on French politics, the most telling answer to questioning adults may have been that of a girl named Elizabeth.

Her reply: "Who are You?"

## Professor of Morals

LONDON, June 16 (Reuters).— Britain's first professor of morals, the Rev. Gordon Dunstan, 49, has been appointed at London University. He will take up the Church of England-sponsored post in January and carry out research into homosexuality, abortion, suicide, artificial insemination, sterilization, marriage and divorce.

ICI C'EST UNE RESIDENCE PRIVÉE
IL N'Y A RIEN A ACHETER, RIEN
A VENDRE. MAIS SI VOUS ETES
BIBLIOPHILE FAITES COMME
CHEZ VOUS

**SHAKESPEARE AND COMPANY**

The Free University of Paris          37 rue de la Bûcherie Paris 5

**To Those Who Cherish Freedom, Practice Equality
And Seek Justice — WELCOME**

We wish our guests to enter with the feeling they have inherited a
booklined apartment on the Seine which is all the more delightful
because they share it with others

Reading Rooms and Lending Library. Writers Guest House (Free Accommodations
limited to 7 persons). Poetry Readings And other Events.

A PRIVATE LIBRARY OPEN BY INVITATION TO THE PUBLIC

Top: A sign written by George for the shop's front window: "This is a private residence. There is nothing to buy, nothing to sell. But if you are a bibliophile, make yourself at home." Bottom: A flyer from the years when the shop was prohibited from selling books.

out the beatnik types whom George encouraged and occasionally housed. Recently, the Paris police had begun trying to expel long-haired, guitar-toting youths from the city in a campaign called "Operation Anti-Beatnik." Or maybe the reason for the shop's closing was more prosaic; maybe the slow-moving wheels of French bureaucracy had simply caught up with the shop's license.

Although George was barred from selling books, he kept the space open as the "Free University of Paris: A Private Library Open by Invitation to the Public," and he continued to host literary readings and discussions. There were anti-war meetings, Marxist study groups, women's collectives, and more. Jazz poet Ted Joans — who'd been coming to the shop since the 1950s — brought his mentor, Langston Hughes. The two men read poetry, and Joans played beats on his trumpet. The Black Power–activist Stokely Carmichael came by the shop, as did writer Alba de Céspedes, who in the 1930s had been jailed in Italy for her anti-fascist activities. A shop regular was Michel Mendès-France, son of the country's former prime minister who, in 1954, had withdrawn the French military from Vietnam. Other visitors included American poets Anne Waldman and Elizabeth Bartlett; the Moroccan writers Mohammed Khaïr-Eddine and Abdellatif Laâbi (the latter had been tortured and imprisoned for eight years for "crimes of opinion" in Morocco); the blacklisted screenwriter Paul Jarrico; American anti-war leaders Carl Oglesby and Thorne Dreyer; eminent Joyce scholar Stuart Gilbert; the artists Jean-Jacques Lebel and Yoko Ono; and Allen Ginsberg, who was back in Paris and staying at the bookshop. Interviewed by the *International Herald Tribune*, Ginsberg brought attention to George's plight, saying, "He's a saint, lives on nothing, gives shelter to everybody. Helps young poets, too, but he's very poor. Someone should do something for him. His only income came from books."

French authorities didn't outright prohibit George from housing Tumbleweeds, but they made it exceedingly inconvenient. George was now required to register his guests in the same manner that hotels did. Each Tumbleweed had to complete an official *déclaration d'hébergement d'étranger* (a foreign-lodger form), which required the guest's name, address, date of birth, and passport number, as well as the dates of arrival and departure. Unlike the hotels, however,

Shakespeare and Company

## FREE UNIVERSITY OF PARIS

**Monday — May 15**
4 PM The War in Vietnam — 'PACS'
8 PM Poetry Reading — Black Power

**Wednesday — May 17**
8 PM Reunion des Poets Francais
de la revue *Poesie Vivante*

**Thursday — May 18**
4 PM The War in Vietnam — PACS
8 PM Cultura y Sociologia en Hispanaamerica
Grupo de la Revista Morgen

**Friday — May 19**
6 PM Exposition of paintings by
Annie Faivre and Yves Paoli
(presented by Jean Fanchette of The Review
"Two Cities")
**Saturday — May 20**
8 PM Seance de Poesie
Steven Goldstein
Skander Daoud

Opposite: Langston Hughes reciting his poetry, accompanied by Ted Joans on trumpet.

A weekly event schedule from 1967.

George wasn't able to submit the forms in batches to the nearest Préfecture. Instead, the authorities required he deliver the forms daily to a station located across the city.

If the officials had hoped to dispirit George, they failed. He bought a Mobylette and, rather uncharacteristically, abided by the new rules. In addition, for his own records, George began attaching "observations" about his guests. One girl, he noted, "likes the rain and the night and French contemporary poetry."

George pursued every avenue toward receiving his *carte de commerçant étranger*, which would allow him to reopen the bookstore. He wrote French president Charles de Gaulle (whose secretary sent a bland reply, with regrets), and he circulated a petition to André Malraux, the celebrated French novelist and the country's minister of culture. His open letter to Malraux, which accompanied the appeal, read:

"Since the deaths of Adrienne Monnier and Sylvia Beach, the type of bookstore that welcomes young writers and book-lovers, that acts as a meeting place, risks disappearing. At Shakespeare and Company, I humbly try to maintain this tradition, one which once helped to contribute to Paris's charms...I don't like to defend the little utopia I'm trying to create here to bureaucrats, who are by their nature pragmatic and conservative. But in remembering some of your

NOM:         Robert
PASSEPORT:   Anglais
NE:   28-7-67
PROFESSION:   poete et pi
DOMICILE:
        Sparkhill Bir
ARRIVE:   23-8-66
DEPART:   31-8-66

Il a publiee des nouvelles
et des poesies dans plusieurs
revues anglaises.  Il suit
des cours d'anglais et de
sociologie a l'universite de
Birmingham.

NOM:         Stephen
PASSEPORT:   Americain
NE:   27-7-67
PROFESSION:   etudiant
DOMICILE:
        New York, N. Y. USA
ARRIVE:   23-8-66
DEPART:   24-8-66

Sa soeur fait des films d'
avant garde qui traitent de
rythmes et de couleurs. Etu-
die à l'université de Buffalo.

NOM:         Caroline
PASSEPORT: Anglais
NEE:   4-3-41
PROFESSION:   professeur d'art
DOMICILE:
        London 8 E
ARRIVEE:   23-8-66
DEPART:   25-8-66

Elle a ete envoyee par Jim
Haynes, libraire, ecrivain
et directeur de Theatre a
Edinbourg. Ecrit des poemes.

NOM:         Robert
PASSEPORT:   Anglais
NE:   26-11-39
PROFESSION:   technicien de films
DOMICILE:
        London
ARRIVEE:   23-8-66
DEPART:   25-8-66

Technicien du fil

NOM:         Marie
PASSEPORT: C I HI
NEE:   15 Juin 1948
PROFESSION:   etudiante aux Beaux Arts
DOMICILE:  Montlignon (Val d'oise)
ARRIVEE:   25-8-66
DEPART:   31-8-66

        OBSERVATION
    Jeune Fille enthousiaste qui
    se lance dans la peinture;
    vend deja avec succes ses
    premiers dessins. Projette
    de faire le tour du monde
    en auto-stop.

NOM: MARGARET
PASSEPORT: Canadian
NEE: 10-1-40
PROFESSION: infermiere pediatrique
DOMICILE:
            Toronto, Ontario, Canada
PERE: Engineer
ARRIVE: 8-11-66

Elle a prit une année sab-
batique pour connaitre le
monde. C'est une refugiée
du déluge de Florence de la
1er semaine de Novembre, '66.

---

NOM: MARY                    5029
PASSEPORT: Canada
NEE: 12-11-38
PROFESSION: dietian. Assistante
            sociale a Toronto
DOMICILE: Claytonville, P.O. Prince
          Albert, Saskatchewan, Can.
PERE: W. J. Spademan
ARRIVEE: 9-11-66
DEPART:

Elle part le tour du monde
pour elargir sa culture ge-
nerale. Avec Mlle. Gray
elle a survéiu du deluge de
Florence.

---

5029

NOM : JANEY Irene
Passeport :
Nee : Le 10-11-46
Profession : Professeur
Pere : Inconnu
Domicile :
        : Detroit.
Arrivee : le 20-11-66

Aime la pluie et la nuit
aimsi que la litterature
française contemporaine.

( A détacher et à remettre au déclarant )

laration faite le : 2 Aout

HLTMAN

37 Buch

nger : SUGARMAN

1.8.66

Le Commissaire de Police,

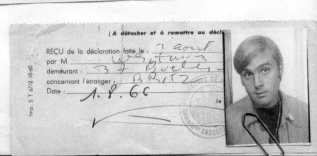

( A détacher et à remettre au décl

REÇU de la déclaration faite le : 2 aout
par M
demeurant : 37 Buch
concernant l'étranger : BRITZ
Date : 1.8.66

Imp. S T 6/2 10-60

confreres — French writers, such as Claude Seignolle, who so loved our atmosphere that they gifted to us their complete works — I believe I can say to you, a book-lover, certain things that would carry little weight with a civil servant at the Préfecture. In my mind, I am less a businessman than someone who demonstrates friendship through books…Karl Marx wrote 'live for humanity,'° and this idea imparts the spirit of the bookshop, along with Pascal's '*quelle chimère est-ce donc que l'homme*' (what a chimera then is man), and Blake's 'everything possible to be believed is an image of truth.' I could have dedicated my life to being a campaigner in a political party, or writing a novel, or living for one great love; instead I gave myself to serving the community…The tides of humanity that arrive each day in our bookstore enchant me when I see them in communion with Spinoza and Tolstoy and Rabindranath Tagore… The family inheritance that allowed me to open a bookstore has, in a way, been passed on to others. And so I find this business with the Préfecture a poor repayment, as they're trying to snatch away some-thing that I only wanted to give to Paris."

While awaiting a reply, and with the bookshop unable to sell books, George finally had time enough to realize his dream of publishing a literary magazine. In 1967, the English critic Cyril Connolly had come →

° This quote can be found in Leo Tolstoy's book
*The Kingdom of God Is Within You*; we were
not able to locate it in Marx's writing. —Ed.

"You think your pain
and your heartbreak are
unprecedented in
the history of the world,
but then you read.
It was books that taught
me that the things
that tormented me most
were the very things
that connected me
with all the people who
were alive, or who had
ever been alive."

JAMES BALDWIN

INGRID BENGIS
*Tumbleweed*

It was June 1967. I was twenty-three and had just arrived in Paris from Israel, where I'd spent a year on a kibbutz, picking bananas and working on a fishing boat. I didn't expect to stay in the city for more than a few days — but then I discovered Shakespeare and Company, a popular place filled with young Americans, many of whom were activists against the Vietnam War. Discussions were always going on upstairs about how to stop the war, the best ways to resist, whether it was better to go to jail or to Canada. I spent my time talking, reading, feeling grateful for not having to buy books, sleeping, sweeping the floors, and taking care of the laundry (which was abundant).

My parents had lived in Paris during the thirties, and my uncle had been an orchestra leader at La Coupole, a brasserie frequented by Josephine Baker and Man Ray. But then the Nazis marched into Paris, and my parents fled, eventually landing in America, where I was born. All of this was coming together in my mind while I was living in the shop. I wrote constantly, insatiably — poetry, short stories, a journal that I worked on for several hours a day — typing out drafts on my portable Olivetti, which I had carried with me all the way to and from Israel. I wrote so much that I started to feel a little giddy. I wanted to have the kind of life I was reading about in *A Moveable Feast*, and I thought I was starting to have it. Then, suddenly, everything changed.

News came over the radio that war had broken out in Israel. The kibbutz I'd lived in was on the border, at the foot of the Golan Heights. All of my friends — were they dead or alive? How could I be in Paris having a good time while they might be dying? I was desperate for information and consumed with guilt. I didn't care anymore about living like Hemingway. I just wanted to be in Israel, doing something useful and important, saving lives. But Israel wasn't interested in volunteers like me, people who would simply arrive and then have to be taken care of by the government — civilians wandering around the country in the middle of a war. It didn't matter that I had just come from there. I should have stayed …

I didn't know what to do with my frustration, so I sat down and wrote about it, and I gave what I'd written to George. He decided to include it in his *Paris Magazine*. That was the first thing I ever published. It gave me the sense that maybe I really could be a writer.

to the bookstore with Panna Grady, a legendary New York socialite. She was known for mixing her wealthy uptown world with bohemian writers — like Burroughs and the Beats — along with Lower East Side artists, including Andy Warhol and his Factory cohorts. Grady, presently living in France and married to the writer Philip O'Connor, offered to fund George's publication. *The Paris Magazine* (or, as George referred to it, "the Poor Man's *Paris Review*") debuted in October 1967. It included an article by Jean-Paul Sartre critical of the American war in Vietnam, poetry from Pablo Neruda and Allen Ginsberg, and an interview with Marguerite Duras. George wrote of his publishing endeavor: "If we can achieve a little humor and explore the universe together, this magazine may be an adventure even though we are not as creative as the avant-garde reviews. Unlike the big anonymous publications, we can at least go back to the days of personal journalism when a poet, carpenter, bookseller, printer, and journalist like Walt Whitman would publish manifestos or set the type for his own book of poems."

In May 1968, the force and passion of France's youth movement erupted onto the streets of Paris. French students had been radicalized by the wars in Algeria and Vietnam and were frustrated by university overcrowding, apathetic school administrators, →

Opposite: The cover of George's 1967 *Paris Magazine*.

# The Paris Magazine

OCTOBER 1967   20F   N° 1

Man With A Hat. Portrait
In Bronze By Kosta Alex

### LETTERS OF
### LAWRENCE DURRELL

### KANSAS CITY TO SAINT LOUIS
### ALLEN GINSBERG

### PICTURES OF VIETNAM AT WAR
PHOTOGRAPHS BY ROGER PIC
TEXT BY JEAN-PAUL SARTRE

### THE LITTLE PRESSES OF ENGLAND
EDWARD LUCIE - SMITH

### INTERVIEW AVEC MARGUERITE DURAS
JEAN-MICHEL FOSSEY

APPEAL FROM VIETNAMESE
TO AMERICAN STUDENTS
AN AMERICAN REPLIES
BRUCE FRANKLIN

### LETTRE A ANDRÉ MALRAUX
GEORGE WHITMAN

Editorial Offices :

# SHAKESPEARE AND COMPANY
### kilometer zero paris

# THE PARIS MAGAZINE

**Publisher**
G Y FOREAU

**Editor**
GEORGE WHITMAN

## SHAKESPEARE & CO.

37 rue de la Bûcherie
Paris 5

## CONTENTS FOR N° 1    OCTOBER    1967

SUBSCRIPTIONS : 8 francs (U.S. $ 2.00) for 4 quarterly issues. (Library Edition 15 francs (U.S. $ 3.00) checks payable to Guy Foreau. Single copies 2 francs, 3 shillings, 50 cents. Contributors should enclose stamped self-addressed envelope with manuscript.

In forthcoming issues : HENRY MILLER On The Theatre of Ionesco, H. J. POLLOCK : Reminiscences of James Joyce In Paris, Also A Series On The Foreign Colonies of Paris (American, Vietnamese, Latin-American, Russian).

### By GEORGE WHITMAN

God who watches over children,
drunkards and fools,
With silent miracles and other
such esoterica,
Suspend the ordinary rules
And take care of the United
States of America.
ARTHUR GUITERMAN.

In the years when France was « the sick man of Europe » I was to all appearances a Frenchman. Now when England stands out as the muddlehead of the occident (despite the remarkable figure of 80 tons of false eyelashes exported every year) I ask myself if perhaps I am not after all an Englishman. But on due consideration I feel the only country which is said to have gone from barbarism to decadence without an intervening period of civilization, has the most just claim to me. I am one of those some-

what unique individuals who go from prolonged adolescence to premature old age, without anything very remarkable in between, so I am at last reconciled to being an American.

As an American bookseller in the heart of Paris I supposedly lead an ideal existence. When I want company I open the doors and people of all nationalities and occupations wander in, showing as much diversity within the family of man as between widely different species of the animal kingdom. When I want solitude there are always 25,000 books on the walls, each one waiting like a faithful mistress to be taken to bed and read all night. However because of the fascinations of reading at all hours I have probably not realized the 2 % of my potential, which psychologists estimate as average. My figure is probably more like 1 % which should make me a 100 % American.

### A MILLIONAIRE ON SKID ROW

Everyone who opens a litera[l] bookstore thinks it will be a congeni[al] occupation but strangely enough a[c]cording to figures published a fe[w] years ago, of every ten bookstore[s] opened in America, five go out o[f] existence within a year and only on[e] lasts ten years.

This bookstore has lasted 16 year[s] although for almost a year I have n[o] sold a book, since I was condemne[d] by the courts for running an illeg[al] business. However Shakespeare an[d] Company still keeps open house as [a] free library and Guest House f[or] writers from abroad. In the apartme[nt] upstairs the Free University of Par[is] has poetry readings, courses and d[e]bates on everything from Vietnam t[o] a seminar in great books. If you wou[ld] like an honorary degree of LSD pleas[e]
*(continued on page 2[9])*

2

(continued from page 2)

ask our dean, Bruce Franklin. Our diplomas this year were Make-Love-Not-War buttons.

I have applied for a foreign businessman's card in order to be allowed to sell books again and hope to receive a favorable response before too many years have passed. It is gratifying to have been tolerated so long by the public powers and every time I hear of a man being arrested in Times Square for handing out dollar bills, or of a wife impounding her husband's bank account because she has heard that he is giving away $ 100 tips to rickshaw boys in Hongkong, I think, there but for the grace of God go I.

Investing your capital in a bookstore like this one is just like giving it away. A literary bookshop is always a quixotic enterprise, and now that we have expanded into 13 rooms on 3 floors, our overhead has gone up so that we don't make any profits whether we sell books or not. I am in the upper fraction of 1 % of Americans in terms of capital ownership and in the bottom fraction of 1 % in terms of income. Statistically I live on less than the average American family spends on tin cans and other containers.

So why do people always come in and ask me is this your bookstore ? I consider it is as much yours as mine, even more so because you can do what you please while I have to keep things in order. Do you know the story about James Gordon Bennett, who was not satisfied with the service at a restaurant on the Riviera so he purchased it, fired the manager and after dining gave it away to his waiter. When you visit Shakespeare & Co. I would like you to feel the way that waiter did. Go ahead and raid the ice-box or kick off your shoes and lie in bed and read. But sometimes, when I am scrubbing floors at 2 o'clock in the morning, I am torn between the wish to lock everyone out because it is so much trouble to pick up after people, or lock everyone in because my guests are so congenial.

An excerpt of George's letter from the editor, alongside the magazine's table of contents.

Deborah Hayden
*Tumbleweed*

*November 1967–April 1968*

On the Cité Universitaire bulletin board, this notice: "For *Paris Magazine*, submit articles to Shakespeare and Company, 37 rue de la Bûcherie." I type a story and drop it in the post before leaving for a brief trip. The following week, on my return, the concierge hands me a note from George Whitman: "I like your story very much. Can you come to dinner, say Friday?" But Friday has already passed.

I find rue de la Bûcherie on a map and go by the next evening. I'm just finishing a warm crêpe *beurre-sucre* in a cone from a street vendor when I get there. The store appears to be closed. Scraps of paper are posted on the door. A penciled note: "Jean-Michel, I'm leaving at midnight and need my luggage. Be here." A printed note inviting browsers to come in and read, then handwritten below: "Read used books only, please." Notes announcing meetings: a Vietnam study group, a Mensa group. Peering through the grimy window, I can make out a room full of books.

I return the next day. Jean-Michel's note is gone. In the window is a stack of *Paris Magazines* with articles by Sartre and Lawrence Durrell. What was I thinking, sending my story?

A man with a goatee emerges from the shop, locking the door behind him. "Mr. Whitman?" He glares at me. He's wearing a baggy suit with holes and has no raincoat. I tell him my name. "Oh yes." He fumbles in his pocket and hands me a ring of keys. "I shouldn't give you these. I don't have copies. Oh well. I have to trust you. There's chicken soup on the stove." He points up, then gets on his moped and peddles into the street as it starts to rain.

165

I try all the keys and finally figure out there are two locks on the heavy door. Upstairs, a timer turns out the light just as I walk in, and I'm startled to see someone moving across the room. But it's only myself, reflected in a dark mirror with a gilt frame. I can see Notre-Dame through the window. A red table, a radio, an armchair, a bed, and books, books everywhere. The carpet's plush dark red. And dirty. Everything is very, very dirty.

I find a light switch, and the room warms. The kitchen is in a hallway between the front and the back rooms. A gas stove, a refrigerator, a jumble of dirty dishes, dried-up food, and a pot of chicken soup.

Then he's back, putting parcels on the table. His watery blue eyes make me think of an opium pipe. "How are you, dear?" His voice barely audible. I match it with my own whisper. I heat the soup and pour some into two bowls. He finds butter and matzo crackers. Then he tells me about the magazine, about the bookstore being closed by the French government. He shows me the back room with his desk, papers piled high and spilling onto the floor. I smell something burning. He spins into the kitchen and heaves the remaining soup, forgotten and now smoking, into the sink. He smiles, revealing missing lower teeth.

Somehow I find myself agreeing to help him reopen the store, publish the next magazine, and find some order in the general disarray. "Noon, Wednesday," he says. "When you come back, knock like this: *tap tap tap* — wait — *tap tap tap* — wait — *tap tap tap*. Well. Good-bye."

I begin spending most of my time at the bookstore, often staying overnight in whatever cot isn't taken by someone else. A number of students come and go with no regularity. I clean,

cook, help George balance his disastrous ledgers and prepare for his tax meeting, turn away people who come at all hours wondering where is George, why is the bookstore closed? Mostly I read in the immense library. Amy, a friend from home, comes to visit and moves in. She buys a new, clean, red bedcover and a notebook to schedule George. It doesn't work. When she catches him cutting his hair by burning it off with a candle, she throws a towel over his head.

We celebrate Thanksgiving. George, Amy, and I cram into the small kitchen area, cooking a turkey, stuffing, applesauce, cranberry sauce, chestnuts, carrots, gravy, three kinds of homemade pie, and homemade ice cream. George's niece from Smith, Eliza Jane, shows up. George wears a formal suit from a rummage sale. He isn't happy when I heat water to wash the greasy plates: "Cold water will do." The meal is delicious. We eat everything, except for the chestnuts. They had fallen on the floor, and George had scraped them off the carpet and put them back in the bowl.

Slept poorly. Street noises. Street lights shining through the window. Thoughts of applying to the University of Chicago. At midnight a couple bangs on the door below and yells up that George has their mail. I find it in a pile in the back room and throw it down to them. On the landing between the first and second floors, a broken Turkish toilet sprays water all over ten years of literary journals, which now smell moldy.

Wake up to the cold air and the smell of George's freshly brewed coffee. I play French songs on the radio, heat a pot of water, and search for vinegar and towels. Then, a startling moment: looking through a swipe of clean window to see a sky of black storm clouds and a single beam of light breaking onto Notre-Dame.

A parade of horses and carriages and men in red uniforms. People passing by smile at me. I'm rained on while washing the outside. I'm like a child in a children's story playing bookstore. Happiest day yet in Paris.

George wanders off with his knapsack. He says, "Don't open the door for anyone but Anaïs, Larry, or Henry," coming back to add, "or Allen Ginsberg." Yesterday someone told me he'd seen Henry Miller pacing around in front of the bookstore late at night, looking at the dark upstairs window. In the pile of hundreds of unopened letters, I see one with Lawrence Durrell's home address. George returns three days later.

We type George's correspondence on a French typewriter, awkwardly learning the foreign order of the letters. George says there's an electric American typewriter in the "catacombs," which reminds me of Poe's "Cask of Amontillado." The key to the Turkish toilet works for the basement door, too. I light a candle. The steps are narrow, and the candle doesn't illuminate much. The "catacombs" turn out to be damp rooms opening one onto another. I'm afraid to venture too far in case the candle goes out or I get lost. Mark showed me a picture he'd taken of a heavy iron door at the end of one of these corridors. He'd tried to pry it open with a crowbar. He thinks the door leads into a tunnel going under the Seine and ending at Notre-Dame. I find the electric typewriter and bring it upstairs. It doesn't work.

George is circulating a petition to André Malraux requesting that the bookstore be allowed to reopen. Amy borrows George's moped to take the petition to Henry Miller's gallery for his signature.

Vietnam rally. I show up and am surprised to see George marching at the front of a group. Stokely Carmichael, with a woman to translate, sparks a wildly enthusiastic crowd.

George returns in the evening in a good mood, burns a pot of chicken soup, and tells stories about the history of the building that include the white slave trade and a woman who fed her husband arsenic in order to inherit the property. I found a used book in the store that identifies it as having been a brothel and a safe house for persecuted monks from Notre-Dame. George is delighted. He brings the electric heater from his room, and we huddle around it while he tells us of his adventures and travels. About ten o'clock, he shoulders his backpack, pockets a handful of cookies, and disappears. The man who owns the shop next door says of George: "*Il vient, il part, comme un éclair.*"

and the sharp divide between their generation and the aging, more conservative one. On May 3, a group had gathered together in a courtyard at the Sorbonne, considered the heart of the University of Paris system, to protest the threatened expulsion of a few politically active, anti-establishment students from the University's nearby Nanterre campus. At the request of the Sorbonne's rector, police entered the courtyard and tried to break up the protest; it marked the first time police had entered the university in its seven-hundred-year history. Outraged, hundreds of other students soon joined the demonstration. The police responded with clubs and tear gas. In the end, six hundred people were arrested, dozens were injured, and the Sorbonne was closed for the first time ever as police moved in to occupy the university.

On May 6, teachers joined with students, converging peacefully on the Sorbonne to protest the police action. The Compagnies Républicaines de Sécurité (CRS) — the French riot police — suddenly charged demonstrators, shields and batons raised, leaving many injured in their wake. The students erected barricades and threw cobblestones. The police threw tear gas. With every show of aggression by the CRS, the students became more determined. Over the next few days, the Latin Quarter came to look like a war zone — battered barricades, overturned cars, →

LA BEAUTÉ EST DANS LA RUE

From top: One of hundreds of posters created by L'Atelier Populaire, the artistic collective that occupied Paris's École des Beaux-Arts during the protests; demonstrators fill Paris's streets. *Photo:* Jean-Pierre Rey; students lobbing cobblestones at approaching gendarmes. *Photo:* The Image Works/Roger-Viollet

Molotov cocktails flying through the air, fires bursting open on the streets. Hundreds of people were arrested. Hundreds were injured.

The majority of clashes occurred in streets near the bookshop, including Boulevard St.-Michel and rue St.-Jacques. The police ran through the *quartier*, banging their truncheons, overrunning cafés, arresting everyone in sight. Throughout the violence, the bookshop was a refuge. George hosted all-night talk sessions, and he hid those who were trying to escape the CRS.

The fighting in Paris was reported live on the radio to the whole country. Photographs appeared in the morning papers, and the television news broadcast images. Across France, workers were incited to join the protests, both because of the police attacks and because of their own dissatisfaction with labor conditions and wages. On May 13, more than a million people marched through Paris in protest. All the major trade unions called for a general strike. Soon, more than ten million people throughout the country →

LAWRENCE FERLINGHETTI
*poet/owner of City Lights bookstore*

It was Paris 1968, and by the eternal corner where the Boulevard St.-Germain cuts across St.-Michel, by the tall iron gates of the Cluny gardens, a band of three violinists, each with his cup, fiddled disparately. The separate screeching strands of music fell upon the curled iron gates and wound around them like snapped violin strings or rubber bands, only to dissolve at once in the swelling carnival sound of the street, while just inside the wrought iron gates, three silent stone-winged griffins sat in darkness, unmoved.

Meanwhile, in the real world of '68, just up the block from the Cluny in its medieval dream, a huge crowd of students and workers was forming in front of the Café Dupont-Latin, some waving signs reading TOUT EST CON CHEZ DUPONT. They were beginning a great parade proclaiming a new ideal society of liberated youth and total freedom from the chains of the status quo. Streaming down the boulevard, they gathered momentum, carrying off stray bewildered tourists, Sorbonne professors, concierges, dowagers, streetwalkers, dance instructors, pale poets and artists with easels, guitarists and street sweepers and girls with books and flowers.

And the horde turned right onto the Boulevard St.-Germain, heading toward the place Maubert, now thousands marching and singing in the street. But when they reached the place Maubert, suddenly, hordes of black-helmeted gendarmes descended from squad cars hidden along side streets and threw themselves upon the students and workers, firing tear gas and wielding horned truncheons and swinging leaded capes, the Establishment descending with all the blind brute force of the entrenched state. Students fell like tin soldiers before the assault, but many rose and started tearing up the paving stones of the place Maubert and making barricades with them. Still, the armed *flics* kept coming on and on in waves, some hiding behind huge shields emblazoned with coats of arms of the imperial state.

Meanwhile *le grand général*, President Charles de Gaulle, was on the radio, calling for calm and for *grandeur* and for *la gloire*, for the eternal glory of *La France*.

173

# The Sidewalkers Moved…

JIM MORRISON

The sidewalkers moved faster
We joined the current. Suddenly
the cops, plastic shields & visors,
wielding long thin truncheons
like wands, in formation,
clearing the street the other way.
To get near or stay away.
Cafes were taking in tables
putting chairs on upside
down, pulling the steel playpen
safety bars. Whistles as
the vans arrive. Moustached
soldiers. We leave the scene.
Eyes of youth, wary, gleaming.

they attack from behind,
Pressed against cafe tables.
Subway & news Kiosk–A
girl beaten, her cries. Can't
hear blows.  Rain.  (Man w/bottle)
Join me at the demonstration

We join groups under trees
& rain. Tall public buildings.

Join us at the demonstration

The church. A pastoral scene
of guitars, drums, flutes,
harps, & lovers. Past
Shakespeare & Co., the restaurants
w/ elegant patrons, cross
street, the small Jazz
district (Story Ville) a
miniature New Orleans.
Negroes in African shirts.
A street brass band.
"Fare well to my web footed friends"
Crowd smiles, jogs, & sings.
Move past. San Michel Blvd.
The Statue. The Seine. Bonfires
of cardboard buzz evilly,
down the blvd. Fire-tenders.
Smell of smoke. Approach closer
nearer. Suddenly screams
long warhoops & the crowd runs
back. And as we flee,

CHRISTOPHER COOK GILMORE
*writer*

It was nine o'clock at night, and I was running for my life down rue de la Huchette. There was a cloud of tear gas behind me, and in the middle of that cloud were about a dozen CRS goons, the biggest policemen you've ever seen in your life, with huge batons and helmets. They'd just stormed the barricades that we'd built at place St.-Michel. Every shop was closed, and every door was locked, and I was hoping that I could get to the Seine and jump in. But when I reached St.-Jacques, there was a whole bus full of CRS guys. So I cut across the street, and now I'm in rue de la Bûcherie. I see a light, one light, and I run down, and I see this light inside a crazy old bookstore — there's an old man with a goatee there. I run in the door. I'm wearing an American football helmet. I have a scarf across my face, an old trench coat around me. I look at the old man and say, "CRS!" And he says, "Get upstairs!" He flicks off the lights, shuts the door, and we both run up the stairs. We see the police go by screaming and pounding the cobblestones. And then I look up and there, across the Seine, is Notre-Dame. On top of one tower, these students are up there, and they've hung the biggest red flag you've ever seen, blowing out over the place Notre-Dame, Kilometer Zero. And the old man looks at me, grabs my arm, and says, "Isn't this the greatest moment of your entire life?"

(roughly two-thirds of the work force) had walked off their jobs. For two weeks, France was virtually shut down — there was little gasoline, no traffic police, and no garbage collection. De Gaulle seemed about to lose power. He secretly fled to Germany. Then, quickly, he was back in Paris and calling for the dissolution of the National Assembly and new elections. And — just like that — it was over. No one ever learned what exactly de Gaulle had done in Germany, but workers returned to their jobs (many to assurances of significant pay increases), and students went back to school. When the National Assembly elections were held in June, the Left was divided and de Gaulle's right-wing party triumphed. It became the first party in the republic's history to obtain a parliamentary majority.

The full consequences of the May 1968 protests are debated by historians, but it's generally agreed that, despite de Gaulle's win in the National Assembly elections, the explosive month marked the beginning of a transformation in French culture, when the spirit of the younger generation began to emerge as the norm, and the French people became, as a whole, freer, more liberal, and less traditional. →

By late 1968, the bookstore was permitted to sell books again.

JEAN-JACQUES LEBEL
*artist/poet/publisher*

In 1960, I made a collage called *Parfum grève générale, bonne odeur* — in English, "general-strike perfume, nice smell." That was eight years before the protests. I wasn't the only one who'd seen it coming. I can't speak about the rest of the world, but in Paris it was maybe a few hundred people. We'd been profoundly affected by the Dadaists and the Surrealists and, then, by the Situationists and other extreme left-wing intellectuals and journals, like *Socialisme ou Barbarie*.

Back then, we were having "happenings." Ours were highly political, first against the Algerian War, then against the war in Vietnam. And while the movement had no clearly defined shape, it was absolutely fundamental. It was anti-racist, anti-imperialist, international. We were taking part with all we had, body and soul. From this small outbreak — well, as it's said, the spark sets fire to the plains.

We'd been preparing and waiting a long time for May '68. None of us knew exactly when or where or how or what, but we knew something was going to happen. We could feel it. Cracks were appearing everywhere. *Le monde va changer de base*, as goes "L'Internationale." The world is about to change its foundation.

We weren't surprised by what happened after May '68 either. We saw the bureaucrats at work. We saw guys like Louis Aragon who came to the Boul' Mich' to say: "Yes, my children, I am with you!" It was bullshit. We saw the Communist Party doing everything in its power to crush the movement, to throw a wrench in the works. We weren't naive or ignorant. We'd read history. We knew what had happened at the Paris Commune and in the Russian Revolution. Bureaucrats took over and stopped the revolutionary momentum. During the Spanish Revolution, in '36 and '37, when the anarchists were the majority, wage labor was abolished, everything was free, society was completely transformed — then Franco's troops and the Stalinists broke it up.

It's the same old story, so we know it by heart. But this isn't a reason to give up. We can't give up. As Ginsberg wrote, we must each put our "queer shoulder to the wheel." Push on.

As they say, it's more about the journey than the destination. In art, it's the emotions we experience when we paint a picture, when we write a poem. Our purpose is not to produce something to be sold or bought. Our purpose is to experience what happens within us during the production — *that* is the real poem.

Painting, music, poetry, philosophy — culture plays a key part in awakening minds and in transmitting a contagious desire for revolution. That's a fact. It wasn't for nothing that the Surrealists called their journal *La Révolution surréaliste*. And culture has a long-term social function. Gilles Deleuze put it very well: culture works as a rhizome, meaning that it goes via the summit, via the canopy, not by the roots. If we go by the roots, we're nailed to the spot. We're prisoners. With a rhizome, we float throughout the world, transcending generations and geography.

Nineteen sixty-eight wasn't just some small electoral event. It was a historic, fundamental moment. Minds were greatly transformed. And it's still going on.

Text was adapted from an oral interview with M. Lebel and translated from the French.

A few months later, on July 4, 1968, George suddenly received his *carte de commerçant étranger* — without explanation — and the shop was permitted to return to bookselling. While George had been politically and personally invigorated by those two years when the shop was shut down, he was now also financially broke, having spent all his savings to keep the lending library and the Tumbleweed Hotel open. From 1968 to 1970, he was forced to rent out the first-floor rooms, and he couldn't afford any staff.

"We've had to make out the best we can," he told a reporter for *Holiday* magazine. "I've put $40,000 into this place, and now I'm down to my last $1,000… I'd never do it again, but now it's my life's work."

He continued optimistically: "I've got to get back the upstairs, and I'm going to open a literary café. Everything will be cooked under my supervision. There's only one way to make a good lemon pie, you know. What I should do is go lock myself in a room and invent something like the safety pin. I've got to raise enough money to buy the store behind this one. Then we can knock out a wall, and the store will reach right back into the garden of St.-Julien-le-Pauvre. Did you know that the oldest tree in Paris is growing there? Go and take a look. We'll have the first floor back on May 1, 1970. That's the day of our big reopening party. Don't forget! Everyone's invited!"

# the
# 1970s

"This is my commune," said George. "Many anonymous hands have shaped the bookstore…A Shakespeare scholar from Kentucky made our desk. A Danish worker built the stairs. A multitude of transients excavated the cellars… I like to think the bookstore is part of an archipelago of utopias that stretch across the world from Costa Rica to Kathmandu… For miles along the Seine River, this is the only door that is open to strangers every day of the year from noon to midnight… Several million persons have walked in our door like tumbleweeds drifting in the wind, and then walked out, their innocence lost, as free citizens of the cosmos."

By the early 1970s, at least seven thousand Tumbleweeds had slept in the bookstore, and this total would soon skyrocket as young people began backpacking across Europe in ever-greater numbers. The baby-boom generation had come of age at the same time that many national economies were growing and air travel was becoming increasingly mainstream.

With more people requesting beds at the bookshop, George codified the three requirements of

(con't)

People are my stimulus for enjoyment, but I hate it if I feel
they are taking any sort of unfair advantage of me.  I love it
here, and reading.  It's so relaxing.  I would love to
stay here.

---

Christopher Geering
Passport British
Born: 21.8.1946.
Profession: Builder
Father: Entomologist
Address: 26 North St. Beauminster. Dorset , England
Arrival: 1.1.72
Departure: 3.1.72

Left school at 15 with no qualifications and no exams to work
on the land.  Toured the refugee camps of Austria in 1962
with a travelling theatre.  Attended agricultural college in
Dorset, learned farming and building.  Married Helen in 1966-
then a barmaid.  Son Toby born 1967.  Milked cows and did odd
farming jobs for a year.  Turned to building as a means of
earning more money and making a home for my wife and son.
Helped to restore about six country houses, learning all the
time.  Lived in a gipsy caravan for three years until able to
buy a condemned cottage in a small town.  This is now restored
and warm and quite large and people wonder why I want to sell it
and get some money for once and be able to do things unconnected
with making money which I am very bad at and whichdestroys
everything of value.
Various young and old people come and stay with us from time to
time and like the way we live in the country and make things
and restore houses and old furniture and Helen making
such beautiful clothes and being so magnetic and beautiful and
they move in and help me with the house and get something out
of the experience.  Disadvantages of having a hous like water
and car and gas and babysitting get you down and sometimes you
wonder what you are doing there and for who and then you break
and decide to go to Paris for New Year and have no addresses
except for Shakespeare & Company bookshop and there out of
the blue somebody welcomes you and doesn't expect much from you
and you have a really good holiday you will never forget
and you think of England and its a long way away and you would
like to stay and read and learn the language and travel the world

each guest (these are still in effect today): help for an hour or two each day in the bookstore, submit a one-page autobiography and photograph, and "read a book a day."

In Paris, tensions between the younger generation and the authorities remained at the forefront, particularly in the Latin Quarter, where the violence of May 1968 was still fresh. There, and around the world, people were continuing to fight for civil and women's rights, while in Vietnam the war raged on. Counterculture types, including those young American men evading the draft, flooded into the *quartier* and the bookshop, where George —"the staunchest of liberals"— offered "a meeting place for any cause dedicated to human rights and freedom, with no questions asked," as *The Houston Post* reported.

While the bookstore mainly attracted students and studious types, occasionally someone did arrive hoping to take advantage of the shop's liberal-minded host and his loose managerial style. Fortunately, a guest's bad intentions were usually thwarted by George's good ones. "Dear George," begins one letter from 1974, "I have been meaning to write you for some time. To tell the truth, I came to your bookshop to see what I could hide away under my coat. Instead, I found myself sitting in your seat, minding the place while you went out. Amazing. I could have stuffed →

Opposite: Having tea in the upstairs library.

LINDA V. WILLIAMS
(A.K.A., LINDA GRANT)
*Tumbleweed*

The student revolution was on high simmer. Stern-faced gendarmes were omnipresent, and people warned us that the hems of their capes hid chains. The Left Bank was occupied territory.

My husband and I had been at the bookstore less than a week when George announced that he was going to London and that we should keep an eye on the shop. Most specifically, we were to see that no one new came to stay in his absence. Unregistered guests could cause George real problems.

On the first night, two girls from Scandinavia showed up. They'd been sleeping on the quay by the Seine with their boyfriends when some gendarmes rousted them. They were taken to a police station, where they were questioned and harassed for several hours. While the boyfriends were still being held, the girls were released into a bad section of town in the middle of the night. They had to walk for hours to get back to the Left Bank. Clearly, they couldn't go back to the quay and risk being picked up again.

George's instructions were clear: no guests. But after only a few days, Andy and I understood that George Whitman would never have refused refuge to two frightened girls, even if it risked trouble with the cops. They stayed.

my pockets and bags full with books and 'ad it away a bit smartish like … It was one of life's poems, meeting you, something which turned that 'day to a song' instead of being another piece of bog paper." (Of course, George didn't charm everyone who entered the shop. A letter received the following year reads: "Dear Sir, I visited your establishment several weeks ago and found you such a preposterous boor … The next time I am in Paris, I intend to spread cream cheese all over your collection.")

The bookstore continued to be frequented by familiar writers, artists, and politicians. Pablo Neruda, Doris Lessing, and Howard Zinn came by on multiple occasions, as did Jacqueline Kennedy Onassis, who wrote in the guest book: "For George Whitman, whose generosity has made so many people happy." Other visitors included François Truffaut, Jacques Chirac, Roland Barthes, and Bernard Malamud, along with Louis Aragon, Jack Hirschman, and Robert Bly.

In 1973 and 1974, two feature films were shot in the bookstore. The first, *Les Autres*, was directed by Hugo Santiago and was co-written with two other Argentines, Jorge Luis Borges and Adolfo Bioy Casares. The second film, *L'Important c'est d'aimer*, was directed by Polish filmmaker Andrzej Żuławski and starred Klaus Kinski and Romy Schneider, with Schneider winning a César award for her performance. →

Page 191: The bookstore's main room and Aguigui Mouna, a Paris street philosopher. *Photo:* CHRISTIAN ERRATH

Name: James Richard Crotteau

Home address: 1806A E. Kane Pl.
Milwaukee, Wisconsin, USA

Profession: Former student, part-time very futile writer, part-time halfway
decent singer and guitar plick plucker, part-time fugitive from
Justice (?) as a draft-dodger, peace-freak, erstwhile Berlitz teacher
in Paris (duration of employment, two days), full-time human being
(I hope) who sometimes happens to be in the right place at the right
time and who tries to help anyone who needs it.

Passport number: USA --

Profession of father: now retired, formerly worker on assembly line for
Schlitz brewery in Milwaukee (forced to do so kind of against his
will (he certainly didn't enjoy it) because he had to support his
family); typical lower middle class American

Family:   father -- Allan Victor, age 71
          mother -- Annette Agnes (née Bozich), age 58
          brothers -- William Michael, age 16 (high school student)
                      Robert Allan, age 29 (drifter and professional
                          psychotic because of his brief stint in the army)

Observations: It's hard, sitting at this typewriter at three o'clock in
the morning, to put down the impressions of my three months' stay at
Shakespeare and Company. There are times when I think that one has to
be as insane as George to have stayed here so long (or at least that
one has to become completely insane after staying here so long).
But then there are times (like now, when I'm just about to leave) when
I think that George is perhaps the only sane person in the world or
perhaps we all should become as insane as he. I just wish I could have
made it here earlier when Shakespeare and Company was really alive
(and when Paris was still alive) rather than now when both seem to be
in their death throws. Shakespeare and Company has a chance at a
resurrection, but I'm afraid that it will be phoenix-like from the
ashes of the burnt-out intellectual and literary life of Paris. What
form this new creature will take is uncertain; perhaps it will
become simply a home for wandering indigents, refugees and exiles like
me, but one thing for sure, it can never appear as a literary center
because there is nothing for it to be the center of. I wish I could
stay and either bury the so store once and for all or assist in its
new creation, but pressing personal problems are driving me away.
     It's also a hard to write humorously now so close to my
departure because I'm really sad to be leaving paris, not so much because of Paris but more because of the people (mostly Americans) I
have met here and because deep down inside I'm grateful to George for
helping me out when I really needed it. But it's too hard to write a
about anything but myself. I don t really know how it has come bout
but my life has changed radically since coming to Paris. This is
getting bad and boring so I'm going to stop soon; I'm just going to
make a few broad generalizations about life which have very little
meaning perhaps but which may get a larger audience than the people I
know from anyone stupid enough to be reading this. Almost everyone
is alone and terribly lonely and no one seems willing or capable to
do much about it. It's all too easy to say "love one another" or

some such rot but very few of us know all that love entails (I'm not at all sure I do myself) and ~~her~~ even fewer are willing to be hurt (as necessarily happens) in the process of helping someone else. I don't know what to do to make (or rather to get) people to love or at least not to hurt their fellow sufferers. (Philip Larkin in a poem called "Talking in Bed" says something like: I tried to utter words at once both true and kind but found myself unable to speak words not untrue and not unkind.) What a bunch of shit this has turned out to be! Well, I'm going to push on to the bitter end no matter how foolish this may sound.

As a final piece of political nonsense, ~~it~~ let me harrangue the masses reading this. As a future political prisoner (one to five years for saying no to the organized murder of the US Army), I've got a few observations (the last, thankfully) for any would-be revolutionaries. Your violent revolution will fail because you will turn into the oppressor as soon as you have the power. The revolution to be real and possible must be Camus' rebellion -- it is inside -- and unless you start there nothing will change at all. Well enough for now. If any of you are ever in Milwaukee and need something be sure to look me up; I'm one of those stupid people who is always there. Love and peace to you all.

James R. Crotteau

The Drs. Kronhausen present

# THE FIRST INTERNATIONAL EXHIBITION OF

## EROTIC ART

### LUND'S KONSTHALL

MUSEUM OF ART
LUND · SWEDEN

3 MAY-31 JULY 1968 · OPEN: 12-5 PM

BOULEVARD

### Hugo Santiago
*filmmaker*

My first feature film, *Invasion*, was co-written with Jorge Luis Borges and Adolfo Bioy Casares. After its success, the three of us decided to do a second movie together, this one based on an original idea from Borges — the film's protagonist would be a bookseller named Spinoza; the setting, his Paris shop.

The project was partly an homage to Paris, the city that had — at one time or another — adopted each of us Argentines. Borges had great memories of Paris, which he'd been visiting since his schoolboy days in Geneva. Bioy Casares came frequently, too. And I moved here in 1959. Our lives revolved around the Latin Quarter and St.-Germain-des-Prés. Everything was happening here, including the Cinémathèque on rue d'Ulm, before it was moved to Chaillot. When it came to choosing a bookshop in which to film, there wasn't even a discussion. The screenplay was written with Shakespeare and Company in mind. We all frequented the shop. Borges himself had been coming since the 1950s, and he had known the first Shakespeare and Company, too.

The movie was to begin with nine minutes of unconventional opening credits, after which there would be a long traveling shot that moved along rue de la Bûcherie, tracing the pavement, to arrive at Shakespeare and Company's front door. During the opening credits and the traveling shot, the colors in the film would be altered; they would become normal only once the camera arrived at the shop's door. For us, the traveling shot — and therefore filming the exterior of the bookshop — was absolutely necessary. This created a problem — not with George (he was a prince),

but with the Préfecture de Police. Since the protests in '68, filming outdoors in central Paris — including in the Latin Quarter, of course — was strictly prohibited by city officials. This was now in late 1973 and early 1974.

We managed to get a meeting at the Préfecture to ask for special permission to film outside. The whole production team went: Pierre-Henri Deleau, Hubert Niogret, and the Nouvelle Vague–filmmaker Jean-Daniel Pollet, who was the movie's producer. To soften up the *préfet*, we said, "Listen. There's this blind old writer who lives in Buenos Aires. You can't imagine. He really wants the film to be set in this bookshop —" The *préfet* interrupted us: "Gentlemen, just because I'm a cop doesn't mean I'm completely stupid and don't know who Borges is." This must have helped as we eventually made an arrangement with the Préfecture. They let us film outside provided we agreed not to install any heavy equipment.

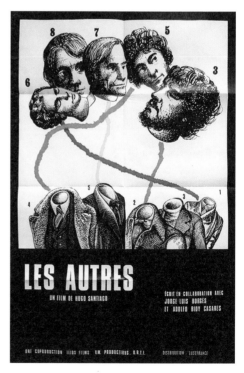

Borges insisted that for the movie we change the name of the bookshop from "Shakespeare and Company" to "Librairie des Amériques." He thought "Shakespeare and Company" was too significant, too evocative, to appear inconspicuously in a film. Though we changed the name, we were careful not to alter the bookshop's decor or personality. When filming, I tried not to touch anything, which was mostly impossible. Things kept falling down all around us from the overstuffed bookshelves.

The most remarkable person on-set, the one who remained most calm during all this, was George. He closed the bookshop for us. He cleared space for us. And he wouldn't come down while we were working. He was adorable. Before production began, I'd known him only from the shop. We'd say hello, exchange a few words in Spanish. Then one day I went to see him about the film. I told him Borges wanted to do this project, that we had the screenplay, and that — in our eyes — it had to be filmed in his bookshop. He said yes immediately, without hesitation, on that very day.

The resulting film, *Les Autres*, competed in the 1974 Cannes Film Festival. It was a scandal. People were screaming from their seats. They were enraged by the opening credits, those beginning nine minutes that play unconventionally with form. The critics and viewers couldn't abide it — but they weren't paying attention. These nine minutes of play generate the whole movie. It's like a toolbox with all the solutions. You can see all the themes of the film unfold.

*Les Autres* did better in Paris, where it benefited from the support of writers, artists, philosophers, musicians, and painters, such as Marguerite Duras, Roland Barthes, and Michel Foucault. There were texts written about it by Jacques Roubaud, Jean-Pierre Faye, and Gilles Deleuze. Books came out in French, Japanese, and Italian — the latter of which was edited and published by Giuseppe Recchia, who worked at Shakespeare and Company.

The movie ended up being a great triumph in the *cinémas d'art et d'essai*; that is, the French independent theater circuit. It was a big and important film at the time. In those days, a little movie could still come out, screen in small theaters, and be a success.

Page 194, from top: The main room on the ground floor, often called the "art gallery"; the back left corner of the ground floor, which was reserved for rare editions; the children's section on the first floor. Page 195, from top: The upstairs front library; two photographs of the Writer's Studio, a room located across the landing from the library, which George added in 1974.

Text was adapted from an oral interview with M. Santiago and translated from the French.

THE ART GALLERY

RARE BOOK DEPT

THE CHILDRENS ROOM

TUMBLEWEED HOTEL

WRITERS GUEST HOUSE

There continued to be regular literary events at the bookshop, including a new weekly series called Lundis Littéraires, organized by a young Italian employee, Giuseppe Recchia. By and large, the series featured French and international writers reading their works in English translation. It drew attention from the French newspaper *Le Monde* and the Italian journal *Il Mondo*, which described Recchia as "the man who brought Italian poetry back to France." →

Opposite: A reading in the bookshop's main room.

GIUSEPPE RECCHIA
*bookstore staff*

I'd arrived in Paris in 1968, a naive young journalist from Milan, exploring the city that so fascinated me. Paris was alive in its streets, in its people, in those who initiated the May student protests. It was during that violent month, while escaping police batons, that I first discovered Shakespeare and Company. George Whitman welcomed me to his bookshop, and to safety, with a typical Italian salute. "Drink," he said, pouring wine into an empty tuna can and handing it to me. "Drink this *vino italiano sincero*." I hesitated. "You're not bourgeois, are you?" he asked. I took the tuna can and drank and, from that day on, I worked in the bookshop.

I began organizing a weekly reading series called Literary Mondays. Among the first to visit us were Jacques Tati, the great director, actor, and mime; Jean-Pierre Faye, the philosopher and poet; Philippe Sollers, a writer and co-founder of the avant-garde literary magazine *Tel Quel*; and Jean-Paul Sartre and Simone de Beauvoir, who dropped in to say hello.

Soon after appeared another great philosopher: François Châtelet, who came with his wife, the actress and writer Noëlle Jospin. Actors Alain Delon and Jean-Paul Belmondo attended several events, including a reading by Alberto Moravia, who talked that evening about his travels in Africa. Brigitte Bardot visited the bookshop once and, just like another great actress, Brigitte Fossey, she gave me the impression that she was a woman fleeing from time. There were still other curious and unexpected visitors, such as John Updike, Gabriel García Márquez, Michel Deguy, Julia Kristeva, Gilles Deleuze, and Jacques Derrida.

One night, at about eleven o'clock, Italo Calvino and Pablo Neruda arrived unannounced. I improvised an evening among friends, as Italo liked to do. Pablo was initially quiet, but he quickly became more talkative, and we began creating poems dedicated to Paris and to love. George was there, too, serving wine from tuna cans.

Our event with Roland Barthes was particular and extraordinary. The French writer and semiotician hadn't wanted any publicity for his evening, so only about twenty people chanced upon his appearance. Giddily, those bookshop browsers situated themselves around a small *puteal* in the center of the room as the native-Cherbourg author began a long monologue about his time in Italy, living in a hotel in Rome with thin walls where he could hear every noise. He described each detail with the meticulousness of a scientist. At the end, he told us that he had once been very poor, and that he had never forgotten this poverty. This was the reason he had remained humble in a sea of vain and presumptuous men.

The writer and feminist Kate Millett was met by a huge audience, mostly women. They murmured and applauded at Millett's every word; sometimes they even shouted out. I let off a scream of my own and demanded everyone speak in turn … or else! The audience was much more alarmed by my yelling than by my threat.

Maria Callas came often to the bookshop. I'd first met her through a mutual friend, the Italian tenor Giuseppe di Stefano, "the Golden Voice." He'd asked me to select a gift for Maria, and I'd brought her a book from the shop. She liked the present and, afterward, she began coming to Shakespeare and Company. She'd wear a large scarf and dark sunglasses hoping not to be recognized — although, of course, she was. Everyone wanted her autograph, everyone except George. Maria Callas wasn't his style. "She wears too much jewelry," he'd say.

Jorge Luis Borges arrived from Argentina, accompanied by María Kodama. Because of his blindness, María was everything to the writer. Borges was then the director of the National Library of Argentina and a sworn enemy of Peronism. For nearly two hours, a tempest of words flowed from his mouth. He spoke of his library and of Buenos Aires, which he saw as a Sicilian city that only by chance happened to be geographically situated in South America. He entertained us with a discussion on tango, which he said was the true nature of the Argentine people, identified through its steps, its passion, and its literature of moving bodies.

In those days, anything could happen. Paris was like a volcano of ideas and fireworks.

Alan Sillitoe stopped in at Shakespeare and Company in January 1973, while vacationing with his wife, the poet and author Ruth Fainlight, and their twelve-year-old son. Sillitoe had been a Tumbleweed in the 1950s, several years before the debut of his acclaimed first novel, *Saturday Night and Sunday Morning*, and his short-story collection *The Loneliness of the Long Distance Runner*.

Having intended merely to catch up with George, Fainlight and Sillitoe were instead roped into giving a reading. "Enthroned last night at George Whitman's Left Bank bookshop, drawing placidly on a small cigar as he prepared to read some of his poetry, Alan Sillitoe could not have looked more at home," reported the *International Herald Tribune*. "Sillitoe, getting into his stride, brought an almost Dickensian manner to his reading, not quite acting out the story but altering his voice adroitly and fleshing the monologue with gestures. The [audience's] laughter was almost constant — toward the end, the author himself in fact was on the edge of breaking-up."

On November 12, 1974, Anaïs Nin was at Shakespeare and Company to sign volume five of her published journals. She'd begun writing her diaries in 1914, at age eleven, but the first volume wasn't released until 1966. Up to then, Nin had been a rather obscure literary figure, known primarily as a friend — and →

Opposite: The S&Co stamp from the 1970s; George stamping a customer's purchase with his bookseller's hallmark. *Photo:* CHRISTOPHE LAURENTIN

Clockwise from top left: Allen Ginsberg (wearing a tie) and Gregory Corso (in hat). *Photo:* FRANÇOIS LAGARDE/OPALE/LEEMAGE; Alberto Moravia; Claude Roy. *Photo:* SOPHIE BASSOULS; Ruth Fainlight and Alan Sillitoe, along with their son; Anaïs Nin; and Lawrence Durrell. *Photo:* CHRISTIAN ERRATH

sometimes lover — of more celebrated authors, such as Henry Miller, Edmund Wilson, and Gore Vidal. Nin's own writing, which included short stories and a book on D. H. Lawrence, had seldom been read. But by 1974, that had changed; Nin had become famous and fashionable, particularly among young women. The queue for her book signing was said to have stretched from Shakespeare and Company to place St.-Michel. →

TED JOANS
*poet*

Anaïs Nin was a delicious woman — eternally young, graceful, straight-ahead, no pretensions. The last time I saw her was in Paris. She was reading at Shakespeare and Company.

George had appointed me and a guy named Hank to be her "sergeants at arms." Hank was an ex-colonel in the American military. I'm a jazz poet. I said, "George, what does a sergeant at arms do?" And he said, "Well, you keep people moving. You don't let them hold up Anaïs."

There was a long line to get inside and have books signed. Anaïs was in the back room. Hank and I stood behind her.

George ran in with a tray of tea. He was wearing that old paisley jacket — the one he's never had properly cleaned — with a paisley tie.

Anaïs said, "I don't want this tea, George."

"Oh but, Anaïs, this is very nice. This is darjee —"

She said, "Yes, served in little jelly and yogurt jars."

George looked disappointed. He did one of his big sighs — *hhhaaaaaa* — and returned to the front of the shop, pushing his way through the crowd.

Anaïs said to me, "What is it you're drinking?"

I said, "I've got some Bordeaux."

She said, "Give me some."

I said, "I'm sorry, Miss Nin. I don't have another glass."

She said, "I know how to do it. I learned this from a Spanish peasant."

She grabbed the neck of the bottle, stuck her thumb out — resting it against her lips — and tilted her head back. She could actually do it! You have to do it real fast. You have to know what you're doing. The wine doesn't touch your thumb. It pours right into your mouth. It works, but when I tried it, I got wine all down the front of my shirt.

Opposite: In 1974, the Shakespeare and Company banner was taken down and replaced with the 3-D lettering that remains today. *Photo:* FRED GURNER

203

STEVEN FORRY
*Tumbleweed*

For two weeks in the fall of 1974, when
I was twenty-two, I slept on a tiny bed hidden
among the Shakespeare and Company
book stacks. Day and night, irascible George
wandered in and out of the store while I swept
the floor, organized books (*could they even
be organized?*), and did odd jobs. George once
tasked me with replacing a ten-inch by ten-inch
windowpane, which I promptly broke
while trying to install. Afraid of his censure,
I returned to the hardware store, bought
a new one with my own scant money, and
stealthily replaced it. When George later found
out, he praised my "quick work."

Anaïs Nin appeared on a Tuesday night
in November. I'd arrived on time — all dusty
and dressed as a ragamuffin from my job as
an apprentice furniture restorer — but the shop
was already packed. I was stuck near the front
door. I couldn't even see Anaïs; however, I could
hear her. I was captivated by her unique voice,
soft yet powerful, a voice full of accents —
American, with hints of French and Cuban.

After the reading, Anaïs patiently
autographed books. I circled her, starstruck, but
I never once got more than ten feet from her.
She stood to leave. Her companion, Ian Hugo,
wrapped a coat around her shoulders and
took her by the hand, escorting her through
the crowd and out the front door. Something
compelled me. I rushed out of the shop, turned
left, and hurried up the street to where Anaïs
and Hugo slowly walked. I ran up behind them,
startling them both.

Anaïs turned. She looked into my eyes.
I tried to say something. Instead, I merely held
out my hand.

"Hello," she said kindly, grasping my hand
with both of hers. They felt thin but warm.
"What's your name? What brings you to France?"

For some reason, tears came to my eyes.
I told her about buying a one-way ticket
from California, starving in Paris while studying
French, and striving to fulfill my dreams.

"We must get together when you return
to the States," she said simply, reaching
into her purse and pulling out a pen and a piece
of paper. She wrote down her Silver Lake home
address and telephone number. Then she leaned
over and kissed me. *Trois fois* on the cheeks.

"When you get back, you can join us
at our gathering of writers." I'd never been
called a writer before. "See you in California,"
she said. She reached for Hugo's arm and
continued up the street. I watched until they
turned left onto rue St.-Jacques… and then
I watched some more.

Nin and George had been friends since the 1950s, when she'd frequented the bookshop. In volume five of her journals, Nin wrote of Shakespeare and Company: "How did George come to have this small bookshop by the Seine? He had read [my] 'Houseboat' story years ago. He had come to Paris to search for a houseboat. He had started his bookshop there, and was happy, but the books mildewed, and he had to move. He moved as near to the river as possible, and often from his window, watching the river, he had the illusion he was living on a houseboat." This story isn't accurate, of course. George never had a bookstore on a boat. It's possible, though, that he did tell Nin this tall tale, one that credits her with the inspiration for his bookshop. Years later, George would playfully hint at an affair. "I might have loved Anaïs once," he'd tell amazed Tumbleweeds.

A few weeks after Nin's reading at the bookstore, a French television program aired a feature on the event. It received an enthusiastic response from one demographic in particular — young women living in the countryside, many of whom were inspired to run away to the capital to try to live at Shakespeare and Company. (George could usually persuade the youngest to at least call home and tell their parents where they were.) As with other countries, the 1970s marked an advance in women's rights in France. A law granting the right to contraceptives, including the birth control pill, was passed in 1967, and then expanded in December 1974 to provide better access. A month after that, abortion was legalized. While it was often the hardline feminists (including those associated with the Mouvement de Libération des Femmes) who worked most vigorously to achieve these aims, the vast majority of French women agreed that the new laws demonstrated progress. Most of these same women, however, didn't identify themselves as "feminists"— or, among those who did, it was as "soft feminists," meaning that they didn't question a woman's primary social role as being a mother or the importance of femininity. This distinction of degree is apparent in an *International Herald Tribune* article about Nin's reading at Shakespeare and Company. "[Nin] has been claimed by women's lib as one of their own," reported the paper. "She seems a trifle uncomfortable in their embrace. 'I have been called "the gentle feminist,"' Miss Nin said, smiling gently."

In January 1976, Allen Ginsberg and Gregory Corso made one of their regular transatlantic visits to Paris and Shakespeare and Company. In the shop's guest book, Ginsberg penned an original poem, which starts "Cold January ends snowing on sidewalks" and concludes with a reference to George's goatee beginning to turn white. The poem also references

Corso's walking off with — then returning — a first-edition copy of James Joyce's *Pomes Penyeach*, a book of poetry published by Sylvia Beach in 1927.

Corso did sometimes help himself to valuable editions without paying for them. Often, he'd try to sell them to other bookshops, though occasionally he'd forget where the stolen books came from and try to peddle them back to George. Other times, Corso would offer George original handwritten manuscripts as collateral for loans. "So I would loan him some money against his notebooks," George said, "and of course he'd come back shortly afterward and steal them from me. He told me that he made more money from selling his manuscripts than from actual book sales. Eventually, I realized why." George continued: "He was banned from City Lights bookstore in San Francisco. Unfortunately, he's a good poet. If he comes around here, we let him in, but we keep an eye on him." →

George dubbed the Writer's Studio his "Little Versailles" and reserved the bed for published authors.

# Inscribed in George
# Whitman's Guest Register

ALLEN GINSBERG

Cold January ends snowing on sidewalks,
Millions of kids cry & sing in Lowell,
Massachusetts is full of bearded pubescent saints,
Notre Dame's lit up white as Whitman's beard,
I got a $1 Wool suit from Salvation Army and a tie
flowered from 1967 and a new round watch
& no beard, & Gregory a leopard spotted coat
on his back returned yr. Pomes Penyeach —
talking of Jonathan Robbins the punk Jersey Rimbaud,
& Brion's operation, & who's been in & out the Bookshop
— This morning acid wakefulness overlooking the Seine
Gregory claimed Death's democracy while the river streets
floated in Eternity eyeballed from the Balcony, solid
evanescent apartments under a grey familiar sky —

Back and forth to Paris, utopian socialists' beards grow longer and whiter — Someday the whole city'll be white as Notre Dame's snow-illumined façade, George's goatee, this page.

A poetry reading with musical accompaniment.
*Photo:* ANNE NORDMANN

211

ED WALTERS
*casino pit boss*

I went to Las Vegas, sent out by a New York mob family to handle something. Frank Sinatra and I met in the Sands Casino, where I was working as a pit boss, and he took a liking to me, wanted to help me, offer me advice on life. He started giving me books to read. What few Sinatra fans know is that he loved books, especially history books. He was in the casino at a twenty-one table, playing blackjack and talking with his friends. He told the guys, "I'm giving Eddie some books to educate him. He needs it."

He asked about a book he'd given me, was I reading it. He said, "Eddie, you must travel and when you do, go to Paris, go to the Shakespeare bookstore. I know the guy there."

I thought he was kidding me in front of his friends because I knew that guy Shakespeare was in England. I laughed him off and said, "Yeah yeah, I'll go there."

Sinatra said, "Go see the guy George — he's a guy that lives with the books."

So I read the books Sinatra gave me, and I listened to him about going to Paris and going to Shakespeare and meeting George. Let me say, these are two interesting guys. Sinatra and Whitman.

By the mid-1970s, France had started to become less welcoming to long-term expatriates. The country was experiencing double-digit inflation, rising prices, and increased unemployment. To protect jobs and resources — and also in response to the protests of May 1968, which some thought were overly influenced by American culture — the government passed a series of measures making it more difficult for foreigners to live in France. It was now almost impossible for expats to secure paid employment legally, while at the same time new laws required unsalaried foreigners to have "personal resources" equivalent to France's basic minimum wage. Furthermore, exchange rates were no longer favorable to British and American expats, as both the pound and the dollar had been devalued.

Fewer and fewer noted anglophone authors resided in the French capital — William Burroughs, James Baldwin, Lawrence Durrell, and James Jones had all departed. (Often, when writers left, they'd sell their books to George. A customer once came across a *Complete Shakespeare* with Baldwin's signature in it.) One of the few authors who remained was Mary McCarthy. The first time she came by the bookshop, she asked George if they might talk privately. In reply, George said he could to speak to her there at the front desk, neglecting to mention that he'd just spotted potential shoplifters. McCarthy left, feeling snubbed, according to George, and never came back.

Of course, short-term travelers continued to pass through Paris and the bookstore, including several young Tumbleweeds who'd later find public success. A. M. Homes visited the shop as a teenager obsessed with the Beats: "I used to think Jack Kerouac was my father," she later told a journalist. Anthony Horowitz, then only twenty-three, worked on an early novel in the upstairs library, and Hanif Kureishi arrived "under the influence of the Beats and Henry Miller and Ferlinghetti." Actor Geoffrey Rush and author Kate Grenville both frequented the shop. Grenville later described, "I arrived a young woman from the outer reaches of the cultural world, as Australia was in the late '70s, feeling like 'stout Cortez' on Darien with a wild surmise that there might be another world of writing out there. When George realized I couldn't afford to buy books, he let me borrow them for free. The bookshop expanded my universe in a way that changed my conception of writing. Instead of a reflection of the known, my writing became an adventure into the unknown."

Financially, Shakespeare and Company was doing well, despite the two years when it was barred from selling books, France's recent economic downturn, and George's genuine disinterest in turning a profit. "There are too damn many customers," he complained to a journalist. "It saves me work if they just sit and read and don't buy the books. It's maddening when they insist on buying them." George hadn't taken a vacation in years. →

People often find love at the bookshop. George said he acted as witness for more than a hundred weddings, including this one in the 1970s.

I was seventeen when, for three magical days, I lived in the bookshop. It was open all through the night, hosting writing workshops, groups, meetings, friends. Writers met, drank gallons of coffee, talked, read, slept, drank more coffee, and wrote. During a workshop, one person might lie down on a couch and doze for an hour, then get up and join right back in. Late in the mornings, the doors closed briefly so we could all rest. But even then, those of us who were staying at the bookshop went right on talking, reading, and writing. I was washing out chipped coffee cups in the makeshift kitchen when I realized with profound shock: *This is it. I am a writer.*

One night I was sitting on a couch, reading a story another Tumbleweed had thrust into my hands. I heard a sound and, when I looked up, a man had pulled a chair over to the couch, and he was staring at me. I greeted him. We began to talk. He was older than me, but he had as similarly a confusing a background as mine—was he from South Africa or Scotland? He was certainly a writer but hadn't been published either. He was particularly interested in medical ethics, and much of our conversation was about the sensation of pain and the use (and non-use) of anesthesia during operations. He made me think about things I had never imagined. My relatively peaceful life faded into insignificance in the face of his adventures, his courage in trying to make a difference. He said something I'll always remember: "What is essential is how you respond to any of life's challenges. Whether you're fortunate or unlucky, whether you decide to wage a battle or to stay home and raise children — whatever your life is like, it's responding to it with dignity and love that matters. And then to write about it from your heart."

As we talked, it was as though we were kindred spirits meeting after centuries of being apart. He listened with interest while I spoke about my passion for writing. He took me seriously. And he was funny. I laughed out loud — something I rarely did then.

Dawn overtook the dim lamp by the couch, and someone else came over, pulled up a chair, and chimed into our conversation. I remember the stranger looking at me intently and saying, "The thread is broken. Do you feel it? But it was good meeting you." And he got up abruptly and left.

I didn't learn his name, and I never saw him again. But I do know we'll meet once more, even if it's in another lifetime.

That was my third and last night "sleeping" at Shakespeare and Company. As I said good-bye to George Whitman that afternoon, words couldn't express my gratitude. I hope he understood that. Something marvelous had occurred, an initiation of sorts. George nodded with kindness and let go of my hand. My eyes filled with emotion, and I blinked like mad to clear them. There on the wall, behind George's head, were these words: "Be not inhospitable to strangers lest they be angels in disguise."

Asleep in the children's section, across from the bookshop motto, "Be not inhospitable to strangers lest they be angels in disguise."

In July 1976, he made an extended trip to the Americas. In the U.S., he visited his family on the East Coast, running into dozens of former Tumbleweeds along the way, including four in a single day in Greenwich Village (each of them no doubt shocked to see George out of the bookshop, much less Paris). After the States, he journeyed to South America, where he'd intended to travel on foot in 1936, before being bogged down in the "swamps of Chocó Colombiano," as he'd tell friends.

George had left the bookshop under the supervision of two employees — Chip and Nicole — and a handful of Tumbleweeds, telling them he'd return in September. Within a few weeks, he received a letter from Chip: "There have been many minor crises since you left. One day I came to work to find the whole entrance [crowded] by men with jackhammers, →

DERVLA MURPHY
*writer*

My six-year-old daughter, Rachel, and I were on our way home to Ireland from a three-month mid-winter trek, with a pack pony, through Baltistan. We'd been delayed in France by food poisoning (the Aeroflot meal eaten en route from Karachi). It was a rare Paris pause and our first opportunity to visit Shakespeare and Company, which I'd learned about a decade earlier — though at the time I'd dismissed it as merely one young Canadian's fantasy, the tallest of traveler's tales.

From between cliffs of books, George emerged, a cat riding high on his shoulder. I introduced myself and was agreeably taken aback by his response: Having read my first four books, he already knew that in our attitudes to traveling we were identical twins. He emphasized that, henceforth, Rachel and I must regard the Tumbleweed Hotel as our home-from-home and never stay anywhere else in Paris. It was a promise instantly made and easily kept.

The Tumbleweed Hotel resembled my own residence: the surplus of books, the rudimentary bathroom-cum-loo, and the fact that no one wasted time on maintaining a twenty-first-century standard of hygiene in the kitchen. On this last point, George was pleasingly un-American.

He never attempted to turn his guests into customers; really he only enjoyed *lending* books, sharing them, seeing people make literary discoveries that might influence the rest of their lives. On that first visit, George presented me with Maud Diver's biography of Honoria Lawrence, a love story with a difference published in 1936 by John Murray, my own publisher. He also gave me *Twelve Years of a Soldier's Life in India* by Major W. S. R. Hodson, referring me to chapter six with its mention of the territory from which Rachel and I had just returned: "The Indus is brawling along five hundred feet below us. One's neck aches with trying to see the top of the craggy mountains that shut us in. So wild a scene I have never beheld." It might have been an extract from my own journal.

Two later books from George prompted me to plan an Andean trek. One was *Rough Notes Taken During Some Rapid Journeys Across the Pampas and Among the Andes* by Captain F. B. Head, published in 1826, another John Murray book. George and I agreed with the daring young officer's observation that "to 'rough it' is in fact the only way to travel without vexation in any country." (Like Captain Head, Rachel and I would travel with a mule from Cajamarca to Cuzco.) The other volume was T. R. Ybarra's *Lands of the Andes*, published in New York in 1947. Together George and I scoffed at the author's advice to make "copious use of planes and automobiles to the virtual exclusion of other available means of transportation."

Over the years, George gave me many books, including *Three Visits to Madagascar* by the Reverend William Ellis, published in Philadelphia in 1859. Within a few pages, the perceptive and kindly Rev. Ellis overcame my allergy to missionaries, and this stout volume remains the favorite on my Madagascar shelf. No less cherished are John Foster Fraser's *The Real Siberia*, Cassell, 1902, and such idiosyncratic volumes as *The Failure of Lord Curzon: An Open Letter to the Earl of Rosebery* by C. J. O'Donnell, T. Fisher Unwin, 1903; as well as *The Lily of Life*, a fairy story by the Queen of Roumania, Hodder and Stoughton, undated.

George was no conversationalist, nor was I. An unimportant limitation. We were so on the same wavelength, as vagabond travelers and frugal socialist/humanist oddities, that not many words needed to be exchanged. Instead, we exchanged books.

tearing up the sidewalk. They finished their work rapidly, but have left the sidewalk only half paved. The only problem is the amount of dirt that gets tracked into the store…Sheday misunderstood my instructions [for constructing the bookcase] and built the back part in my absence, so instead of half a dozen shelves as you wished, there is only one. But it doesn't look too bad…About a week and a half after you left, an antiquarian *Ulysses* was stolen…I had already put a notice for people to leave bags at the desk before I got your letter, but that is difficult, too, because people have been robbed of their papers there…Apart from these problems, the store is doing really well. Madame André [the shop's neighbor] says that if I gave you an accurate report of how well the store is doing, you probably wouldn't come back until Christmas."

During George's absence, Beat poet Diane di Prima gave a reading and attempted to stay a few nights in the shop. She lasted only one. Without George's supervision, the bookstore was "quite chaotic," di Prima said. In spite of this and Chip's rather alarming reports, George proved Madame André correct and indeed didn't return for six months. He arrived just in time to serve his annual hot-buttered rum and holiday pudding to everyone who passed by the bookshop on Christmas Eve.

NAME **STROUD, PATSY LORRAINE**
P #
Born **9 JUNE, 1954**
Prof **Student-painter at Beaux-arts**
Father **Raises pigs a mile from Tarboro**
Address: **Rt. 3 Box 4 Tarboro, N.C. 278**
Rec By **Happened to stumble upon you.**

Arr   Dec 77
Dep

   Yes I am a first-year painter at Beaux-arts; in Paris
since June 1977. BFA from the SanFrancisco art Insti-
tute after three years there, the first year of school
having been at the Chicago academy of Fine art. I know
most of the North american continent and have hitch-hiked
from alaska to Panama often with nothing in my pockets
but holes. I am dull of wit, have a fetish for the smell
of ~~therebinthin~~ (an acquired taste) and know a hell of a lot
about castrating pigs. First one-woman show at the
Coffee Gallery, Upper Grant ave. San Francisco in april '76 —
Second at University of N.C. chapel Hill in May '77.
  another words your typical irresponsible long haired
artsy type living on illusions and the fruits and vegetables left in the gutter after the street markets are
over. ✳✳✳
        ✳ My second home is the New Riviera Hotel where
       ✳ I worked as toilet scrubber, stair sweeper and
          all-around excrement remover in exchange for
       my rent for almost three years. across the
       street from Washington Square park in San Fran-
       cisco — 615 Union St. (you can't miss it) a cheap
       funky North Beach Hotel where you can find any-
       thing from burned-out Beat Poets to allen Gins-
       burgs divorced wife (Sheila room # 42) to metal
       sculptors, jazz singers, junk dealers, and dog
         molesters.
            Tell them Pat "the sweeper" sent you.

If you ever come to Paris
On a cold and rainy night
& find the Shakespeare store
It can be a welcome sight

Because it has a motto
Something friendly and wise
Be kind to strangers
Lest they're angels in disguise

Above the wishing well
Is a place where you may stay
In the Tumbleweed Hotel
If you read a book a day

Meet Romeo and Juliet
Tom Jones and Little Nell
In the book-lined walls
Of the Tumbleweed Hotel

the lead in the touring com
000 francs.    of 'Oh, Calcutta'?"

## ANNOUNCEMENTS

ASSI-
KLY
FICE
Y

White,
ienna

R.L.,
Brus-

IF YOU LIKE UNUSUAL places visit the Lido in Mogadishu; the
Himalaya Hotel in Kalimpong,
Quinn's bar in Tahiti & SHAKE-
SPEARE & COMPANY, Paris. (Left
Bank facing Notre Dame. Largest
stock of antiquarian books on the
continent.)
GLAMOUR INTERNATIONAL, the
world's largest escort agency. Over
200 girls await your call. Open 9
a.m.-midnight. All credit cards

E.

Dear George,
    Thank-you for the
lodgings, oysters, ice cream,
and a glimpse of your
imagination. I will see you
again when I can dress
all in gold.
        Love,
            Ellen

From top left: A poem by two Tumbleweeds from Australia; a classified ad for the bookstore; a note left by a departing guest; reading in the library, where benches double as beds at night.

A year later, George was planning another long trip, this one to China. He wrote to his old friend Lawrence Durrell: "Living in the Tumbleweed Hotel has, unfortunately, not brought in all the wisdom I would have liked to attain, but it has kept me young and imaginative … My last letter was written to you from Buenos Aires, and my next one, God willing, will be from some far-off place like the Cocos Keeling Islands or the Kingdom of Hunza."

Durrell responded: "I hasten to reply lest you have already stepped onto your magic carpet and wafted off to China … Who will be in charge of the place when you are away? I hear that the library is at sixes and sevens still and that you can't find a thing in it — that is the charm you will say, but I must add that the Edgar Poe I bought there had a number of pages *torn out* — for easy reference, I spose. All this adds up to the simple fact that you can't sell books *and* go to China for a year at a time."

Durrell's pronouncement turned out to be somewhat accurate. George had entrusted the shop — the entirety of its operations — to a twenty-year-old employee and her teenage "apprentice." Durrell was to have had a book-signing event while George was abroad; however, the event was "mismanaged" (George's word), and the two men were estranged for several years. →

Page 225: A photo collage from a 1970s magazine article.

"By hook or by crook,
I hope that you
will possess yourselves
of money enough
to travel and to idle,
to contemplate
the future or the past
of the world, to dream
over books and
loiter at street corners
and let the line
of thought dip deep
into the stream."

Virginia Woolf

George welcomed the year 1979 from aboard the MS *Lermontov*. His journey took him across the Tropic of Cancer, past Puerto Rico, through the Panama Canal, on to Tahiti, New Zealand, and Australia, where he arrived unannounced at a former Tumbleweed's house, expecting — and receiving — a place to stay. After a stop in Bali, his final call was to Beijing to pursue the Chinese government's offer to open an Asian outpost of Shakespeare and Company. George had been enamored with China since his boyhood days living with his family in Nanjing.

While in Beijing, George learned that two spaces in the bookshop's building were about to become available for purchase: a third-floor apartment and a ground-floor retail space. He was determined to →

BARBARA STAFFORD-WILSON
*Tumbleweed*

Opposite: One of George's maxims painted on a shop step. *Photo:* CYNTHIA COPPER-BENJAMIN

A sweltering afternoon, the heat of summer 1978, with sketchbook in hand and a poem in my pocket, there came an invitation to tea upstairs. Talk ranged around and hovered on American poets, one of whom was my dad, William. George asked what I'd learned from a father who wrote poems. I answered: He has only a few imperatives, but one of them —"make sure to talk with strangers"— had led me to a good life, had brought me to Shakespeare and Co. Clicking his tongue with decision, George insisted I paint a missive on the shop's inside front step. We settled on three words: "Live For Humanity." Big and simple. I prostrated myself on the cool floor before the worn step, brush in hand, and painted the dictum in white oil. Around me, the scent of well-loved books, the soft turning of pages into night, and little pools of light connecting strangers in a dark and good shared world.

add these properties to his growing shop, which now also included a first-floor studio, located next to the front library, that he'd purchased in 1974 and reserved for published writers. George wrote to the bookshop apprentice, Barbara, from China: "Beijing," he concluded, "is unfavorable to opening an international bookstore, so it is all the more important to enlarge our premises in Paris. Please, please do your best to obtain the store and apartment. [The owners] must come down…Try to discreetly bargain with them."

George returned to Paris and immediately launched a fund-raising campaign to purchase the two vacant spaces. He had considered asking Louis Aragon for a loan but, as he explained in a letter to his brother, Carl: "Aragon is eighty-two and hard of hearing so I didn't mention our problem to him." In the end, George was able to come up with most of the down payment for the two spaces using money he'd recently inherited from a family member. The remainder was loaned to him by Barbara. "She took every penny she had out of the bank," George said. "We celebrated with a bottle of champagne."

Outside, on the shop's exterior, George hung a painting of Walt Whitman surrounded by the words *Étranger qui passe, tu ne sais pas avec quel désir ardent je te regarde.* The lines come from a French translation of Whitman's poem "To a Stranger," which in →

My poems book *Sale or Return* was published, and I sent that to George, whom I'd met a couple times before; then I followed up with a phone call. "Who?" George asked. "Oh you, right. Yes, I got it. You should do a reading. Lawrence Durrell will be gone by then. I'll put you up. You can be our poet in residence for a week." *Click*. He'd hung up.

As the poet in residence, I didn't have to help out during the day. I watched others do that, and more, like trotting off with George to a late-night flea market somewhere. Although George mainly went to buy books, he would now and then send his helpers on the most bizarre errands. Such as: "Go find me a pair of shoes. Leather. Brown or black, doesn't matter. Laces. And cheap!"

"What size, George? Won't you have to try them on?"

"Size? Look at my feet. Something that'll fit those. Shoo! And don't take all night."

One bloke was told to score him a pair of eyeglasses.

"Huh?"

"Just look around. Not too thick. Probably what you would wear. Stop making life so complicated!"

George gave me a room of my own, in the Writer's Studio across from the first-floor library. Bed, table, a couple of chairs, window overlooking whatever, a tiny kitchen of sorts, and a lavatory. There was no heating (and it being wintertime, it was cold), but George kindly laid on an electric-bar fire.

My poetry reading went well. Pretty much a full house. To my delight, more than half the audience was female. And dead keen on poetry.

I held forth for about an hour, then circulated, chatted, and flogged a few books (the proceeds from which George wanted nothing; frequently gruff, even cantankerous, he did have a generous streak). I slept well that night, my dreams fortified by a goodly intake of dry *vin rouge*.

The following morning began with a tapping at the door, and then the door opening. It was one of the lovely ladies from the previous night. I remember her name, could never forget it. S., that's what I'll call her. American girl, living in Paris for years, single mother with a couple of kids and an apartment she couldn't afford about five-minutes' walk from the shop. She'd been to India (like me), been a Rajneesh neo-sannyasin (I hadn't but I knew many), and was nice. She bore gifts. Two warm croissants and a ziplock bag filled with strong grass.

"I thought you might like waking up to a joint," she said, smiling coyly. Not what I'd had in mind, but I went for it anyway. I jumped up, put on some coffee, dressed, and started getting stoned with S.

"This bed is exuding all manner of sexual odors," she remarked whilst slipping under the covers. Indeed it was.

English begins, "Passing stranger! you do not know/ How longingly I look upon you,/You must be he I was seeking,/Or she I was seeking/(It comes to me as a dream)."

In the ground-floor space, George opened the Antiquarian, a shop devoted solely to modern first editions and rare books. On the third floor (which is separated from the bookshop by the building's second-floor tenants), George built daybeds in the front room, accommodating as many as four additional guests. George himself moved into the back room of the apartment. He wrote to a friend: "We're slowly reconstructing the ancient monastery that existed here centuries ago, but in the form of a wonderland of books, friends, writers, comrades, such as has never before existed on land or sea, a socialist utopia masquerading as a bookstore."

In 1980, George opened the Antiquarian to the left of the main shop.

# the
# 1980s
# & 90s

George's only child was born April 1, 1981, just across the Seine from the bookshop, at the hospital Hôtel-Dieu on Île de la Cité. "If the baby was a boy, we were going to call him Walt," said the sixty-seven-year-old father. Instead, the child was a girl and was named Sylvia after the founder of the first Shakespeare and Company.

In the third-floor apartment, in a back room, a bunk bed was installed for Sylvia. Downstairs, on the first floor, an aerie-like sleeping loft was built above the children's section and embellished with red-velvet drapes. The curtains parted to reveal the Mirror of Love, where visitors left messages for George, for strangers, for their future selves. "We met here thirty years ago, and now we're back with our two children!" read one message. "Dear Stranger, You may not know me, and I may not know you, but the miracles of this world have helped connect us through this note." And from an Italian mother: "Dear Mr. Whitman, My son Geri ran away from home for a week. Now I know that he's been sleeping in your library that he loves very much. I wish to thank you for the help you give to anybody."

Sylvia's childhood in the bookshop was filled with adventures. She spent her second Christmas with Allen Ginsberg, Lawrence Ferlinghetti, and Gregory Corso eating a supper of baking-powder biscuits and

Page 234: There's always a cat at S&Co, and it's always named Kitty, after Anne Frank's diary friend.

Opposite: George captioned this photo for a page in the 1984 edition of *The Paris Magazine. Photo:* MORT ROSENBLUM

236

LIKE THE PRINCESS MARIE BASHKIRTSEFF, SYLVIA WHITMAN,
SITTING HIGH UP ON HER FATHER'S SHOULDERS, SEEMS TO BE SAYING
« FROM THE HIGH TOWER OF MY DIVINE SOLITUDE I LOOK DOWN UPON THE VULGAR HERD ».

cheese soufflé. Tumbleweeds read her stories and took her to the nearby parks, accompanied by her dog, Baskerville, a large Alsatian. "What's the name for *dog* in French?" they'd ask her. "*Chien,*" Sylvia would reply. "What's the name for *book*?" Sylvia answered, "*Livre.*" And "How do you say *bookstore*?" Sylvia responded, "Shakespeare and Company."

Tumbleweeds who stayed during Sylvia's childhood included Sebastian Barry, Ethan Hawke, and Ian Rankin. Darren Aronofsky slept for two weeks in the bunk above the children's section, where, he later said, "I got my first taste of bed bugs, or I guess they got a taste of me." A twenty-something Dave Eggers visited during that time, as well, while backpacking through Europe; he recalled his first impression of the store as "an absurd place — almost down to the last crooked corner and narrow staircase." It was, he said, "the bookstore of my dreams." →

Name: David Rakoff
Passport: Canadian
Father: Psychiatrist / vivian
Mother: Doctor / GWA
Heard about s+c thru Friends

When my grandfather, David Rakovitze arrived in South Africa in 1911 he bought a banana from a fruit seller. Having heard that this fruit was just one of the boundless pleasures available to him in this new land devoid of snow and pogroms, he no doubt had his hopes up. He hated that banana. Years later my family found out why- he had never peeled it. How must this Jewish man from Neshuiz, Latvia looked? 4 feet tall, his semetic features standing out crude against the dutch noses, blond hair and blue eyes of the Dutch settlers of Cape Town, eating a banana with the peel on, muttering yiddish curses of disappointment? My family has since emigrated to Canada in 1960 where I was born. I have never been to Kuala Lumpor, I have never climbed the Andes, I have never romanticized a drug-addiction and have managed to ~~have led~~ a life devoid of stormy, destructive relationships. I am not a writer- although I have all the pretensions with none of the talent. Like most North American adolescents, I grew up thinking that I was unusual and that I alone understood Salinger like no one else.

   I have since moved to New York where I study at Columbia University. As a psychiatrist's son, I have spent most of my college career performing amateur psycho- analysis for all my friends. Like my grandfather, I have ingrained in myself the scowl of the yiddish curse, and the unintentioned inability to enjoy life's bananas without the peels.

IAN RANKIN
*Tumbleweed*

"You look like a smoker — give me a cigarette!"

These were the first words George Whitman spoke to me. In fact, they were the *only* words he spoke to me during my short time at Shakespeare and Company, though I'll never forget the look of disappointment on his face when I apologized for being a non-smoker.

This was in the autumn of 1982. My girlfriend and I had spent the summer on a vineyard-farm-commune near Castillon-la-Bataille. We had recently finished university in Edinburgh and were enjoying our adventures, including a two-week stint hitchhiking our way to Florence and back. With the grapes all picked and pressed, we were now returning to the U.K. as slowly as we could—bearing in mind that we had almost no money. Miranda (my girlfriend — now my wife) had worked for a while at Shakespeare and Company in the mid-1970s. It was her idea that we stay there for a week or so. We arrived and encountered George. Whether he remembered Miranda or not wasn't clear to me, though her memories of her time working at the shop were vivid. George had even treated her to dinner once or twice at a nearby African restaurant. He took a flask with him, which he would fill with anything left uneaten, saving himself the bother of cooking the following day.

So, anyway, grubby and exhausted, we moved into the shop. We had to work the till in the evening if no one else was around, and we had to be there at closing time (anywhere between 10 P.M. and midnight) to sweep and wash the floor. In exchange for our labors, there was an uncomfortable bed of sorts in an alcove upstairs where we could sleep. We were sitting in our little space one evening, while in the room next to us — separated only by a curtain — a writing group was holding its regular meeting. From the voices, these were predominantly young Americans, enjoying the excitement of being unshackled in Europe. They seemed to think they were the direct descendents of Ernest Hemingway, and spoke loudly and confidently. At this time, I was writing short stories and poems, none of them published, but that didn't stop me snorting and giggling with Miranda — until the group told us to leave. And for some reason, we obeyed.

We had both studied English literature at Edinburgh, including James Joyce's *Ulysses*, so we were aware of the shop's history and of Sylvia Beach. We had also read Walt Whitman, and George did have the bearing of a poet or a distinguished (if impoverished) man of letters. I don't think we encountered him again after our arrival. Maybe I had failed his audition.

Pages 242–243: George's contribution to the debut issue of *Paris Passion*, an English-language magazine published from 1981 to 1991.

NOVEMBER 12 – 25, 1981

**FIRST ISSUE**

# PASSION

- Interpol sur Seine • Paris Day & Night •
- Paris for Free • Dispatch from N.Y.
- George Whitman's City of Desire
- Fassbinder's latest • Jazz Guide

## A CITY NAMED DESIRE

# My Paris, Mon Amour
## by George Whitman

*The proprietor of Shakespeare & Company presents his feelings on the city in which he's lived for 35 years*

WHEN I WAS A seaman on the beach in New Orleans living off poor boy sandwiches, I saw the streetcar named Desire arrive at its terminal on Canal Street. Ever since the age of twelve, when I made my first trip around the world, I have been riding the streetcar named Desire from city to city. It finally came to a stop for me here, in Paris.

Paris, City of Desire, you have

Just after the war most Americans traveling to France came by ship to Le Havre and then took the boat-train to the Gare Saint-Lazare. In those postwar years Paris was a mutilated Madonna.

aftermath of war, seeing Paris for the first time was like being reborn.

Almost my first night on the town I wandered into the Café de l'Odéon and was befriended by a

cially in Mexico, where one family in Mexico City adopted me for a month and another family in Guadalajara found me feverish with dysentery on the streets, and took me home until I was cured.

For the last thirty years Shakespeare and Company has been able to reciprocate this hospitality by giving refuge to many hundreds of writers including Allen Ginsberg, Paul Ableman, Gregory Corso, Allen Sillitoe and Lawrence Ferlinghetti, who was last with us for two weeks in October. Our Tumbleweed Hotel has expanded into three apartments upstairs above the two bookstores on the ground floor. Our housemothers have included Hemingway's granddaughter and one of Lawrence Durrell's children.

Many of the world's cities are

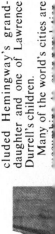

humanity, the city of light whose universities draw students from darkest Africa, from the rice paddies of Indochina, from the rain forests of South America. James Joyce called Paris "a lamp for lovers hung in the wood of the world." Perhaps the ideal human situation is that of a 17-year-old girl in Paris, in the springtime, ready for her first love.

If you look up Paris in a hundred-year-old encyclopedia you will be referred to *Lutetia Parisiorum*, stradling the banks of the Seine at 48 degrees, 50 minutes north latitude. "It is the finest city in the world and the second largest one." Today a dozen cities have surpassed Paris in population. Not everyone would agree it is still the finest city in the world. Of the two-and-a-half million Americans living abroad, about 50,000 reside in Paris. The same number lived here during the Golden Twenties before the depression reduced this figure by half.

I myself arrived in Paris in 1946 when it was host to only five or six thousand Americans. I planned to spend a summer – as a volunteer in a camp for war orphans – but have now spent half my life here in a little bookstore that has mysteriously grown into an institution. Some people say it is the most Parisian of all the things they expected to find in Paris.

*George Whitman in front of Shakespeare and Company*

Under the dim street lamps people, myself included, were picking up cigarette butts. We were rationed a few hundred grams of bread each day and a few ounces of butter and sugar each week. But despite the grim

French couple who had been active in the Résistance. They invited me to dinner, baked me a cake out of their meager rations and took me to the Bobino music hall. I have experienced similar hospitality in many lands, espe-

crime, bad architecture and a generally dehumanized environment. Many quarters of Paris are contaminated by this blight. But is Paris losing its soul? I think its artistic patrimony is too great for this to happen. I think its legend will live on in the imagination of mankind. I think there will be more writers like Henry Miller tramping on foot across Paris thinking in their sublime madness that they are "surrounded by insects masquerading as men for some diabolical purpose."

And at least in my particular corner of Paris everyday life has a special charm because generations of men now dead have bequeathed us the living poetry of its streets, gardens, squares, churches and bridges. On rainy nights I like reading Flaubert's letters to Louise Colet, knowing that across the city there are other insomniacs reading while the world sleeps.

On sunny afternoons I promenade in the Latin Quarter together with the ghosts of Baudelaire and Balzac. In the evening twilight I walk my dog, Baskerville, along the quais of the Seine, past one of the world's finest museums – the Louvre – and stop to pick up one of the world's greatest newspapers – Le Monde – and return home to one of the world's strangest bookstores – Shakespeare and Company.

243

Until Sylvia's birth, it had been unknown who would take ownership of Shakespeare and Company when that need eventually arose. In France, the inheritance tax for non-relatives is so substantial that it's often financially prohibitive to leave property to anyone who isn't a family member. On top of that, George simply couldn't envision handing off his bookstore to anyone else, a fact that didn't deter several people from trying to position themselves to become his successor. Ferlinghetti later recalled: "There seemed to be a lot of people buzzing around, like harpies ready to pounce and pick over his store." That, fortunately, now seemed to be in the past.

In May 1981, François Mitterrand became the first socialist president of France's Fifth Republic and his government the first leftist one in twenty-three years. George wrote to his niece and nephew in the States: "Today I am catching up on my correspondence while babysitting. All the schools in France are closed. Police were on our rooftop this morning to survey Mitterrand's passage in front of the bookstore. We are waiting to hear the twenty-one cannons fire in salvo from the Tuileries over the Seine, and then we will take the baby with us to participate in the celebrations at place St.-Michel. There will be twenty orchestras playing outdoors within a mile of us." →

RACHAEL HOROVITZ
*bookstore staff*

"I'm here to see George Whitman.
Samuel Beckett said to say he sent me."

I was quickly corralled up to an apartment at the top of the building and handed over to a wisp of a man with a large dog and a small child. George's first words to me were: "Hurry up, will you? Get this gingerbread made. The poet Robert Bly is coming to tea."

It was August 15, 1983. Assumption Day. I had arrived in France only that morning, my last "Incomplete" handed in to my university adviser. My graduation present from my parents in New York had been a one-way ticket to Paris, a place to stay in the Seventh, three hundred dollars, and a date to have coffee with a family friend, Samuel Beckett.

The coffee with Sam had been that same bleary morning. Café Crème cigars cut with cups of actual *café crème*. Sam, inquiring how long I would be staying and whom I knew in town, promptly suggested I go see George at Shakespeare and Company. Apparently, I hadn't given any good answers to his questions about my prospects in Paris, and I suppose he was concerned that he would end up being

responsible for my well-being. This was not, it has been written, one of Sam's strengths.

I didn't know how to make gingerbread, but I was young enough — and good enough company and possibly even nice to look at, despite an unflattering Laura Ashley — that I furtively managed to get someone to help me fix the cakes. George raced in and out muttering the word "Beckett" under his breath and occasionally looking in my direction. I wasn't sure how much more to explain about myself, but suffice it to say that after Bly walked in the door and said, "Rachael, what are *you* doing here?!" (being friends with a famous writer was about as close to a secret password as you could get with George), I found myself locked inside the bookstore for a good part of the next year.

George gave me the Writer's Studio (except for the nights Ferlinghetti came through town) and a job looking after the front desk, as well as after his daughter and usually after the dog, too. He habitually disappeared near dawn on his Mobylette, never saying where he was going or when he would be back. I passed the mornings at the till and the afternoons with Sylvia in the park behind Notre-Dame, reading her stories and dreaming of Paris even though I was in Paris. The evenings I spent falling in love and waiting for the midnight snacks, which meant time with George.

When George liked you, he had no clock, no interest in the world other than the conversation he was having with you at that moment. He made it clear that a non-literary, non-informed life was unacceptable. He was a presence like no other: handsome, witty, attentive, and sly.

Curiouser and curiouser

She would keep through all her older years, the simple and loving heart of her childhood; and she would gather about her other little children, and make their eyes bright and eager with many a strange tale, perhaps even with a dream of Wonderland.

SHAKESPEARE AND CO    ANTIQUARIAN BOOKS

In August of that year, Mitterand's government passed the Lang Law, which established fixed book pricing in France. Shops could no longer discount editions more than five percent off the publisher's cover price. This prevented big-box retailers from being able to edge smaller, independent shops out of the market, as they would do in many cases in the U.S. and other countries. The result was that France had — and continues to have — one of the strongest, most diverse bookshop cultures in the world. (Today the Lang Law is not only still in effect, it was extended in 2011 to protect e-book pricing and in 2013 to regulate online sales.)

George was determined to build an everlasting institution. He once said: "The whole idea is that we booksellers, well, we're just errand boys for the writers and the readers. Sylvia Beach used to say she was Shakespeare's errand boy." George now prioritized publishing endeavors, with the intention of using revenues to buy more apartments in the building as they became available. His first project was the autumn 1984 resurrection of *The Paris Magazine*, sixteen years after the journal's first and only edition.

"Whitman explained the time gap between issues as a combination of both his perfectionism and procrastination," reported the *International Herald Tribune*. The magazine featured an interview with

Pages 245–253: Drawing and paintings by Neil Packer for Shakespeare and Company; text adapted from Lewis Carroll's *Alice's Adventures in Wonderland.*

Ionesco, an essay by poet Edouard Roditi, and an article about Margaux Hemingway's recent visit to Paris, walking in the footsteps of her grandfather. There was also a guide of Lost Generation haunts in Paris by William Wiser, and in another article, John Train, one of the founders of *The Paris Review*, recounted the 1950s literary scene in Paris.

Back in 1975, a profile of the shop in *The New York Times* had mentioned that "Mr. Whitman is working on the story of Shakespeare and Company since he became its 'ill-starred host.'" There'd been immediate interest from publishers, including Houghton Mifflin and Harper & Row. In truth, George hadn't begun his book at all. Now, in 1985, he was determined finally to put pen to paper. In December, he boarded

# "All the characters in this bookstore are fictitious so please leave your everyday self outside the door."

GEORGE

the MS *Taras Shevchenko*, journeying to Australia, India, Yemen, and Egypt, all the while attempting to write a biography of the bookshop. He explained to a friend: "I am on a four-month leave of absence, traveling around the world…plodding away at writing a book with some faint hope it might earn enough to help purchase the other half of our house that does not belong to Shakespeare and Company." He had already settled on a title — in fact, he'd known it for decades: "The Rag & Bone Shop of the Heart." It comes from the last two lines of the poem "The Circus Animals' Desertion" by W. B. Yeats: "I must lie down where all the ladders start/In the foul rag and bone shop of the heart." But George couldn't seem to make much progress beyond the book's title. "It's such a great line," he said. "Anything I write would be anticlimactic." In the early spring, George returned to Paris and refocused on publishing other writers' works.

He brought out *Ballads Exchanged for Bread: Children of Hunger*, a booklet of poetry by Andrew Oerke, in the spring of 1987. The two men had met the year prior when the poet's daughter was a Tumbleweed. George was already an admirer of Oerke's poems, which had appeared in *The New Yorker* and *Poetry*, among other magazines, as well as of Oerke's humanitarian work. →

# SHAKESPEARE AND COMPANY  kilometer zero paris

DEAR MIKHAIL GORBACHOV:                                             June 16  1986.

　　　This letter is being carried to Moscow by a friend who is a member of the African National Congress. I myself am an American bookseller in Paris who recently made a world cruise abroad the TARAS SHEVCHENKO. I wanted to write a book, which would be difficult while working in my busy bookstore. So I took a working holiday— spending several hours every day writing and studying in my cabin— with time off to visit ports scattered along the shores of five continents. Now that the time has come to say goodbye to my travels, I would like to submit to you my idea for a floating university.

　　　Not so many years ago some Americans inaugurated "The University of the Seven Seas". This university had a curriculum for students travelling by ship and visiting the countries whose history they were studying. It was soon bankrupt. Perhaps it was too utopian to succeed without the support of some philanthropist or government.

　　　Every year an English company which makes cruises to various destinations charters its ships from the Black Sea Shipping Line. Perhaps you might like to reserve one of your ships in order to invite the youth of the world to repeat the voyages of discovery of Magellan, Vasco da Gama and Columbus.

　　　Such a floating university would stand for peace and friendship as it sailed between the warships of nations that foolishly believe they are enemies when the issues that separate them are trivial in comparison to the interests they share in common. I like to think the floating university would be an omen of a better world for all mankind as we go forward into the third millenium.

　　　　　　　　　　　　　　　　　　AMITIE SINCERE


　　　　　　　　　　　　　　　　　　George Whitman.

## Where  Streets  Of  The  World·Meet  Avenues  Of  The  Mind

OVERTY DARREN PETER

Passport No:
Place of Birth: Leicester England
Date of birth: 7 January 1965
Profession: trained as an Actor
Father's Profession: Plumber
Mother's Profession: Hosiery cutter
Date of Arrival: 7 October 1985
Date of Departure: 15 February 1986
How I came to know of 'Shakespeare & Company': I simply stumbled upon the
shop during a previous visit to Paris

My past was 'typical' English working-class until I reached the age of 16
when, while my ex-classmates went into factories, I went to Melton-Mowbray
College to get 'A' Levels and thus defied convention. My parents came from
large families, so they knew from an early age what it was like to be poor.
My mother's schooling suffered as a result of her not having any shoes to
wear to school. My father used to steal coal from the passing coal lorries
to keep his family warm during the winter. Both went into factories immediately after school, and my mother, for one, has stayed there ever since.

I was born after my parents married in their early twenties. Two years later
a sister, Nicola, followed. We lived in the slums of Leicester and, just as
Dick Whittington before me, I remember rats running over my bed as a tiny
child. Our house was the last to be pulled down during a programme of urban
(suburban) renewal. I can still remember my sister once pointing out of the
window, seeing a white layer covering the garden and thinking it was snow.
This is not a peculiarity in England (ev en in July) but my father walked out
to find the garden alive with a mass carpet of maggots. Such were the cir-
cumstances of my infancy; spent under the oppressive dictatorship of poverty
amidst the indistinctive pallor of Leicester.

During those days I was taught the value of money, and though that  lesson
has since be re-evaluated, it is still one that I'll never forget. School
came and went, and with it I suffered the agonies and frustrations of a
thousand and one other rebellious youths. But my kick against establishment
soon turned into a kick of a different kind, as I found myself rejecting the
Monetarist and Materialistic values put forward by my parents regarding my
career choice. I held out, but my contemporaries all succumbed to the pres-
sures put on them by the generation above them. Now the people I schooled
with all have factory jobs, wives, mortgages and young children. Such sad,
grey depressing lines. Leicester has so much to answer for.

In July 1980, after a prolonged illness, my father died of cancer at the age
of 38. The wall tumbled down and, after being painfully rebuilt, I realized
how precious little time we really have. So, with the backing of my mother
I  set my schemes and dreams into action so that I could live life brilliant-
ly and to the full. Thereafter began a process of education and change.

In 1981 I went to college to study Theatre Arts, Dance, Psychology and English
and, after a childhood of cruel neglect I began to read books more or less
for the first time. 'Howard's End' by E M Forster soon became my bible during
a richly rewarding two years which, in retrospect, did much to alter my ideals
and focus my philosophies.

In 1984, at the age of nineteen and with my time at college now ended, I found
myself teaching Theatre to African schoolchildren in the troubled Pearl of
Africa: Uganda. This was a period of living dangerously: machine-gunfire kept
me awake at night; friends of mine mysteriously 'disappeared' only to turn up
later as headless corpses washed up on the shores of Lake Victoria. I soon
came to understand a little of the power, greed and madness that provide the
common ruin for so many African countries.

Yet, for all its atrocities, I ultimately found Uganda a country of brilliance
and potential, and the rewards for living there were great. I found a people

of great beauty, with such strength and purity of spirit despite their immense difficulties and incredible poverty.  I learned about dreamers moving the
their mountains while helping a priest build a church and a school on a tiny
African island.  For a young boy of nineteen, those days in Africa were quite
an education.

Following Uganda came more education and discovery through time spent in the
United States, and through lengthy sojourns spent travelling around Europe.
It was at the end of a summer spent travelling in Greece that I first came
into contact with the 'rag and bone shop of the heart': Shakespeare & Company.

The story goes that I arrived in Paris with a mere 15 francs to my name.  I
desperately wanted to stay in Paris and not return to the greyness of England,
and more specifically the paralysis of Leicester.  I caught the Metro to St
Michel and, after failing to find a job at the numerous cafes and bars of the
Latin Quarter, I turned up at 'Shakespeare & Company' to check the notice-
board: no luck there either, so I tried inside.

"Excuse me, are you the owner?  Yes?  Oh.  Do you by chance need any staff?"

"Sure we do, boy!  Can ya work twenty-five hours a day?  Do ya like scrubbing
floors?  Can ya go without sleep for three weeks?  Do ya love books?  Do you
know how <u>not</u> to run a bookstore?  You do?  Then what are you waiting for?
Take over!"

And with that introduction I came to stay and be a part of the dream for the
winter of 1985/6.  Out of an act borne from sheer desperation, George entrusted me with the running of the shop during the four months he spent travelling and writing in Australia and touring around the world on a Russian cruise
ship.  As one can imagine, running 'Shakespeare & Company' has been quite an
experience: one that I'm sure I'll never forget.  I hope to move on soon
after George returns, and handing him his bookstore back, relatively safe and
sound is probably the best I can do as a means of saying "thankyou" for all
he, and everyone connected to the bookstore, has done for me.


PATERSON MATTHEW: The mundane essentials

Passport NO:
Date of birth: 10 June 1967
Place of birth: Moseley, England
Occupation: presently unemployed
but Leeds University in October
Father's profession: Geography teacher
Mother's profession: Music teacher
Address: 145 Park Road, Loughborough, UK
Arrived: 4 April 1986
Left: 7 April 1986
Heard of 'Shakespeare & Company' through Darren Overty who was (is) a friend
of mine from England

My early life was relatively uneventful apart from spending my first year in
Ghana where my parents were teaching.  In 1977 we had a holiday on the East
Coast of the USA and Canada with friends who were there at the time.  My most
vivid recollection was that of collecting absolutely every free pamphlet that
I could lay my hands on.

Other than this, my first memory is of having a fight at the age of three
with a boy from down the road, just after we moved to our present address in
1970, who was friendly with the previous owner's daughter, and, being only
four, didn't understand the ins and outs of moving house, and thought I was
an intruder.  He later went on to become my best friend for many years.

Otherwise, the usual male child's pastimes - train sets, toy soldiers, Action

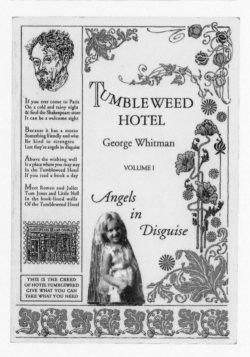

In 1988, George started on two more publishing projects. The first was *The Tumbleweed Hotel*, a collection of autobiographies from some of those who'd stayed in the bookstore. The second was volume three of *The Paris Magazine*, which came out in the summer of 1989. Noël Riley Fitch, the foremost expert on Sylvia Beach, contributed an article about the original shop's founder and her relationships with members of the Lost Generation. There was also an interview with Lawrence Ferlinghetti and a posthumous interview with Henry Miller, who'd passed away eight years earlier. "To me, feeling is everything. The brain is the least important part of the body," said Miller. "You should surrender completely to emotions without reservation. Do it gladly and be willing to die for it."

In his editor's letter for *The Paris Magazine*, George wrote: "In old age, it is hard to give up one's home and livelihood to make way for a new generation…I may yet linger on a while longer, however, among the books and ghosts that haunt these walls — percolating coffee in the morning for the guests and strangers in our midst…After all, we are only a few centuries behind the times. Let the Tories, the Capitalists, the Communists, and the Republican Party be dragged kicking and screaming into the third millennium. We will linger in our monastic twilight treasuring the world's patrimony of books." →

Opposite, from top left: The 1984 and 1989 editions of *The Paris Magazine*; the poetry collection by Andrew Oerke published by S&Co; the cover of *The Tumbleweed Hotel*.

261

Erica Lowe
*Tumbleweed*

An old man emerges from the bookshop's front door, his hair wisping wildly off his head. Holding a ratty broom, he looks about. "Here," he says, thrusting it at the closest person, a young British gentleman who'd been thumbing through a bin of books with his wife. "Make yourself useful. That side of the walk is a mess."

A bit incredulous, the gentleman gingerly accepts the broom and starts to sweep, shrugging at his equally surprised wife. The old man turns to her and smiles warmly. "I made some lovely broccoli with cheese sauce. I hope you will both join me for some later." He picks up a paperback and hands it to her. "Have you read *The Idiot*?" The woman shakes her head. "But it's Dostoyevsky's *best* novel," he says with a small hop. "Nobody ever reads it anymore! It's the same with Theodore Dreiser — everyone knows *Sister Carrie* even though *Jennie Gerhardt* is clearly his greatest work!" The old man insists the woman keep *The Idiot* free of charge. "The hero is me. I'm the idiot, lost in the labyrinth of existence —"

A boy sticks his head out a first-story window. "Hey, George!" he calls down in a thick Scottish accent. "Where's the typewriter ribbon?"

The old man squints up at him. "How the hell should I know? I'm not your supplier! Is the cat up there?"

The kid shakes his head and disappears.

"You must be George Whitman," I say, extending my hand.

"Yes, but you must call me 'dear,'" says George.

He asks if I'd like to share a treat — he has homemade strawberry ice cream upstairs. Before I can answer, he leads me into the shop and seats me in his chair. "I'll run and get it. Watch the till," he says, pointing to a wooden cigar box filled with franc notes.

A few minutes later, he returns with a frozen glass of pink ice cream and a bent spoon. "Guess what, dear?" he says. "You're going to run the store while I go pick up a load of books. Don't sell anything that isn't marked." He ducks out the front door, then sticks his head back in. "And tell all the customers about tomorrow night's tea party!"

From the large window, I watch him kick his moped into gear and zoom down the street, scattering pedestrians, his tie flying over his shoulder.

"Wake up," says George, holding a tray up to the top bunk. "Thanks for helping me out in the shop yesterday. I made you breakfast because it's your first morning here. From now on, you're on your own." The plate of eggs, blackened potatoes, and cardboard toast is the first American-style breakfast I've seen since arriving in Paris three weeks ago.

"Are you really related to Walt Whitman?" I ask, poking at my eggs.

"It's too early for interrogations," says George. He scrapes his plate into the cat's dish.

From my bunk, I can see Notre-Dame through the window.

"This is delicious," I say.

"Good," he says. "You can clean up the kitchen when you're done. The others are up and gone already. You're welcome to use the Writer's Studio. It's on the first floor. And I hope you'll serve tea at tonight's party." He raises his voice, and his eyebrows fold inward:

"I don't care if you stay here two days or two months, but you're not leaving until you've written me an autobiography — at least two pages! I'm publishing a book about everyone who's stayed here."

"No problem," I say. "Thank you."

"Don't thank me — just do it," George says, finding a candle in the cupboard and lighting it. He touches the flame to his hair in several places. It catches fire. He then quickly swats at his head to put out the blaze. "Beats a haircut!" he says, tossing the candle into the sink. I'm not sure whether to laugh or hide. "I'm off to pick up a load of books."

"I'll see you at the bookstore later," I say.

"Yeah, yeah," he says, as though he doesn't believe me and walks out of the apartment, leaving me with a sink full of greasy dishes and the smell of burnt hair.

George's red Mobylette, which he used to transport books from various estate and charity sales to the shop. *Photo:* ORLA THIERRY

FRANCES ANNE SOLOMON . BRITISH PASSPORT
DATE OF BIRTH 28 6 60
FATHERS OCCUPATION LAWYER; MOTHERS OCCUPATION MANAGEMENT CONSULTANT.
DATES OF STAY AT SHAKES PEARE:  6-9-85 to 23-9-85

my father's eyes are opal green.he's a big red man_with alot of
red curls and covered from head to toe in freckles.his mother was irish
her name was eileen.she sang and had a temper.she would stand on the
veranda in her bra and slip her arms folded across her chest squinting and
wait for me to come home from school everyday.she drove a volkswagon at
60 mph around the town til she was sixty years old.she was an alcoholic;
one night she fell down drunk in a gutter in london and died.when my grandfather got the cable saying theyd found her body what should they do with it,
he said: tell them i dont know who she is.

when eileen died my father gave me her engagement ring,but he never spoke
to me about her.its an opal,green xxx like the colour of his eyes.i wear
it on a chainaround my neck.

my father married three times and dragged me through each marriage with
him.i remember:that he worshipped my mother,beat my stepmother and threw her
down some stairs, and kept his third wife at a suspicious and calculated
distance.i came to know his passions like theback of my hand, or the inside
of my stomach.sometimes i thought we were the same person.whenever he hurt,
he would break, destroy, everything around him,while i shed all his tears.

where we come from and where i grew up is a place called trinidad, an island
off the coast of venezuela.at one time it was virtually being run by my
grandfather.hes a black man,smart,cultured,and driven.once i asked him
why with all his power he didnt do something to stop the ugly stupid things
that were happening around us, and he got sad and distant and also angry
and said: why dont you do it.

i left my father when i was eighteen.

paris is nice,its better than toronto where i was for seven years.toronto
was a womb,it was safe, i came of age there.paris keeps me on my toes; after
a year it still enchants me:it sparkles it gleams, it seduces,its rich,
it has many secrets.

i do miss the sea.i miss the way black people move when they are in their own
element,the way they express themselves,the relationship they have_with the
hot green land.i miss my father like an awful cut that won't heal.

i fell off my motorcycle and opened my knee.all night i thought about
the way my blood poured down my leg onto the street,it was so red.the
next day i sat up in the hospital bed and watched while the doctor sewed
up my leg.the doctor said:stay in bed for three weeks,but i know myself,
i cant do that.id rather be here where there are people and books and things
to do.i'll stay till i'm better.i like george, he reminds me of my grandmother
eileen.

At 5:00 P.M. on July 18, 1990, a fire broke out in the bookstore's first floor and quickly engulfed the front room. The building was evacuated, and hundreds of people, including George, gathered across the street where they could only stand and watch as flames burst through the front-library window and crawled up the outside facade. Firefighters arrived, mounted the building's central staircase, and kicked down the library door. A backdraft roared forward. Two firemen were badly injured. Only after the flames were finally extinguished did it become clear that all the shop browsers and Tumbleweeds had escaped the blaze unharmed.

With the danger passed, firefighters began clearing refuse from the library, throwing sodden books and beds from the first-floor window onto the esplanade below. What hadn't been devoured by flames had been destroyed by water. Unable to watch his life's work reduced to wet rubbish, George told everyone he was going to sleep and locked himself in the ground-floor Antiquarian with its lone mattress.

While no one knows what caused the fire, at the time speculation abounded: it was surely the ancient electrical wiring or it could have been an errant cigarette from a careless customer or was it the rejected poet who'd been lurking about? It didn't matter. The Tumbleweed Hotel and three thousand uninsured

Page 265: A literary menu, conceived by George, and illustrated by Jean Paul Briquet, which appeared in the second issue of *The Paris Magazine*.

Opposite: The fire in the first-floor library.

books, including one thousand antiquarian editions, were ruined. In their place were muddy soot, shattered glass, a hole in the ceiling, and no electricity.

"Don't mourn. Organize," George said, quoting the American labor activist and songwriter Joe Hill. George opened the shop for business the very next day.

Friends and patrons arrived to help clean up the mess, although nothing could be done about the smell of burning, which would remain in the bookshop for months. Writer-in-residence Christopher Sawyer-Lauçanno (who'd recently published the first English-language biography of Paul Bowles) scrubbed the library alongside Richard Hallward, a Tumbleweed. The two devised a plan to raise funds for rebuilding: they would organize literary events in multiple cities, inviting writers to read their works and audiences to donate money. →

LINE HOECK
*Tumbleweed*

"Shakespeare's on fire!" I don't remember who screamed it, but I'll never forget the words. We were in the adjacent park — three seventeen-year-old Danish girls traveling through Europe on InterRail. We stood up and ran to the bookstore. Smoke and fire were streaming out the windows.

Firemen arrived right after us and ran inside the building to search for people. We watched their ascent through the stairway windows, then — suddenly — fire and heat surged forth. All the firemen scrambled out of the building…

but one of them was trapped! He was hanging out of the stairway window on the second floor. He screamed the most horrible scream I've ever heard. His voice was loud and light, like a woman in deep pain. We screamed, too, all of us watching from the street.

Frantically, the other firemen collected plastic tables from the next-door café so that the man could fall on the tables rather than on the hard ground. But just as he was about to jump, a ladder truck arrived and he was helped down.

At the same time, a medical helicopter landed on the square in front of Notre-Dame to fly him and another firefighter to a burn hospital.

While this was happening, all of us — the Tumbleweeds and the hang-arounds — were trying to locate each other. Who among us was missing? We couldn't find two German girls who'd earlier been seen asleep in the room behind the library. Were they still in there? We were almost certain that a little boy had been trapped in the bookshop. He was staying at Shakespeare's with his family, and he was eight or nine years old, and not even his parents knew where he was. There were rumors that the firefighters had found a body.

The firemen had to evacuate the building entirely — meaning them, too. All they could do now was pour water through the smoking windows and onto the flames. George stood in front of the bookstore. He stood very still. Just looking. He seemed calm, but I think he must have been in some kind of shock.

The German girls turned up after some time, not even knowing they'd been missing. The boy turned up, too, which was a huge relief.

As the fire eventually came under control, the firemen began dragging out thousands and thousands of burned books. Surprisingly, one of the men called out my name. "Line! Line!" He'd found the remains of my backpack — my nametag was the only thing intact. My passport and my money were on me, but I'd lost everything else. Being a teenage girl, I had brought all my clothes.

Later that night, we were allowed to go inside the bookstore. I thought it might be dangerous to walk on the scorched floors but, of course, we wanted to see how bad the damage was. On the ground floor, nothing had burned but all the books were soaking wet and water dripped from the ceiling. On the first floor — especially in the front library, our bedroom — everything had been destroyed, and the walls were black with soot. None of the books remained, and the bed on which we'd slept the night before had burned away entirely. There's a photo of me standing in its place, and I'm smiling, which seems strange, but I was just so relieved that everyone was alive and that everything was over. Afterward, I called my parents from a pay phone and cried.

That night, my friends and I crashed at the apartment of Lee the Juggler, a former Tumbleweed. Someone gave me clothes. The next morning we returned to Shakespeare's. It wasn't the same. No one could sleep in the bookstore anymore. But we did what we could. We gathered together all the wet books and placed them outside, in front of the shop, hoping they would dry in the sun.

Opposite: Ginsberg visited shortly after the fire and photographed George, as well as renovations to the recently burned-out library. *Photos*: ALLEN GINSBERG

George offers damaged books to customers — in a shop tradition, patrons were encouraged to "give what you can; take what you need."

Just three months later, in October 1990, simultaneous benefit readings were held in Boston, London, New York, San Francisco, and Paris. In total, one hundred and forty writers read to more than five thousand attendees. Allen Ginsberg spearheaded the benefit in New York, where he received such an enthusiastic response from poets and writers that the proposed one-night event was extended to three nights. Eileen Myles, Ann Lauterbach, Bradford Morrow, David Ignatow, Wanda Phipps, and Lynne Tillman were among those who participated. In San Francisco, Lawrence Ferlinghetti and City Lights bookstore staged an exhibition of Shakespeare and Company memorabilia, along with a day of spontaneous literary readings. The Boston event, organized by

Sawyer-Lauçanno and hosted by the French Cultural Center, featured poets Frank Bidart, Lucie Brock-Broido, and William Corbett. In London, the Poetry Society and the Poetry Library co-sponsored an event that included readings from Carol Ann Duffy, Eric Mottram, and Andrew Motion, among others.

The London benefit had been organized by Hallward, who also coordinated the Paris event at Shakespeare and Company. Here, the readings occurred over twenty-one straight hours with writers such as C. K. Williams, Ted Joans, and Jean Fanchette, as well as numerous local poets, patrons, and Tumbleweeds. George provided the finale. Bursting through the front door, a burning pine branch held above his head, he marched through the crowd to the wishing well, where a shimmering liquid reflected the flame. George threw in the branch, and a fire roared upward and out toward the audience. People were more alarmed than charmed, and one person quickly rushed forward to put out the blaze.

In addition to audience donations, many far-flung friends and former Tumbleweeds sent unsolicited offerings in the mail. One man gifted two first editions by Mark Twain. The Abbey, the Canadian bookstore around the corner from the shop, raffled off a first-edition *Ulysses*. Furthermore, two publications were released to subsidize the rebuilding effort. The

Thursday; October 1, 1987

Indian Passport :          Arrived 1 October 1987
NAME:   JEET THAYIL
ADDRESS:   Rm 312 Central YMCA, Bombay, India
PERMANENT ADDRESS:   'Akshara', 166 A  Rajmahal Vilas Ext
                8th B Main Rd., Bangalore, India
JOB:  Poetry Ed., Indian Post; otherzise unemployed
FATHER: Journalist (founder Editor, Asianweek Mag; HK)

---

Poets are the most desolate of God's sad creatures.  To be a poet
dark-skinned, writing in a decidedly palefaced language is to be
doubly damned, as I confessedly am.  Should I maintain that English
is an Indian dialect -- one of three hundred plus?  That it no
more belongs to the English than, say, raincoats or roast beef?
I might, and then again I might explain why I'm in Paris France.

I'm here to get this city out of my system:  It's not that I've been
here before, no, this is a first visit.  But having grown up on
the french 'damned poets' -'les poètes maudits' as Verlaine's
famous; if slightly trite, phrase - this is a city I dad to visit.
This is zhere Baudelaire so wretchedly lived and died; the city
Lautréamount's 24-year-old ghost must undoubtedly haunt; here
the scene of Rimbaud's bitter disappointment and zhere Jim Morrison
(certainly Rimbaud's most dubious child) finally slipped into the long
sleep.  This;,by now it should be clear, is the city of poets.

One avowed intention in coming to Paris was to visit Baudelaire's
grave:  This I did and still can't believe the injustice France
has done to her greatest poet.  While  travelling through the open spaces
of the French countryside on my way up to Paris from Madrid, I
often wondered at the number of cemetaries the train past.  They
are especially noticeable because, being so crammed zith graves;
there is a shock of contrast with the surrounding countryside:
I would keep seeing hundreds of gravestones squeezed into a tiny area
and find myself unable to take with equiminity these profusions
of the massed and lonely dead.  I wondered then zhy there zere so
many cemetaries in France.  Did the French die more than other
races?  Or did they perhaps bury their dead more ostentatiously,
if less comfortably?  I had no inkling then of the shock awaiting
at the Cemetrière Montparnasse in Paris.  The French had buried
Baudelaire zith his hated step-father, General Aupicle,
(a man  he had attempted to murder on more than one occasion)
and his mother.  All three in one small,  completely
unprepossing grave.  What an unfortunate trianlge, an eternal
unholy trinty.  On a grave nearby I found a line of graffiti that
expressed my own sentiments:  POURQUOI AVEC SON PERE?
Indeed, pourquoi?

This morning; around opening time, I was in the front room
brooming the floor, There was one customer in the shop.  He
was Chinese and looking through the contemporary fiction.
He turned to me, grinned, and said, "Are you Indian?"

I said, "Yes."

"Congratulations", he said:

Needless to say, I was more than a little surprised and must
have looked it.  He went on:  "Congratulations on your victory."

I wondered what victory he might have been refering to --
a victory over the forces of evil? Death? The English language?
What for god's sake?

"India beat Austrailia in the Davis Cup, it's  the first time
you've made the finals:"

I tried to look suitably impressed.  How  to explain to this beaming
Chinese that I had no interest whatsoever in the fortunes of two
men -whatever their countries of origin- who spend hours in the
hot sun beating all hell out of  a soft ball?

In Morocco, a land I visted with my family before proceeding
alone to Paris, a land that in my mind had always embodied the
exotic, there were even more bizarre encounters.

I was walking through a market in Marrakesh overwhelmed by
the smells of burning meat and Moroccan women.  A little
boy sitting outside a shoe shop came running up pointing at me,
shouting to his firends, "Indian, Indian!"  This began a regular
occurence:  It happened that in Morocco they watch a lot of the
worst kinds of Hindi movies; full of cheap sex; gratuitious
violence and raucous music

What I'm trying to say, I think, is thqt the American
writer in exile is no exile at all:  He, at least, is the right
colour.  Think of theAsian writer who writes in English, his
entire state of being is a state of exile,

first was a book published by the literary journal *Frank*, which had its editorial address at the bookshop and boasted contributors such as John Berger, Mavis Gallant, and James Salter. The special edition, entitled *Fire Readings*, included some of the stories and poems read at the various fund-raising events. The second publication was the booklet "Shakespeare & Company: Biography of a Bookstore in Pictures and Poems," released by the bookshop and credited to nine-year-old Sylvia Whitman. George gave his daughter a commission on all the copies she sold personally, thus marking Sylvia's debut as a bookseller. →

MARK ZELLER
*journalist*

A peculiar addendum to the fire happened one night a few summers later. I was in the bookstore doing research on a story I was putting together, sitting in the middle rear of the shop, flipping through some books. A rather rotund gray-haired man with black plastic-frame glasses came in and started looking around the shelves. He moved beside me, scanned the lower levels, and asked, "Is this the science fiction section?"

"This place is pretty disorganized," I told him, "but that's mostly sci-fi down there. Looking for anything in particular?"

"No, not really," he said. "I was just wondering if they have any of my books."

"Your books…Did someone steal your books?"

"No," the man laughed, skimming the titles. "I'm a writer."

Normally, when people announce that they're writers, I'm a bit skeptical, especially when they're young. This guy, however, had to be around seventy, so I figured he was on the level.

"Written anything I might have heard of?" I asked.

"Well, I've published quite a few, but *Fahrenheit 451* is probably the most famous."

And thus I met Ray Bradbury. We talked, and I told him about the fire. He was, after all, a man famous for writing about firemen burning books, himself now wandering around a place where firemen threw burning books from the windows.

It took money, book-scouting, and a couple years, but by August 1992 the Sylvia Beach Memorial Library had been mostly restored. George wrote Sawyer-Lauçanno: "The burned-out apartment has been rebuilt to such an extent that we feel no writer is too distinguished to be offered a bed here. Old friends Ferlinghetti and Ginsberg have written to say that sometime soon they plan a long feast of reading, writing, painting, and meditation."

Ginsberg arrived in 1994 to give a reading on the bookshop's esplanade. George introduced him: "Walt Whitman said, We hear of miracles. But what is there that is not a miracle? I believe a leaf of grass is no less than the journey-work of the stars. And a mouse is miracle enough to stagger sextillions of infidels. When Walt Whitman said, who touches this book touches a man, he could have been speaking for me and my bookstore because I like you to open my →

PIA COPPER-IND
*bookstore staff*

It's been three days since I arrived in Paris. Following a stroll along the quays, I decide to take refuge at Shakespeare and Co. and read Granet on the *pensée chinoise*. I am well hidden among the children's books, wrapped in my chocolate-brown shawl and with my Chinese jacket to keep warm. I think to myself, No one will ever know I passed through here, not even M. Whitman himself.

A certain happiness at being incognito takes hold of me, and my heart is light. Then, in the other room, I hear my name. I stand up and speak. M. Whitman appears and says that we must have a talk. He says: Would I like to work at the bookstore? Starting tonight from eight to midnight?

I bite my tongue a few times to see if I will agree and then say: Yes.

The next thing I know, I'm headed into the Latin Quarter for a pizza, then I eat a *crêpe au sucre* from a cone while sitting in front of Notre-Dame, that big church whose shadow looms over the pink water. Why is the water so pink in Paris? I watch a young man with a suitcase devouring a baguette with nothing on it. I am counting the seconds until my shift begins.

Soon enough, I'm being given a lesson on how to manage the bookshop. It lasts two minutes, then M. Whitman vanishes. The books are in chaos. There are no prices on some. I can't figure out how to open the till. I drop it into the furnace by accident, start a fire, and put it out with a cushion — all to the amazement of the customers at large. Then the sales-slip machine bursts open. Abandoned to my own devices, I have to calculate everything by hand.

I also have to work without any money from the till, which I still can't open. Some drunken authors stumble in at eleven (I have thus far managed entirely on my own — M. Whitman is surely sleeping, nowhere to be found, imagined, lost, real, a ghost?) to give a running commentary on the books people are buying.

Miracles happen here, I think. This is a place in which miracles happen. It's like having sipped from a bottle of rare liquor marked DO NOT DRINK; bitten deep into a cake, DO NOT EAT. Composers coming in with messages for Hugo "because we can trust you;" the till hanging by a thread; the impression that everything — your present employment, your present situation — is transitory; that the yellow tree reflected in the front glass is perhaps only a reflection and does not exist at all. And then the idea that you are somehow imprisoned in this imaginary world where M. Whitman sometimes appears, his hair combed back, dressed for dinner, with a twinkle in his eye saying: Tomorrow you must come to the rummage sale at the American Church. You can find a Christian Dior gown there.

M. Whitman likes adventurers and revolutionaries. He was friends with Patrick Leigh Fermor, who walked across Europe around the same time M. Whitman was walking across Central America. Bruce Chatwin returned from "Patagonia to Shakespeare and Co., from the end of the world to the center of it," as he wrote in the store's guest book. Today Dervla Murphy comes to the bookshop — a shy, wiry, gray-haired lady who, when prodded, will tell you tales of Laos, Cuba, Madagascar.

Many of M. Whitman's heroes are women: Rosa Luxemburg, Louise Bryant, Angelica Balabanoff. The pictures of his other loyalties, Sacco and Vanzetti and such, adorn the third-floor rooms. He tells me stories of how the police closed him down in '68 for *aide aux révolutionnaires*. Later, he funded some students who wanted to go to Detroit and protest globalization. He is always on the cusp of the next revolution. Secrets and conspiracies. In love as in life.

A beautiful Irish poetess mysteriously arrives at the bookstore at the perilous age of ninety to live in an apartment on rue de la Huchette. She says she's come to be close to M. Whitman "before she dies." She still has the blond, angelic hair of youth and bright blue eyes. She feels sorry for the old radio announcer who's been kicked out of the bookstore for embezzlement, who ends up sleeping at the foot of her bed. I think M. Whitman may also curl up there from time to time. Anyone would. She said she wanted to die in Paris, and she does, shortly after arriving.

Ginsberg returns to the bookstore. I have his credit card. I discovered it one day in the till. It was there from his last visit, when M. Whitman claimed to have lost the key to the Writer's Studio. He borrowed Ginsberg's credit card to pop open the lock. Then he pocketed the card. This is a trick he uses on his guests to keep them "good Communists."

When Ginsberg arrives to reclaim the Writer's Studio, I give him the credit card. This is greeted with a rant: You're the one! He shouts. He calls me obscene names. (M. Whitman is probably peeking from around the corner, laughing.)

That night Ginsberg reads "Howl" in front of the bookstore. The echo of his voice reverberates off the crowd, off the passing Bateaux-Mouches, off Notre-Dame. A throng of people surround him. The night is suffused with wild youth. We believe anything is possible. We are breathless. We are fearless.

After the reading, Ginsberg invites some of us to the corner café, Le Petit Pont, a big table, the biggest table there, all men, and me. (Perhaps he feels bad about the rant earlier.) Ginsberg exudes sexuality, despite his being rather ugly. We talk about Corso, there's a whiff of inspiration, poetry is alive.

door the way you open a book — a book that leads into a magic world of the imagination. And when Walt Whitman said, I sound my barbaric yawp over the roofs of the world, he could equally have been speaking for Allen Ginsberg because both Allen's book *Howl* and *Leaves of Grass* a century earlier were great poetic manifestos that could almost make you believe what Shelley said, that poets are the unacknowledged legislators of the world... In the 1950s, Allen Ginsberg, Gregory Corso, and William Burroughs lived in the Beat Hotel, a few doors down along the river from our bookstore. One day Allen decided to give a poetry reading, but he was so shy he had to have a few drinks before he could face the miniscule audience that was all that could crowd into our little bookstore. Since then, the world has changed, Allen has changed, and the bookstore has

Allen Ginsberg's reading on the esplanade in front of the shop.
*Photo:* Michelle Campbell

changed. In those days, our little bookstore was a hole in the wall where the proprietor slept in the back room. Now we have joined together three stores and three apartments to create an institution that has become part of the artistic patrimony of Paris. Allen, too, has changed — changed most of all from a tyro

The actress Jeanne Moreau photographed through a window in the Antiquarian.
*Photo:* PATRICK SWIRC

to a paragon who is accustomed to addressing vast audiences from Paris to Prague to Peking and beyond. Tonight we welcome him back to the bookstore where he gave one of his first poetry readings almost forty years ago."

By the time George had finished speaking, a crowd of more than one thousand people had gathered in front of the bookshop, pressed closely together, completely filling rue de la Bûcherie, and near-rowdy with excitement. →

MARY DUNCAN
*academic/writer*

He was in a buoyant mood that wintry morning. "George," I asked, "why so cheerful?"

Looking up from the front desk, he replied, "I'm going to Simone de Beauvoir's to see her books this afternoon. You can come if you want." George had been contacted by Sylvie Le Bon de Beauvoir, Simone's heir, who wanted to sell her late mother's English-language library. Complex French inheritance laws had persuaded Simone to adopt Sylvie, an adult, only a few years before her death in 1986. Without a family heir, a sizable amount of de Beauvoir's estate would have been acquired by the government. Sartre had adopted Arlette Elkaïm for the same reason.

De Beauvoir's apartment was at 11 bis rue Schoelcher, a white Deco structure facing the ivy-covered walls of Montparnasse Cemetery, where de Beauvoir and Sartre are buried together. The wrought-iron and glass entrance opened onto a courtyard, which was guarded all around by large, high windows. Inside

de Beauvoir's apartment, light filtered through sheer drapes and into the sitting room where George now knelt, peering into books, placing many into his oversized canvas bags. The room had an international flair — exotic fabrics, American Indian blankets, small statuettes, and once-brightly colored pillows, now faded. Perched on the edge of a bookshelf were two bottles: vodka and vermouth. Into George's bags went paperback, hardback, and bright-red leather-bound copies of *The Second Sex*. I also saw *The Mandarins* and *Force of Circumstance*, books which had caused a breach in de Beauvoir's relationship with Nelson Algren, the American novelist.

From 1948 to 1955, Simone de Beauvoir had lived at 11 rue de la Bûcherie, on the same street as George's bookshop. Her apartment had three rooms on the top floor, a view of Notre-Dame, a leaky roof, and no bath. It was here she and Algren had been lovers. She'd vowed that "this will be our place" and "no man but you will ever sleep here," yet she broke her promise in 1952 when she met Claude Lanzmann, then a young journalist. In 1955, de Beauvoir bought the apartment on rue Schoelcher with prize money from the Prix Goncourt, which she'd received for *The Mandarins*.

Back at the bookstore, I volunteered to help sort the collection. George agreed and set me up in the Antiquarian. With a partially made bed tucked into a corner and thousands of books lining the walls, I began the pleasant task of cataloging Simone de Beauvoir's English-language library. I made five stacks. The first contained books written and signed by de Beauvoir. The second was her unsigned books. Works by Sartre constituted a third, smaller group. Fourth was miscellany. The fifth, and final pile, was possibly the most fascinating: books inscribed to de Beauvoir by other famous authors, including Gloria Steinem and Kate Millett.

Over the coming weeks, customers would buy up much of the collection, but George kept many precious volumes for the shop's own library. Once, years before, I'd asked what motivated him. "Inertia," he replied. "You throw a stone, just as Spinoza said, and it goes in that direction because it wants to. I believe in determinism. I don't believe that we are living but that we are being lived by cosmic forces. I suppose I have a tragic sense of life." Having watched George with de Beauvoir's books, handling them with such infinite care, it was hard to believe he had a tragic sense of life. Books give us life, don't they? George's love of them, as well as his desire for his shop to go on, clearly motivated him to keep living.

As night drew over Paris, I stepped out of the Antiquarian and washed my dusty hands in the Wallace fountain — the four women forever raising the large dome above their heads. I was half in the past and half in the future. I walked home.

A Wallace fountain was installed in front of the shop in the mid-1980s. There are more than a hundred such fountains in Paris, each one dispensing potable water. *Photo:* CARA TOBE

The view from the south tower of Notre-Dame includes Square René Viviani, the church of St. Julien-le-Pauvre, and the bookshop. *Photo:* CLAUDE TOURNAY

"We are torn between nostalgia for the familiar and an urge for the foreign and strange. As often as not, we are homesick most for the places we have never known." Carson McCullers

Allen Ginsberg passed away three years later, in April 1997, followed by William Burroughs in August of that same year. Anaïs Nin had died in 1977, three years after her last bookstore reading, Henry Miller in 1980, James Baldwin in 1987, and Lawrence Durrell in 1990. George, Ferlinghetti, and Corso were among the few who remained from the early bookshop days.

George, now eighty-four, wrote privately to a friend: "The fact is the future of the bookstore is a life and death matter to me since it is only recently that I realized my daughter will not participate." Sylvia had been living in the U.K. since the late 1980s, in order to experience a less chaotic childhood, one where the front room of her apartment wasn't "carpeted with Scandinavian hippies," as Ferlinghetti described it. A journalist at the time noted: "Life at the Paris bookshop can be somewhat frenetic, and some of the more unscrupulous visitors have abused the hospitality and trust on offer. One visitor funded her trip round Asia with money stolen from the cash box." Furthermore, for a child, the continual leave-taking of favorite friends and babysitters could be confusing, sometimes even heartbreaking.

In the years immediately following, Sylvia journeyed often to her father's bookstore in Paris — returning for birthdays, summer holidays, and long weekends, sleeping in her third-floor bunk bed.

RAMON VIVES XIOL
Muntaner 537 atica
08022 Barcelona
Since & Economics student, Uni. de Barcelona

I was born in Barcelona in February 1973. Long time ago...
I have had a very happy childhood sharing my life with my parents,
two brothers and one sister. I studied in the University of Barcel
ona and I learnt to play guitar and a sit of msuic. My real passions are music
(all kinds), friendship, humaan communication and the powerful and wish
fulfillment: sense of human. I am stronglydecided to not betraymy deepest
feelings and live according to them. I came three years ago to study an academic
year in the university of Paris and this time I discovered Shakespear & co. My
Italian friend worked here and I came many times to read and buy same books in
the mervellaus place you have built. This time I have came with my girlfriend
and we are spending beautiful days in Paris. The possibility of sleeping
surounded by the mmagic of library mkes me shiver. We will be able to have so
many different and beautiful dreams...

JOANA COSTA KNUFINKE
Major de Sarria 142 bajos berecha
08017 Barcelona

I was born in Barcelona in 1979. Now I am 21 years old nad it is
not my first time in Paris. I was here three years before in a
school travel. This time I have come here with my boyfriend Ramon, who loves
Paris and is sitting here, at my side, also writing to you. It is so difficult
for me to explain the story of my life in just one page that I amgoing to
explain just four or five relecant facts that have happened to me during this 21
years of experience and that I think that changed my life someway. When I was
four my parents got divorced and I now remember it as a shock, although it took
me one year to realize about what had happened to my family. I went on going to
school and I really was a very good student. At the age of sixteen I began to
interess me of reading books, a lot of books , as much as possible: Henry
Miller, Gabriel Garcia Marquez, Perez Reverte, Paul Auster and another unkown
writers. It just lasted two years since that moment of my life I am really
interested in literature. Of coures I have read a lot of books since that moment
but I have not eaten three books a week anymore. I began to study pharmacy . the
university when I was eighteen. Something very important happened to me this
last year: I decided to leave science and begin to study letters: Arts,
Philosophy, Litreature and History. I will study it next year and I am sure I
will love it. The brain and the bones are very interesting but are not able to
fill my life at all.

SARA LECKNER, TOMAS LANDFELDT
Robertsviksvagen 1
1B2 35 Danderyd
Sweden

The tired travellers of this story are Tomas nd Sara, both from
icy country called Sweden. Tomas is studying Architecture at the moment, but
that is not very important. The important thing is the fact that we are here in
this place that we just found by chenc. Sara had heard about it somewhat before,
the idea ofr travelling we guess, is to meet people and if more places would be
like this one, you would not need traveling. We do not really know where this
journey will takes us and neither where our lifes will, but wa recomand all you
other people out thre who read this to pop by at the shakespear and company, for
tea or a month; that is up to you.

But after Sylvia started boarding school in her early teens, these visits became less and less frequent until a time came when father and daughter hadn't seen one another in several years.

Throughout, it had remained George's ardent desire that his daughter grow up to helm the bookstore, but that decision had to be Sylvia's. In the late 1990s, she was still a teenager, happily studying history at University College London and surrounded by friends.

George was desperate for the shop to continue, to be "more than just a project of one man's personality, which has been the case with most literary bookstores, almost none of which have outlived their owners," and began seeking something like an angel of his own. "If I was to put a classified in the papers," he told a journalist, "it would say this: 'Eccentric bookseller

289

in his eighties looking for a philanthropic person with five million dollars and a progressive attitude about capitalism to take his Paris institution into the twenty-first century.'" George already had such a wealthy, progressive philanthropist in mind. "Perhaps ironic for a Marxist, through an intermediary George Whitman has asked George Soros, the billionaire financier, to become the next owner of the bookstore," reported *Book* magazine. "Whitman says his reasoning behind selecting Soros as successor is that he is a great humanitarian with the financial means to help expand the bookshop." →

Opposite: A draft of the letter George sent to George Soros in hopes of giving S&Co away to the famous financier.

KATHLEEN SPIVACK
*writer*

It was a particularly freezing, dismal Christmas Eve. My son Marin had been staying in town with me, playing his saxophone in all the lonely places — a special kind of melancholy thrives in Paris beneath the bare trees and bridges. We'd spent the evening in a crush, awaiting the midnight service at Notre-Dame, and now we were retreating across the Pont au Double. The damp and cold crept into us while, on the other side of the Seine, Shakespeare and Company gleamed and glowed. We went upstairs and found George in his little jewel-box room. It was almost two in the morning. Marin watched as George dictated to me yet another letter to George Soros, reading aloud from ones he'd previously started then discarded. There were many. George hoped Soros might be moved to fund the continuation of Shakespeare and Company. He was fixated on it. In fact, everyone was quite concerned about what would happen to the bookstore. The American Center on Boulevard Raspail had been closed and moved to Bercy with much fanfare, but it lasted less than two seasons. The bookstore felt like the last remaining harbor for anglophone culture in Paris. Marin and I stayed up all night working. In the morning, we ate George's famous pancakes, then doddered out into another cold winter's day.

# GEORGE SOROS -- -- PHILANTHROPIST

When Frances Steloff was President of the American Booksellers Association she told me that my bookstore had drifted into being the sort of place that might have been designed by the world's greatest architects. I have let my imagination run wild with the result that a stranger walking the streets of Paris can believe he is entering just another of the bookstores along the left bank of the Seine but if he finds his way through a labyrinth of alcoves and cubbyholes and climbs a stairway leading to a private residence then he can linger there and enjoy reading the books in my library and looking at the pictures on the walls of my bedroom.

When you were a student living in London and spent the holiday hitchhiking in France you would not have been impressed if you passed by my book shop. It was just a hole in the wall. But since then I have combined three stores and three apartments and built up a business to subsidize cultural activities not usually associated with the cash nexus. For the past half century I have held thousands of poetry readings on the esplanade in front of Shakespeare and Company, played host to many millions of book-lovers from all over the world (more and more from Eastern Europe and Russia) and given free lodgings to more than all the people living in my home town of Salem, Massachusetts -- population 40.000.

All this is the merest trifle compared to what someone like you could achieve if you would please accept the bookstore as a gift. I believe you have the vision as well as the wealth to capitalize on the opportunities which have suddenly materialized -- three floors on the other side of our building have suddenly become vacant. Plus another possibility in the near future -- a small picturesque hotel with nineteen rooms. All these and other minor expansions could be joined into one emporium by breaking down a few partitions.

How can I presume to add to your far-flung commitments ranging from Argentina to Eastern Europe, and Russia, London and New York? Expanding Shakespeare And Company may strike you as picayune compared to projects like the Central European University. But for me it has been fun and I think you might find it one of the most fascinating of all possible philanthropies, that is if you still have any money left. In the year 1600 the building where Shakespeare And Company is located was a monastery called la Maison du Moustier. In the middle ages each monastery had a monk called the *frère-lampier*, whose function it was to light the lamps. When I disappear I would like to be remembered as the *frère lampier* and I would like to pass this function on to you because of your endearing belief in your own fallibility. Here at kilometer zero in one of the most beautiful corners of one of the most romantic cities anywhere on earth someone like you could build another Taj Mahal or Villa Medicis and add one more historic monument to the world's patrimony.

George Whitman,

37 rue de la Bûcherie,

75005 Paris.

Robyn Hillman-Harrigan
born 1981 Teaneck N.J.
USA

I say that I'm a writer, but today as I am asked to write this, the prospect makes me very nervous. I say that I'm a writer because I know that I am. I know it deeply because of how writing amazes me, how it affects me, and draws me in to write and flow and write nearly everyday.

When I was 13 I needed an outlet for my problems so I began to write. My notebooks became a place of respected  truth; open helplessness and vanity. Truth that wasn't pretty and didn't have to be appreciated by the outside world. Yet I would read it aloud, perform it and revise and correct it, all through the outside world. I found that I needed the appreciation; I wanted other people to tell me what I was worth, because secretly, I did not think that I was worth much. My mother is a therapist and she taught me self-confidence and assurance and giving the semblance of safety from traps of adolescent girls - eating disorders and make-up and bleaching their hair. Sadly, to meet society's standards of beauty I would fail my own ideas, and although intellectually I knew and could talk for hours about feminism, I could not apply these ideas to myself. Still, I became the "voice of reason" among my friends, and felt I had to maintain this appearance of strength as an example. Plus I just wanted to be that perfect; I wanted to help people and make them feel that everything was alright. But my inner self could not handle the pressure from my own brain and it still can't.

From age 13 I return to here, to this point. Now I am sitting in this Shakespeare and Co. on the couch in the children's nook, and I am here because I am broken inside, and I am trying to heal myself. I left my home in suburban New Jersey, comfortable and materially complete 3 moths ago, because I begrudged myself that economic dependency. I felt myself a hypocrite because my ideals were anti-capitalist, and I knew that the materialistic society was fucked up, but I was a member of it, and knew nothing about a having to work for what comforts I had. I decided I ought to stop taking money from my parents, get a job, save money and go travel, live simply and support myself. This was a bit much for me to take on though, considering the confused and volatile state of my emotions.

You see, there were other reasons that made me decide to travel. I was angry and hurt at having spent the last three years in high school. (I graduated early) American public high school to me is this place where kids are taught to follow orders  and repress individual expression. Then we are supposed to learn the one right answer, receive the best grades in order to get into the best colleges, to step into the high-paying jobs and make ourselves a part of capitalist society.

Another reason I came to Europe is because my beautful father Bill is dying of cancer. I dont give a damn about what anyone thinks of that. I dont want to respond to the outside opinion of what that means, because it is too personal and besides I can already guess what you will say. This is why I didn't want to write this, because it is difficult to commit to telling the truth. Its become hard to believe in good, in fact hard to believe in anything at all, when a love that is so fundamental to me, a love that has been present since birth, that sustains my every breath is suddenly threatened. My father is dying, and there is a shadow across my life. Right, so who said life was fair? But I used to believe that it was somewhere deep inside. Now I cannot even believe in myself and I am fragile, nervous, paranoid and fighting for hope. This is why I am here now. For hope.
                                        — Robyn

George hung a photo of Soros on the Mirror of Love and awaited a reply. In the meantime, he and Ferlinghetti renewed a discussion about officially joining together City Lights and Shakespeare and Company. Several years earlier, Ferlinghetti had written George: "I'd like to form an association with you to save our bookstores for after we croak. We have just formed a nonprofit City Lights Foundation to ensure that City Lights will continue. Join us!" George was intrigued but, at the time, too skeptical to accept the offer. He replied: "All [your lawyer's] talk of coming to Paris this winter to tell me 'what is possible legally under both U.S. and French law' sounds like his way of humoring a utopian socialist in Paris and an anarchist utopian in San Francisco." Now in 1999, growing more anxious about the shop's continuation, George revived the conversation with Ferlinghetti, one of his most trusted friends. He wrote: "I won't last much longer, and the bookstore would all go in taxes. To avoid this, Shakespeare and Company needs the foundation, and I will pay your lawyer to enlarge yours to include us."

George came very close to signing over Shakespeare and Company to the City Lights Foundation; he even contacted his bank, instructing it to transfer his savings. In the end, however, the deal didn't go through. First, Ferlinghetti's lawyers advised against →

# Darkness Chez
# George Whitman

LAWRENCE FERLINGHETTI

Sometime toward four A.M.
softly on the stone rooftops
softly on the old skylights
I could hear the separate drops
falling like soft pellets

When the rain at last gave up
an owl somewhere
started up its glum complaint
and when a cat got its tongue
gave a croak and rolled over

which caused a single bird to fly over
from the gardens of *Julien-le-pauvre*

and start a complicated threnody
a sweet story a sad story
an oh-so-melancholy story
to some old melody

Then back it flew
into some oubliette
leaving only silence to forget
and more silence
with its own tale to tell
of paradise and hell

as I lay there waiting
for the next wing of darkness
to swoop down on me

City Lights absorbing Shakespeare and Company. They didn't trust that George would be able to bring his shop's accounts and operations to a standard sufficient to American auditors. At the time, *Biblio*, a magazine about bookselling, had described the bookstore this way: "Truly old and old fashioned, the place has no computers, no faxes, not even telephones … Apart from Karl Orend, a knowledgeable bookseller, the bookshop usually is manned by one of George's short-term wayfarers — an indifferent poet or student learning survival skills." It was these same wayfarers to whom George entrusted the shop's accounts, not much more than fanciful numbers jotted into

The cherry blossom trees were planted in the mid-1980s.

a ledger. One astute Tumbleweed, for example, was quite astonished to discover the impressive sales figures for February 30th and 31st in the previous year's account book.

For his part, George also backed away from the agreement. He was much less interested in decoding international nonprofit law than he was in his ambition to continue expanding Shakespeare and Company. In the midst of attorneys' letters, George wrote to Ferlinghetti: "As you say, I am the most eccentric person you ever met so perhaps my ideas are too fey, too far-fetched, for our brainchildren to ever marry."

Soon after, Ferlinghetti told a journalist: "George had a single-minded vision to have a great bookstore in Paris, and he's succeeded. At enormous personal cost…He sacrificed everything for the bookstore… The trouble is, if he dies and doesn't make any provision, the store is jammed full of signed books from Anaïs Nin, Henry Miller, Gregory Corso, Allen Ginsberg, Lawrence Durrell, and plenty of others. And all that ephemera will disappear."

At the top of the stairs on the first floor.
*Photo:* TOBIAS STÄBLER

# the
# 2000s

"You and I age now," wrote poet Desmond O'Grady, one of the early Tumbleweeds, to his friend George, "but Shakespeare and Company will never grow old. It's like an evergreen tree that blooms daily every year."

Many longtime customers and friends shared O'Grady's optimistic sentiment, but the truth was the shop's future seemed grave. Despite the uncertainty and his ever-increasing age, George remained determined to expand his little kingdom of books. It was a difficult ambition to achieve. Only rarely did an apartment in the building come up for sale. The last had been in 1979, when George purchased the third-floor flat. Now, twenty years later, the apartment opposite it had become available. George intended to buy it and, as he grandly described, "make the apartment a sort of annex to Notre-Dame, where poems could be composed and books written, where boys and girls on their way to dig wells in Namibia or plant trees in Malawi or open a bookstore in Hanoi or teach

Page 300: Nighttime in front of the Antiquarian, with a sign in the window for a lost Kitty. *Photo:* Esther Schubert

George emerges from his bedroom, in the back of the third-floor apartment, to Tumbleweeds waking up in the front room.

English in Shanghai or fight disease in the hinterlands of the world could be enchanted by the beauty of Paris — Paris the golden city spread out beneath our windows."

George contacted the seller's notary and accepted the asking price. Unfortunately, his own notary was slow in finalizing the deal, and another tenant in the building quickly acquired the apartment instead. George was heartbroken. "I am eighty-eight years →

Jonathan McNamara
*Tumbleweed*

At times, some of the Tumbleweeds resented customers coming in to buy books. There were grumblings of *How dare they? This is where I live, this is where I sleep, where I eat and drink, where I have romances.* There was a poet who lived in the Antiquarian for five years, and he wouldn't open the door even to George, who'd bang on the window to be let in. Naturally, the bookshop had a bad reputation when it came to customer service.

The shop itself was practically in need of a bulldozer. Nothing worked. There was no fire exit. No toilet. The electricity was pre-War. The back stairs were forty-five centimeters wide and went up at a sixty-degree angle — every now and then someone would slip down them. And the big, clay pipe in the short-story section had a gaping hole in the middle. When it rained, water came gushing out and sprayed over the books. We'd sweep the water into a stream, going from the pipe and out the front door, all to the amusement and alarm of customers.

Then there were those who wanted to make Shakespeare and Company their personal cash cow, those with designs on its ownership or management. George would never hear of it. This mental toughness was matched only by his physical strength. At near-enough ninety, he single-handedly installed those heavy, unwieldy benches in the front library, rigging up a pulley system and raising each bench from the pavement, up to the first floor, and through the window.

It was stunning to be invited to live in his shop, and his own bibliophilia inspired all of us at the Tumbleweed Hotel. In the morning, we only had to reach out to take a book off the shelf, and we all did so because we looked up to George. It was at Shakespeare's that I got acquainted with the idea of first editions and the book trade — though that didn't matter so much at the time. The books were invaluable because everything I could ever want was there.

old," he wrote in a pamphlet about the shop in 2000. "It can't be long before the bookstore is broken up to pay inheritance taxes…[and sold] to some millionaire who will probably leave it empty most of the year."

It had become more and more difficult for George to manage the shop's affairs in recent years: the government claimed he was behind in taxes, many accounts were overdue, and the bookstore itself was more run-down, dirtier, than ever before. Though still physically robust, his strength legendary, George now spent most evenings sequestered in his third-floor back bedroom. "Growing old is such a weird existence," he was overheard muttering to himself.

Downstairs, the Tumbleweeds numbered as many as twenty-five a night and were without the type of authoritative supervision that inhibits young people from fully enjoying being young people. A journalist-guest noted: "Today the shop is the site of rumbustious nocturnal revelry, much to George's dismay.

Opposite: When it rained, there were often massive leaks through the skylight — which never caused George to close the shop.

A note left for George on the Mirror of Love.

amanda lewis/age 25/virginia usa

when I was three years old I looked across the parking lot of the preschool at tommy and his mom climbing into their car and the door handle of my dad's car was level to my cheek and I asked my dad why I could not hear Tommy's thoughts but could hear my own thoughts and I do not remember the answer but I know that on the way home I slid off the backseat and played on the floor of our white Pontiac, pretending that we were a race car, in a race with the other cars on the highway.

when I was six I watched a television program about a little girl, an orphan, who ran away from home to search for her absent father. she hopped freight trains and carried a little hobo sack on a stick and had a dog to keep her company. I became obsessed with running away from home and would ride my bike all day constructing complicated escape plans in my head, and felt this great sense of urgency to do it while I was a little girl, because I imagined it would be quite easy to trick adults into taking care of me if I appeared young and helpless. for years and years afterward I would badger my friends to leave home with me in the summertime, but did not actually follow through because I didn't want to cause my parents any concern.

I am always riding a bicycle, but not a fast one in any sporty sort of way. a one speed, with the brakes at the feet. I ride in circles and figure-eights and wrap up neighborhoods around and around in vague patterns, daydreaming and having conversations and singing songs.

being in motion is my only, only solace.

when I was sixteen I found myself one evening driving around in a blue car with a new boyfriend who played the viola and had radiant olive skin; I tested him with the question I had posed to every friend since age six, do you want to run away from home with me this summer? and when he said yes without hesitation I was quiet for a long time. and then I said, well do you want to run away tomorrow?

I packed every musical instrument in the house, including the violin with only two strings and the oboe I stopped lessons for at age twelve, and I can't remember if I even brought a change of clothes. And with my arms laden with essential objects I strolled past my parents with a casual see-you-later and climbed into the blue car and we drove that night to zanesville, ohio before finally falling deeply asleep against each other's shoulders in the backseat; every morning we would wake up and with sore backs and sun coming through every window we would ask each other, where are we today, and reply, this is memphis, or this is saint louis, this might be jackson, I'm not sure lets look for a sign. it was early march and very cold and together we took a short tour of dull Midwestern cities, always arriving somewhere at three in the morning when the only thing open would be a church with its organist practicing and then we would sit very still in the balcony listening in absolute rapture.

this is the moment when I gave in to restlessness. restlessness does not stop, does it? I feel like it only gets worse. for I can't seem to be normal unless I am an arrow pointed towards somewhere else. A trajectory. I do things, I have great lists of things I have tried, like learning to read music and ride an unicycle and flying airplanes and working as a janitor and artists' model and bus driver and graduating art school and making films and baking cakes and having boyfriends and girlfriends and everything else, but the only thing that makes me happy is walking down an unfamiliar street in a place where I do not speak the language.

so I bought a standby ticket and flew to the first place available which was paris and was too shy to ask to stay here for 3 days and instead I read paul bowles the sheltering sky in the library until finally gathering the courage to speak up and when I told you my name was amanda you said it was your least favorite name and then yelled at me for making an error in the accounting book in ink.

I am leaving here December 16, 2002. I stayed exactly a month and slept in the children's section surrounded by picture books and went to the soup kitchen and walked around looking at churches and drank red wine in the library and fell asleep at night in the middle of paragraphs and was so, so content. the bookstore circled back perfectly to my image of grown-ups taking care of runaway children. thank you for having me

The first thing that strikes one about it is the 'aroma'—it smells like hell." Another guest compared the atmosphere to *Lord of the Flies.*

Carl Whitman tried to encourage his older brother, writing in a letter: "I wish your daily activities and responsibilities could be lightened with a greater

From an independent movie filmed at the shop. *Photo:* PIA CAMILLA COPPER

list of participating characters, sharing and lifting the load … I do hope some of your dreams for the bookstore come to pass, even as obstacles seem formidable. Life can be mysterious, and a response may come from an unexpected source." →

Standing at the entrance to the Sylvia Beach Memorial Library. *Photo:* CYNTHIA COPPER-BENJAMIN

SOPHIE KHO
*Tumbleweed*

I've come to Paris to live the life of a bohemian, the kind of existence that is unavoidable at Shakespeare and Company. I've made a network of friends here from all over the globe. We spend our time together in search of ourselves. We stroll barefoot by the Seine, taste French wine and cheese in the park, charm street musicians into playing a tune so good that it will tempt us to dance in public. We always succumb. I feel myself mature here even more than when I first visited England, fresh from my life in Kuala Lumpur.

We are walking along the edge of the river Seine. It's about three in the morning. It starts to get chilly, so we all head back to Shakespeare, where we sneak in. Philip does a neat trick where he uses a long stick to reach inside the window and press the button that opens the front door. It's Jenni's first night so I give her my bed. I grab a spare sleeping bag and lie on the bench next to Philip. He awakes during the night. I lean over and kiss him on the top of his head. It's rather forward on my part. Perhaps it's just Paris itself, and Shakespeare. Nothing else happens. He doesn't stir again. That was his last night.

In the morning, I change into my blue dress. I want to look nice. I want his final memory to be of a carefree, romantic spirit. We walk with Kalem and DJ, who buy beers from the Franprix. We all sit in the park beside Shakespeare. Conversations start and stop. The topic turns to massages. The next thing we know, we are giving them to each other. Philip to Kalem, Kalem to DJ, me to Philip (I walk on his back as he lies sprawled on the grass), and Philip to me. His hands are firm on my bare shoulders.

I feel the pressure on my skin. I think to myself that maybe, for him, it isn't just a casual massage between friends. At some moments, it feels as though he wants to touch me, just like that. Afterward, he leans himself against me, and we remain like this for a long time.

We return to the bookstore, where Philip gathers his bags, ready to leave. He's going to the Metro station. I offer to go with him. As we walk, I take his hand. He clasps mine back. We are walking through Paris together, hand in hand. We talk…we talk about the most random things…about philosophy mostly. He says we have a connection. He tells me he hopes to direct a documentary about philosophy someday, and I tell him I would be happy to be in it, or to be his muse.

Then we're outside the Metro station.

A hug and a few little kisses on the side of my mouth and he's walking toward the front doors. I decide there and then not to let myself regret this. I call out, "Hey!" and he turns around. I run to him, take his head in my hands, and kiss him hard on the mouth, in front of all the people. He drops his bags, wraps his arms around me, and kisses me back, for a long time. I taste him, and him me. As he holds me close, I whisper, "And that's how they do it in Paris." He laughs. These are the last words I say to him. With a kiss on my cheek, he walks back toward the station. I watch him as he moves away, passes through the doors, turns a corner and — just like that — he is gone.

That winter, in 2000, Sylvia visited the bookshop. Over the past several years, she'd seen her father only once, briefly. On this occasion, she stayed for a week, sleeping among the Tumbleweeds. "I was nineteen, and my father was in his eighties. I wanted to get to know him, before I regretted it forever," said Sylvia. "He introduced me to everyone as 'Emily, an actress from London.' I understood. Our reunion would have been too shared otherwise. It wasn't in my mind that I might return to the shop to stay. Still, there was a strong feeling that I was coming home. I had abstract childhood memories of the streets, the smells, the texture of life — the Metros and the *boulangeries*. When I returned, certain experiences fit perfectly into those memories."

In April, Sylvia visited again, this time for her twentieth birthday. George hosted a tea party on the third floor to celebrate. After the cake was cut, he handed his daughter a gift, stuffed into an old, used plastic bag. Opening it, Sylvia discovered George's own first-edition copy of *Ulysses*.

Three Tumbleweeds in the children's section, including a mother and daughter.

That summer, between her second and third years of university, Sylvia spent several months in the bookshop. At night, she slept in her old bunk bed. During the day, she busied herself around the shop, making small improvements here and there. From four to eight o'clock each evening, she worked at the front desk. She also programmed a series of events that included several poetry readings and a fete for Lawrence Ferlinghetti, who'd arrived back in Paris to commemorate the fiftieth anniversaries of the sister bookstores. The centerpiece of Sylvia's event schedule was a performance of *A Midsummer Night's Dream* staged in front of the bookshop. She and a half-dozen Tumbleweeds performed the roles, dancing and singing, some hanging from the library windows, calling out their lines.

George tossing flower petals on the cast of Sylvia's *A Midsummer Night's Dream*. *Photo:* MARGO BERDESHEVSKY.

I am the last of 6 children born to parents who lived in a tiny redneck town in Oregon in the US. My parents' parents were sons and daughters of the pioneers of the West and they didn't think much about literature; they were farmers and owned stores that sold farm implements. Somehow because of the movies, and a drama teacher, and the Second World War, my parents both grew up to care only about words.

My father loved Shakespeare and my mother loved Henry Miller. I grew up mooning over Hamlet or leafing through The Tropic of Cancer looking for the best parts.

My father wanted to be a drama teacher, but his father said to him "only sissies do that." My father was a sissy. He became a dry cleaner.

My mother wanted to be a writer. She was a writer, but she had six kids, so she never finished anything she wrote. She named me after a character in one of her plays. She always said, "I had you instead of finishing that script." This was the kind of equation that we lived with as children.

I didn't want to be a writer, but I married one and I teach other people who want to be writers. This is a strange equation too. I'm not a writer, but I teach people about writing.

Now in the middle of life, in the middle of a load of grief about a lost child, I find myself in the middle of Paris with my husband and son, who is in the middle of his childhood. We are no longer young backpackers or a young couple just married. We are in the middle and we carry a heavier load. Even my son, because he is the middle, is carrying a heavier load.

George Whitman offers us a place to stay at Shakespeare and Co. My husband asks me, "Shall we stay at Shakespeare and Co.?" The answer to this question is not a matter of money for us; since we can afford a cheap hotel if we need one. Staying at Shakespeare and Co. is much more for us than having a place to stay…it is about being in love, about being in love with Words, with Hamlet, with Miller, with my parents, with each other.

I'm reading Woolf and Joyce and Hemingway and Stein on this voyage. They have been travelling with us. I have been in love with them, but I need to teach them in the fall, and that wears my love out a bit. But here, in the room where we are staying, there is a picture of Stein and Hemingway and many of Joyce… When I call my mother who is 83 and tell her we are staying at Shakespeare and Co. and she says, "Did you ever read the script I wrote about Sylvia Beach." I had forgotten that she wrote a script about Sylvia Beach and I guess I never read it. She hasn't finished it yet, but I'm sure it will be good.

Perrin Kerns Stafford
Sept. 7th, 2004


I live in Oregon. My name is Guthrie. I'm named after Woody Guthrie. My real name is wind. My other real name is William. I live in a house. I have long hair. When I grow up I want to get a motor scooter. I am in a trip in Paris. Here are some things I like in Paris:
The Mammoth museum
The hamburger I got at McDonalds
The black lab puppy in the pet shop
The feather I see floating down out of the sky right now
Making my parents go up the Eiffel Tower
Looking at books

William Guthrie Stafford
Sept. 7th, 2004

George and Sylvia making
pancakes in the third-floor kitchen.
*Photo:* GILLIAN GARNICA

George was deeply pleased, as well as relieved, by his daughter's return, and he did his best to keep these feelings a secret from everyone, especially from Sylvia. He was continually complaining, barking orders, and undoing all of Sylvia's innovations around the bookstore. As it turned out, he had finally met his match. "My father and I had a real tug-of-war," said Sylvia. "Even small changes I made — like moving overstock books from under a table to a closet — he would sneak down in the middle of the night to undo. In the morning, I'd return things to where I wanted them. It went back and forth like this." →

A "classified ad" written on the shop's shutters, which George called the Paris Wall Newspaper.

KATHLEEN SPIVACK
*writer*

I knew how much George cherished Sylvia even though, when she first came back, he'd shout and mutter, complaining to me, like always, as he initiated his daughter into the ways of the store. Sylvia, so like her father, stood right up to him, using her sweetness and wiles and laughter. "Oh, Daddeeee," she'd say in her proper British accent whenever he yelled at her. "*Daddeeee*," she'd say, and I'd watch George melt. Sometimes I would come upon the two of them sitting in one of the red-velvet, sagging-sofa rooms, huddled together over an old copybook, George telling Sylvia which titles to order, the two of them concentrating intently, their bodies mirroring one another, the same shrugged shoulder, the same tilted head.

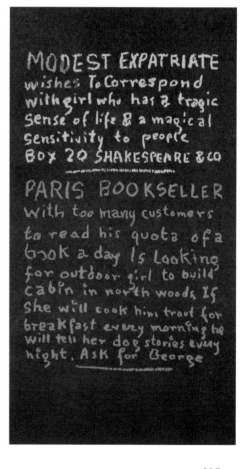

MODEST EXPATRIATE wishes To Correspond with girl who has a tragic sense of life & a magical sensitivity to people BOX 2Q SHAKESPEARE & CO

PARIS BOOKSELLER with too many customers to read his quota of a book a day Is Looking for outdoor girl to build cabin in north woods If she will cook him trout for breakfast every morning he will tell her dog stories every night. Ask for George

One night Sylvia came home late to the bookshop, where she discovered a stranger sleeping in her bed. She roused him, asked him what he was doing in her bunk. "I'm a writer from New York. I used to know Allen Ginsberg," the man argued. "Your dad said I could take this bed!"

Sylvia returned to London in the fall for her final year of university. "The bookshop is magnetic," she later said, "and people are always coming back to it. I found that happening to me, too. After my first visit, I went back and back and back — for holidays and long weekends — then I returned after I graduated in 2002, planning to stay only for the summer and autumn."

Before Sylvia's various arrivals, George would herd all the Tumbleweeds together to scrub the bookshop, inside and out. George even became moderately interested in the store's finances. He now made bi-weekly trips to the bank, and customers were less likely to find large sums of money stashed away — then forgotten — in books. He wanted to make the bookshop seem steady and solid, secure enough that his daughter might stay and make her life there. He'd written to her during her final year at university: "In the last century, mankind has probably acquired more knowledge than in all the millions of years before the existence of the printing press and libraries and →

Jacob Mitas
Born : 1976
Adress: 33500 SE Stevens Road, Corbett, Oregon 97019

Education: Bard College, Ammandal, NY
BA in Asian Studies
Intensive Chinese, Tianjin University

What I do: write, play violin, erhu, guitar, drums, make
murals, ride bikes, carpentry, dance

I was 4 years old when an elderly woman approached my sister
and I in a Dallas, Oregon supermarket and asked what would you
like to be when you grow up? I said I wanted to be a turtle
and my sister said she wanted to be a mortician. Today my
sister is a performer and writer living in London and I am a
turtle. I travel with my house on my back. I want peace and
longevity. When I was born I screamed for two years straight
according to my mom. She says I was a warrior in the past life
and came back to make peace with the world. I do things
slowly.

My father built a house in the countryside of Oregon outside a
town with more churches and bars per capita than any other in
America: Dallas. We had a community out there in the woods
known as Oread but it was broken apart by a scandalous affair.
My father turned to the bottle, and we moved to the city:
Portland, Oregon. Father quit drinking and I started doing
graffiti and learned to play the violin again. I did a mural
of the pope and sold my handmade jewelry in galleries.

After graduating I travelled through Europe for 3 months. I
met a Chinese man who didn't speak any English and at every
new site he threw his hands in the air in awe and shouted in
Chinese. That might have been partly what inspired my decision
to start studying Chinese in college, along with music and
anthropolgy. To graduate I wrote a book about Chinese
musicians living in New York and the history of the erhu, and
gave a concert playing that instrument before my master came
on and made the audience cry. It was my dream to work in a
violin shop after graduating. I found a job back in Portland
at a big shop and learned how to tell how old a violin by
sniffing it. Old violins smell like chocolate. After two years
I moved to Shanghai, got a room in an old house and taught
English to 1,200 students in a public high school. My students
called me Jack and I called them by number. At the school I
earned Chinese family members: An uncle who petted the hair on
my arm when he spoke to me. A mother who bought me a yellow
rain jacket and medicine, and a brother who said I was even
more an idiot than him and thats why he likes me. He was also
from the countryside. Then came a mysterious epidemic that
everyone came to fear. People wore masks and kept their
distance while Ting Ting, my comrade, and I got close and made
a film about Shanghai. We're going to edit the film this
summer in London and at the same time I'm going to create a
zine combining my students writing with my own.

On one of the makeshift beds in the upstairs library. *Photo:* SARAHLYNN M. PABLO

schools and bookstores like Shakespeare and Company. We have a wonderful profession — the dissemination of knowledge. So let's go together hand in hand, heart and soul, on the road to victory over superstition and militarism."

Sylvia wanted a relationship with her father, but she was unsure about comanaging the shop. "At the time, I was more interested in acting. I had performed in a few plays at university. George knew this, of course; he'd say to me, 'What do you want to be an actress for? The shop is a theater! You could be the star of the show at the till!'" He wasn't entirely joking. One day, for example, the local authorities came to the bookstore; George tried to evade them, but the officials soon had him cornered. He'd been disposing of boxes in the wrong bins. Sylvia remembered: "George yelled out, 'I'm not in charge! My daughter, she's in charge!' He was acting the eccentric old man, his white hair falling into his eyes. I joined in, playing innocent. 'Oh, lovely, yes, thank you. We'll try our best not to do that again.' The officials became so frustrated by our act that they simply walked off."

It was this summer, in 2002, that the battle over bookstore improvements truly began. George was adamantly opposed to any changes; Sylvia was committed to bringing the shop into the modern era. "When I first arrived, we didn't even have a telephone, and a publisher was threatening to cancel our account for not paying invoices. I had to ring their collections department in England from a pay phone, depositing more and more coins so we wouldn't be cut off," said Sylvia. "I wanted to improve the book stock, too, and we needed a computer system to keep inventory."

Sylvia soon installed a telephone and a computer. Then came a credit card machine and a cash register. She put in a proper bathroom, too. "We're *girls*, Daddy!" she said when George objected. Until then, Tumbleweeds had had to make do with the Turkish toilet on the stair landing leading to the second floor or venture out to a restroom in a nearby café. Over the next few years, Sylvia would make other changes, including replacing the steep, ladder-like staircase that led from the ground floor to the first-floor library; the French safety inspectors had been insisting on the retrofit for years. George was scandalized by his daughter's capitulation to the authorities. "This is a traditional bookstore, but the police want to make it look like Chicago," he said. "They've made us build these huge long stairs; they ruin the room … People liked [the old staircase]. It was right for Paris. Maybe it's not right for Chicago, but is the whole world going to look like Chicago? I hope not."

Sylvia took a more diplomatic view: "There are many places to buy books in Paris and on the internet, too. If the bookshop doesn't innovate from time to time, we'll become a museum. Change is inevitable. The new staircase and computer system are a part of this. We're also renovating the tumbledown bookshelves, but we're reusing all the old wood. With each change, I'm trying to enhance both the style and spirit of the bookshop, not disturb them. It's a fine balance." →

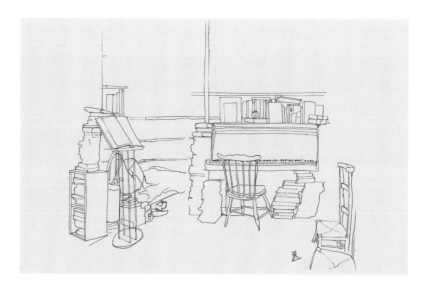

In the mid-2000s, Sylvia moved the piano from the ground floor to the back library room.
*Illustration:* ARIANE CHANG

**JAMES GREGOR**
*bookstore staff*

Sylvia wanted a professional staff to greet the multitudes who flooded into the shop. I was one of those hired, and I was grateful to have Sylvia as my boss. She was sweet and even-tempered, while George was known to be unpredictable and irascible. At one of his heralded Sunday pancake breakfasts, he spied a single boy among the crowd of young female admirers and remarked, with narrowed eyes, "There's a weed in my flower garden."

My shift lasted until midnight. Sylvia warned me that George often came down in the evenings, after she'd gone home, to engage in sabotage. Father and daughter were embroiled in a simmering conflict over "improvements." Under orders from the French authorities, the famously treacherous staircase, the one described by Anaïs Nin as "unbelievable," had been taken down and replaced by a wider, more conventional thing. Enraged, George would wait until night, then attack the stairs with a hammer. He'd previously been successful smashing up the shop's new toilet, as well as ripping out a computer.

My first night on the job, I sat at the register, nervous that George would renew his assault on the stairs. What would I do if he suddenly appeared with that hammer? When he did turn up midway through my shift, it wasn't the staircase he had in mind. A friend was coming from Atlantic City, he said. We needed another bed. Ignoring the line of waiting customers, George ordered me to climb out onto the dilapidated roof of this seventeenth century building and retrieve a piece of rotting plywood skewered with nails. I obliged, of course, and later he brought me his gluey pancakes in thanks.

George was uninterested in anything convenient, orderly, or efficient. Phones? Computers? Cash registers? No thanks. When we organized the books, he disorganized them. When we called in the cleaners, he was livid. The wishing well was constantly raided by vagrants. George didn't care. As long as people had books.

Stephen Pain
*Tumbleweed*

One night, outside an old lamplighter's house, there was a noisy clunk of a car door, the clanging of keys, and then nothing. Someone had entered the building. The *who* was a mystery. The *why* was not, or at least not for long. In the morning, the person who captained the shop for the first shift found that the new cash register was missing. Alarmed by its disappearance, the guy went in search of the shop's proprietor. At this moment, George was cooking a stew in the studio and did not seem to be in the mood to be disturbed. The guy stood before the open door, no doubt a tad nervous. He started with a tentative "George…" and there was no response. This was rather typical of George when preoccupied. The guy gathered up more courage and walked inside the studio, at which point George made eye contact: "What do you want?" The guy replied: "Mr. Whitman"— scared Tumbleweeds often resort to formal address —"I think the cash register has been stolen." "What?" "The cash register." "What's happened to the confounded thing?" "I am afraid it has gone." "A damn nuisance." "Should we contact the police?" At this, George gripped the guy's wrist with the force of a boa constrictor and said to him with a growl: "Are you a complete lunatic?" "No, Mr. Whitman," the guy replied, trembling now. George said: "We have no insurance, and the police are useless." Letting go, George waved the guy away, signaling with this gesture that he had much more important matters at hand, namely the stew, which was starting to boil over. A waft of beef trailed after the guy, followed by the sound of a slamming door.

Further investigation — including interviews with witnesses both on the ground floor and in the library — pointed to one conclusion: it was an inside job. To corroborate, one had only to rewind to several weeks before. The new cash register — while offering the clear advantages of accurate sales reporting, and while giving customers the impression of a normal, semi-efficient bookstore — went against the very grain and credo of the founder of this book empire. George detested technology. And it seemed the feeling was mutual. Every time George was at the till, the cash register revolted. It opened and closed on its own. The paper roll jammed. It did everything in its power to annoy and provoke. The thing that irritated George the most was that it occupied space, space that quite rightly was allocated for his lunch and his little yogurt jars filled with tea. George hit the register with his hand now and again. He never to anyone's knowledge actually spoke to it, but curses were clearly on the tip of his tongue.

It should be noted here that the cash register was just one battle in the internecine war between George and his daughter, Sylvia, who was fully in favor of such fancy things as registers and computers and fire alarms. George had judged that the best way to prevent the new order from taking over was anarchy and sabotage. George, in everything he did, was an old-fashioned anarchist and saboteur. While talking to a customer (rather, that is, arguing with a customer, usually about bags — George believed that you should either bring your own or be prepared to accept a recycled one, any recycled one, whatever seeping thing it had previously contained), he might inadvertently knock over a coffee onto the machine. This would help the cause greatly. *Vive la Révolution!* Another tactic was to recruit allies. George would silently spy on those working at the till; if something went wrong, he'd jump out and blame the person for incompetence. "What do you mean it's the register's fault? You damn nincompoop!" he'd shout. Using this clever strategy, George incited several Tumbleweeds to disdain the register as much as he did. Of all George's allies, the one most like him in temperament was Kitty the cat. Kitty hated the register, which was not as comfortable as the usual pile of books, and once even attacked a poor Tumbleweed as she used it. A Kitty attack is *memorable*, but that's another story.

The conflict had reached the stage at which one of them — man or machine — had to go. George was, of course, not leaving. So he phoned a taxi company and ordered the car to wait outside. He then entered the front door, shining the same flashlight that he used in the middle of the night to see who *exactly* was staying at the Tumbleweed Hotel. Seizing the register, he hurried off into the cab, taking the machine to some unknown destination, its fate probably unmentionable. George had stolen his own cash register. Happy as a Marat or Robespierre, he came home and went to his room, Kitty the coconspirator trotting behind.

Eager for her own project, one in which George couldn't interfere, Sylvia began planning a literary festival to occur the next summer, June 2003. Explaining its origins, Sylvia and her friends, festival cofounders Emily Randall and Tara Mulholland, wrote: "That Paris, mythical refuge for aspiring artists, should have no event to celebrate the haven and inspiration she has provided for some of the world's great writers seemed like an anomaly that needed to be rectified."

The theme presented itself easily: "Lost, Beat, and New." The Beat Generation, of course, had a strong connection to George's shop, the Lost Generation →

An illustration from the program for
the shop's 2008 literary festival.
*Illustration:* JEAN-BAPTISTE MAROT

TARA MULHOLLAND
*bookstore staff*

It was August 2002, and Sylvia had recently
arrived back at the bookshop. At the time,
Shakespeare and Company had three employees,
one for each shift: I was midday to four, Sylvia
was four to eight, and a lovely Scottish guy,
Colin, was "the night man," as George called
him, from eight to midnight.

Sylvia saw straight away that Shakespeare
and Company could be used theatrically,
as a stage, as a setting. Within the first months,
we'd produced a few small plays upstairs in
the library, held readings, filmed some things.

Sylvia liked challenges and the feeling of
adventure — but I also wonder if she mightn't
have been trying to prove something to her dad,
to show him that she was taking the bookshop
seriously, that she was a viable successor.
She wanted to inject new life into the shop and
to make Shakespeare and Company a center
for international literature again. At the time,
there weren't many well-known writers coming.

I'd worked three summers at the Edinburgh
Festival, so I had a very vague idea of how
an arts festival was put together. Apart from that,

we were complete novices. Sylvia and I did most of the work, along with Emily Randall, a mutual friend we'd both known in London. Other friends, Gilly Thompson and Lucy Cohen, came along later to help with the festival exhibition, the visuals, and event organization.

Sylvia, Emily, and I would walk across the street to Café Panis, drink coffees, and brainstorm about which writers to contact. None of us had internet at home, and we didn't use email much, as it meant having to find an internet café. The festival didn't have a website either. We handwrote letters to all the authors, often with a fountain pen, each very personal and probably far too earnest. To try to make it look official, we put the Shakespeare stamp at the top of each letter. We posted the invitations and then waited to see if we'd get any replies.

It's incredible that any writer agreed to take part, much less the fantastic authors who did say yes. One of the first to respond was Claire Messud — we couldn't believe it!

During the planning stage, we were working flat out. If we paused, we'd get overwhelmed: *Oh! We need somewhere to put it on, we need to book flights and hotel rooms for the participants, and then we have to organize publicity!* It was quite an ambitious project. We knew the bookshop was too small for our events, that people like Jung Chang and Alan Sillitoe would draw a crowd. Sylvia made contact with the Mairie of the Fifth Arrondissement. I think the officials were charmed by her. More formally, they thought a festival might add prestige to the area. They agreed to our staging the event in the Square René Viviani and to our erecting a tent. They even proposed that the opening night be held in the Mairie itself.

It was a lovely, prestigious start. Sylvia and Emily had worked on a speech to read aloud

at the opening — only it was written in English. Right as we sat down, ten minutes before the address, Sylvia leaned over to me and whispered, "And now you'll have to translate it!" It was terrifying, especially with my dodgy French — a simultaneous translation in front of a large audience that included French officials. But it had to be done. Sylvia or Emily would read a couple of lines in English, and I would translate into French. It felt quite representative of the festival as a whole — disorganized right down to the end, but we pulled it off.

The festival's participants were the best part. They included Noël Riley Fitch, the authority on Sylvia Beach; Shusha Guppy, the Persian writer and London editor of *The Paris Review*; and C. K. Williams, who'd won the 2000 Pulitzer Prize for poetry. There was also Alan Sillitoe, who was warm and wonderful, as were Harry Mathews and Jung Chang. The musician David Amram, who'd done the music for *Pull My Daisy*, the 1959 Beat short film, went around making everyone feel positive, saying: "This is amazing! Look at this energy!" When he played his music and read poetry, it felt like we were getting the authentic Beat experience. It was fascinating, too, to hear Carolyn Cassady's side of the story. People at her reading kept saying how incredible it must have been to have had Neal Cassady/Dean Moriarty as a husband, and she'd reply, "Those boys drank too much. They didn't know how to look after themselves."

We did a whole week of events — actually, it was eight days. It was crazy. It was too long. By the end, we'd each experienced a moment of total meltdown, of bursting into tears. Still, I don't think the writers minded the running around. There was a nice vibe, a true feeling of people coming together.

to Beach's. And Sylvia was hoping that a more coordinated event schedule, which included the festival, would attract a new generation of writers to the bookshop. When Sylvia told George about the festival, he said, "But who's going to cook for all those extra people?"

Dubbed "FestivalandCo," the event was held for eight days under a big white tent in Square René Viviani, the park between the bookshop and the church of St.-Julien-le-Pauvre. The festival had just the effect Sylvia had hoped. Having received flattering coverage in *The Sunday Times*, among other journals, it helped the bookshop reconnect with an international community of writers.

Soon after, Sylvia hired an events director, Jemma Birrell. The two began a campaign to lure the day's leading writers to appear in the shop's weekly reading series. Among the hundreds who came in the following years were Dave Eggers, Kate Tempest, Sarah Hall, Will Self, Jonathan Safran Foer, Saul Williams, and Marilynne Robinson.

Jeanette Winterson also arrived around this time. Winterson was in a dangerous depression, though Sylvia and the staff didn't know it then; they thought she simply had the flu. Sylvia extended Winterson's travel arrangements and booked her into the nearby Hotel Esmeralda, where she brought Winterson pajamas, hot soup, and books, as well as George's dog, Colette, to keep her company. Winterson later wrote of that time in her memoir: "I was safe. I was surrounded by books. My breathing became deeper and steadier and I was no longer haunted." →

LINDA FALLON
*bookstore staff*

Dave Eggers is coming to read at the bookshop, an unexpected treat, all arranged at the last, heart-stopping minute. The shop staff is small, only eight people including Sylvia, so we have to go into overdrive. Before tonight, most readings were given in the first-floor library but, judging by the number of phone calls we've received, this event will be much, much bigger than normal. The main room on the ground floor has to be dismantled and hundreds of books removed to create a temporary event space. To customers, the staff must look like book-wielding dervishes. We're ready on time, thank God, because the queue is like nothing we've seen before. Somehow, who knows how, we find room for everyone. It's like loaves and fishes, but instead it's seats and standing room.

Dave is an inspiration, an avowed fan of indie bookshops, adamant about their role in society. He isn't just galvanizing, he's also funny and charming and lovely. He's like that book-loving boy-next-door, and we all develop instant crushes. He says that e-books are no substitute for real books, Amazon's algorithms no substitute for a conversation with a good bookseller. It's exciting and reassuring to hear someone speak so passionately. For me, books are like Proust's madeleine. The sight of an e-reader could never waltz me down memory lane in the same way.

After the Q&A, George comes downstairs to greet Dave. He's now in his nineties, and it's rare for him to descend from his third-floor apartment. It's a touching moment, and there's applause from the audience at the meeting of these two humble, generous devotees of the literary world.

Everyone lines up to have their books signed. The queue weaves in and out through the shop's little labyrinth. Dave talks at length with each person. Finally, it's my turn. I have an armload of books. While he writes, we chat and he comments on the fact that I'm Irish, saying I must therefore know lots of McSweeneys. I know only one, I reply. His name is Daniel. He was my first kiss.

Above: Sylvia, Colette, and Jeanette Winterson; Marilyn Robinson with then events director Jemma Birrell. *Photos*: LAUREN GOLDENBERG

Clockwise from top left: Jonathan Safran Foer reading on the esplanade; Marina Warner in the bookshop; Dave Eggers, Sylvia, and George. *Photos:* LAUREN GOLDENBERG

331

In 2004, the film *Before Sunset* was released. Its opening scenes, with stars Julie Delpy and Ethan Hawke, had been shot at Shakespeare and Company. The movie's director, Richard Linklater, had thought George might play the role of the bookstore owner. "But he was too shy," said Sylvia, "though he's been known to set his hair on fire with a candle when he finds a reading boring." George spent most of the film shoot hiding in his upstairs apartment, and an actor had to be found. →

Opposite: Ethan Hawke and Julie Delpy filming a scene for *Before Sunset*. *Photo*: WARNER BROS

ETHAN HAWKE
*Tumbleweed*

"What can I do? Please, tell me. Is there anything I can do that will push you to be a better student?"

It was 1985, a few days before Christmas, and I was halfway through my junior year of high school. I had been grounded since October for my barely passing grades.

"Yeah … You could do something …"

"What?" she asked skeptically.

"Let me go to Europe by myself for the summer."

"If you make the honor roll and don't ask me for any money, you can do whatever you want this summer."

"Can we shake on that?"

Six months later, when she found I had made the honor roll and bought my own ticket to England, my mother panicked and decided to give my step-brother (one year older than I), for his graduation present, a ticket to London to be my chaperone.

So, at sixteen, I flew to Europe for the first time. I'd purchased the cheapest flight, some dubious charter destined for Heathrow, which ended up making an impromptu fuel stop at the Orly Airport. My brother, elated, wanted to get out in Paris. After a brief and surprisingly civil discussion, we elected to part ways, deciding that the best way to rendezvous would be to meet in exactly one week at noon in front of a famous Parisian landmark.

"How about the Notre-Dame?" I said, and it was set. If one of us didn't appear after an hour, we would try again at midnight, and so on — noon, midnight, noon, midnight — until we found each other.

One week, a shitload of theater, an all-nighter on the boat from London to Calais, and a train to Paris later, I was in front of the Notre-Dame. I waited an hour but, through the crowds, I couldn't find my brother anywhere. With eleven hours to kill before midnight and zero

French under my belt, I was a lost lamb. As luck would have it, not one hundred yards away (and open until twelve A.M.), the greatest English bookshop in all of Europe glistened across the Seine.

Fifteen years later, when Richard Linklater, Julie Delpy, and I decided to make a sequel to *Before Sunrise*, the initial concept of the film centered on a chance encounter at a bookstore. Immediately, I knew where we would shoot. When time for production rolled around, however, I discovered that the hero bookshop owner, George Whitman, hated cinema. After many approaches, word came down that Mr. Whitman was unmovable: there would be no shooting of any Hollywood bullshit in his shop. He'd worked too hard to have his reputation tarnished by a team of American populists. Rather than accept this answer, I went to the bookstore myself. George wouldn't talk to me, but he did have a daughter, twenty years old and, to my good fortune, a *Before Sunrise* fan. I met with her, explained the situation and, miraculously, George's fatwa was lifted. This is

how I became friends with Sylvia Whitman, who was eventually hired by *Before Sunset* production to run lines with me. Richard Linklater felt I was soft on my dialogue and knew I would take any opportunity to meet with the booky blonde.

Over the years, I've spent many nights in the Hotel Tumbleweed and while I thought nothing would ever top the experience of shooting *Before Sunset* in that holy place, the truth is that the bookshop has given me countless experiences that have carved themselves deeply into my consciousness. Spending the night in the bookshop for my daughter's birthday, listening to her play Bruce Springsteen on the piano. Lawrence Ferlinghetti upstairs, holding court about Henry Miller. Marilynne Robinson downstairs, reading from her new work. Every day, countless tourists line up to visit the Notre-Dame. My church is Shakespeare and Company.

George celebrated his ninety-second birthday on December 12, 2005, with a party on the shop floor. He brought down his keyboard and led everyone in the singing of the Shakespeare and Company song. "If you ever go to Paris, on a cold and rainy night, and you find the Shakespeare bookstore, it can be a welcome sight …" At its conclusion, he stood, threw up his hands, and said: "One hundred years ago, my bookstore was a wine shop hidden from the Seine by an annex of the Hôtel-Dieu hospital, which has since been demolished and replaced by a garden. And further back, in the year 1600, our whole building was a monastery called La Maison du Mustier. In medieval times, each monastery had a *frère lampier* whose duty it was to light the lamps at nightfall. I have been doing this for fifty years. Now it's my daughter's turn." He was officially handing over the reins of the shop to Sylvia.

"I think he's come round to the tidying up," Sylvia joked with one journalist. To others, she said: "I'm very determined and quite adamant about doing things my way, which means taking what George has created and slightly adjusting it to meet the present day. Fortunately, we have a very good relationship, one that's based on humor… He still gives a lot of advice. To be a really good bookseller, you have to have years of experience. I only have three!" →

Opposite: George set the Tumbleweed Hotel poem (which was actually written by two sisters) to music, for which he would play the keyboard.

334

# Angels In Disguise

## The Shakespeare and Company Song
### Notated for Piano and Guitar

Sing-a-long style. ♩=72

Words and music:
George Whitman

If you ev-er go to Par-is on a cold and rainy night and you find the shakespeare book store it can be a wel come sight be cause it has a Mo-TTo Thats friendly and wise be kind be kind to strang-ers lest they're ang-els in dis-guise be kind be kind to strangers lest they're ang-els in disguise

Above the Wishing well
Is a place where you may stay

In the Tumbleweed Hotel
If you read a book a day

Meet Romeo and Julliet
Tom Jones and Little Nell

In the book-lined walls
Of the Tumbleweed Hotel

Bevan Thomas
*Tumbleweed*

Several days after I'd arrived at the bookstore, Sylvia sent me up to the third-floor apartment to spend my shift assisting George. To the Tumbleweeds, he was an elusive and mysterious figure. Tales of his unpredictability and cantankerousness loomed over us from above.

George emerged that day from the depths of his boudoir with a cartoonish shock of white hair, well-worn silk pajamas, and a look of mischief about him. I think he missed being at the center of the exuberant bustle below, missed bossing around all the Tumbleweeds. He quickly took to ordering me about. I was to arrange and then rearrange the stacks of ancient wooden wine crates that filled his bedroom, each one brimming with all sorts of papers and ephemera. I humored his wishes. Even when he barked at me, even when he yelled, there was a twinkle in his eyes that revealed a deep and tender soul beneath. We developed a rapport. Seeing our ease together, Sylvia — in her loving effort to bring George happiness — started sending me up to work with him every day.

Each afternoon George had me move these same crates into varying corners of his beautifully crumbling and terribly cramped bedroom — all to no effect, but I did begin to notice what the boxes held. Old newspapers and hoary receipts mixed together with interesting mementos and gorgeous photographs. The closer I looked, the clearer it became that there was a trove of treasure at hand. George had kept everything: every postcard, every letter, every photo, every Tumbleweed autobiography, every journal, every document imaginable. The entirety

of George's life and the bookstore's were housed in these old crates.

For the better part of a year, I lived in the shop and in George's papers. When I wasn't sorting archives, I was George's "secretary," as he was wont to call me. Really, I was more of his companion. Together we took walks hand in hand. Occasionally, when he was able, we dared to cross the Seine to his favorite discount grocery store, where he would stock up on cheap treats for the next tea party. On the city streets, George seemed fragile, otherworldly.

Once in a blue moon, he would allow me to take him out of his insulated world. We would catch a revival film at the Action Écoles (Antonioni's *Blow-Up* was one, to which he remarked, "I meant to see that when it came out," back in 1967), or he'd treat me to Peking duck on the rue St.-Jacques and practice his Chinese with the waitstaff, or we would

hold court in front of the shop, humorously antagonizing the starstruck tourists. But mostly we just sat together, reading, and in silence.

Bill Clinton visited the bookstore with his daughter, Chelsea, and about a dozen Secret Service. I ran upstairs to summon George. I knew he was a fan of the former U.S. president, so I was surprised to encounter real resistance. After some frantic prodding on my part, George — in his characteristic midday pajamas — reluctantly agreed to descend. As our distinguished guests browsed the Antiquarian, we flew down three very precarious flights of stairs while simultaneously trying to stuff George's bare feet into dress shoes.

One night I found George reading in bed with the television switched on at his feet. The screen showed Marilyn Monroe in *The Misfits*, her final performance. I asked George if he would like to watch the film with me. He peered over his newspaper, looked quizzical for a moment, and then asked who the woman was on the TV. Assuming it was a joke, I ignored his question. When he asked again, I said, "That's Marilyn Monroe, George!" "*WHO?!*" he rattled.

I am profoundly touched by this man. Reading his archives, I feel the heartache of lost loves, the sadness of innumerable friends passing, and the irreconcilable changes in the world beyond the shop in the decades since its opening. Our friendship has taught me invaluable lessons — how to free my imagination and open my mind, the importance of community and connecting people. Most importantly, George has taught me that there are many kinds of love, an endless

spectrum that cannot be boxed or labeled. He's crushed my illusion of a singular, estimable life path toward happiness and fulfillment. He's shown me that following my dreams, or simply just believing in them, is alone a worthy endeavor.

George is unquestioningly and unapologetically himself. He loves what he loves, and he lets the rest go.

Opposite: "I don't understand why you should spend an hour doing what can be done in a minute," said George. "My way takes no time at all and costs nothing." *Photo:* Gillian Garnica

Sam Riviere

A not outlandish but still haphazard set of coincidences had to slot together for me to be here, now– June 29th 2007 –my laptop propped against an obsolete typewriter, a jammed window, beyond which Notre Dame uses its tested intimidation tactics, and the dregs of a protest swirl around the square. I arrived from London yesterday, a day after the Blair/Brown handover, and 3 days before the smoking ban is implemented. I am hoping, I suppose, to find a small corner of time to quietly slink into.

There's a light mist of rain (umbrellas pop up like poisonous mushrooms), and the cathedral looks over-exerted, pitting itself against the sky. I'm watched over by 2 massive ornate mirrors, and share these quarters with a few 1000 books– as long as they keep to themselves, I can't see us causing each other any problems. What else... The tree opposite cranes it branches surreptitiously at my window, then pretends it has other business.

Some background, then. I'll turn 26 in just over 2 weeks, on Bastille Day. 'Between jobs'. I was born on the 2nd highest floor of the Norfolk & Norwich hospital, which has recently been reborn as a giant mall. That was the 1st coincidence. And my gradual slipping into poetry (a cluster of smaller, yet nonetheless explosive coincidences) almost accounts for my presence here. I am an absurd example of the state of British higher education: a graduate in creative writing. I've been effectively cornering myself like this for years: within a decade I expect to be unemployable. I have worked as a warehouse serf, kitchen underling, short-order cook, researcher and fundraiser and hit it off with none of them. I blame the poetry!

I forget who said that uncertainty is the only state of mind that does not deceive, but until this year I'd never realised how true it is. Widespread doubt is, I'm assured, a general malaise, but ● uncertainty (paradoxically) proved the decisive stroke that propelled me to France. I hope, without much conviction, that I am at least pointed in the right direction. Like a chess player, I feel my only chance is to gaze (unflinching!) at whatever sequence of chances unfolds in front of me. Wow. I think this outing deserves a higher register, and (fuck it) italics:

*I don't look up to much. I might appear unmarked (apart, that is, from the crescent scar, planted on me like a crown, the fans that open at each eye when I smile). Though I have wept! Openly on the streets of foreign cities! At 4 am! Until, bitterly, I laughed. I have spent innumerable hours bowed over basins... No doubt it takes a little more to move me now. Reader, you're quiet. Like rain breaking in the middle-distance, traffic circling a dark, beleaguered town. See? I'm finally listening.*

My French is, shall we say, confined, but (thank god) I keep having useless flashbacks to high-school classes: *Je voudrais le jambon. Je monte l'escalier.* This is all factual, at least. I have the standard romantic notions about my stay: I want to follow girls around Paris, smoke and drink coffee outside cafes with what I imagine to be an air of Gallic sophistication. So I spent yesterday diligently gathering my 1st impressions– an aimless stagger down the wide and busy boulevards, feeling feckless as a thought in a mind resoundingly not mine. Well, let's have some good old-fashioned comparisons then! Paris is like a stone wedding cake (please!)... Paris is like London with the brightness and contrast maxed-out. I feel like a chess piece that's just slid from a black square to a white one. There. 5:30pm. Let the tolling of these discordant bells serve as my outro. One more coincidence might give me all the momentum I need.

The following spring, word came that George would be named an Officier de l'Ordre des Arts et des Lettres, a title awarded by France's Ministry of Culture to distinguished artists and writers, as well as those who've made significant contributions to the arts. There would be a ceremony and reception on June 17 at the Palais du Luxembourg. Sylvia knew her father would never accept a personal honor — he was allergic to that type of attention — so she told him the award was in recognition of the shop itself. It really wasn't much of a stretch: George and the bookstore seemed inextricably one.

At the ceremony, more than a hundred guests sipped from icy, lime coolers on a pretty summer evening. The French author and diplomat Yves Marek presented the official certificate and pinned to George's left lapel the ornate medal, which hung from a green-and-white striped ribbon. Sylvia stood behind her father, proud and moved. The next afternoon, she had the certificate framed and placed on George's bedroom wall; by morning, it had disappeared. Months later, the frame—empty and broken—was spotted buried beneath George's vast piles of papers; the certificate was still nowhere to be found.

The Officier ceremony occurred amidst the second FestivalandCo, which over the following years would become a biennial event. The 2006 theme was Travel in Words, and participating authors included Geoff Dyer, Ruth Padel, Barry Lopez, William Dalrymple, Jon Ronson, Stephen Clarke, Dervla Murphy, and Andreï Makine.

In June 2008, Shakespeare and Company staged the third FestivalandCo, titled Real Lives: Exploring Memoir and Biography, with writers Alain de Botton, Hermione Lee, André Schiffrin, Catherine Millet, A. M. Homes, Amélie Nothomb, Marjane Satrapi, and Alistair Horne, among others. The participants included a notable increase of French authors, translators, and sponsors — this owing to →

Page 339, from top: Sylvia and George with former U.S. president Bill Clinton. *Photo*: BEVAN THOMAS; George peeking out from the first-floor window. *Photo*: DANIEL STORISTEANU

Opposite: George with Sylvia's fiancé, David Delannet.

# "I'm tired of people saying they don't have time to read. I don't have time for anything else!"

GEORGE

# The Old Dogs Who Fought So Well

KATE TEMPEST

It struck me that morning. I was in Ireland, terrified in a tiny tent.
Outside, a storm was gathering gale force and I was going out of my mind with the guilt.
The drugs had made a monster out of my face.
In my head I was listening to Chopin and I was reading Joyce and I was in love with them for being
    so human and for saying it all so well.
I felt myself shrinking and desperate and worthless and I wondered if they ever felt like the most
    alone and despicable people in all of Poland, or Paris, or Dublin, or the World.
I could see him, Chopin — thin and pale at his piano stool, sicker every day, watching his hands getting older.
I could see Joyce, tearful behind his eyepatch — throwing himself into it in a room as dark as wet earth
    and I smiled to myself, and stopped trying to sleep.
The wind was still making an orchestra out of the tent. But it wasn't a requiem anymore.
Three mornings later, I woke up and reached for one of the books by the bed.
It was Bukowski. I opened him at random and read a poem I'd not read before — it was called
    *How To Be A Great Writer* and in it he said:

remember the old dogs

who fought so well:
Hemingway, Celine, Dostoevsky, Hamsun.

if you think they didn't go crazy
in tiny rooms
just like you're doing now

without women
without food
without hope
then you're not ready

And I laughed out loud. Because it's always the way — when you're alone and feeling like you could
    jump off the edge of the world,
that's when they find you and tell you they all went through the same thing.
And it makes you feel special because you feel like of all the people in all the world, these yearsdead
    writers wrote whatever it was that made the blood run in your veins again, just for you.
And you say their names out loud when you walk the city in the middle of the night, and you feel
    close to something timeless;
you feel like someone just lay you down on your back and showed you the sky.

## ROSY LAMB
*painter*

I worked on a painting of George and Sylvia for about eight months, from the fall of 2009 through the spring of 2010. I sat atop the books and magazines piled on the side of George's bedroom, trying to get as much distance from my subjects as I could. It was difficult in that tiny space, with George's bed taking up half the room, amidst falling-down photographs of writers, his paisley suit hanging ready on the outside of the clothes cupboard, old cups of tea, newspapers, and leftover bits of toast — all of it a pleasant playground for the little cockroaches that dashed through the colors on my palette and then went on to paint racing stripes up and down the walls with their feet.

I felt invisible as I worked, which is so rarely the case when painting a portrait and yet so desirable. A subject's interest in his own image can be a great weight. George never once looked at me or acknowledged my presence in his room. Once in a while, his head would turn in my direction but without focus or the slightest interest in what I was doing. It was wonderful for me, a dream come true. George didn't care that I was there looking at him, or rather — as far as he was concerned — he was alone with his cat and dog. It was as if his mind's eye had become the only eye he chose to see through. He spent much of every day in more or less the same position, propped up in bed with a book or newspaper, his thin arms stretching naked out of the bedsheets, grasping the far sides of a book. The words on the page seemed real to him, vivid in a way that I was not.

On Sunday afternoons, there would be a tea party in the adjoining room, and old friends, writers, and Tumbleweeds would present themselves at the bottom of George's bed. Often they would come armed with magazine articles about the shop. Sometimes people would give George books they'd published and dedicated: TO GEORGE WHITMAN. And once a man came to say that his wife had just had a baby and that they'd named the baby *George* after him. George asked, "Boy or girl?"

Sylvia told me that one day, when the portrait was almost finished, she'd caught George examining it with some interest. He seemed to like it, she said, but he had one critical comment: "Put the dog and the cat in the poster." I would have if the animals had ever settled into the folds of the bedcovers long enough, but they were moving targets. Instead I made George's request the title of the painting.

When *Put the Dog and the Cat in the Poster* was subsequently shown at the BP Portrait Award exhibition at the National Gallery in London, I thought to myself: *This is surely the only portrait here whose subject is still in the exact same spot as when the painting was done.* In my mind's eye, I saw George, across the Channel, reading his newspaper under the light of a solitary bulb, his dog and his cat asleep by his side.

Sylvia's fiancé, David Delannet, a Parisian whom she'd met a couple of years earlier while working in the Antiquarian (and who would later become comanager of the bookstore). On Friday, June 13, Paul Auster and Siri Hustvedt headlined a special event in the *salle des fêtes* at Hôtel de Ville. Their discussion with Faber and Faber editor Walter Donohue was punctuated with readings by the actress Charlotte Rampling. In the end, more than six thousand people had attended the four-day, free-admission festival, making it one of the largest literary events in Paris at the time.

George wasn't entirely satisfied with the shop's projects. He said to a journalist: "We don't consider it a real bookstore unless there's a hundred thousand books. We just have about half of that. But you'll have to talk to my daughter. She's in charge now." He added, "I hope she'll be happy here. I think she will."

The painting *Put the Dog and the Cat in the Poster* by Rosy Lamb.

"What a piece of work is a man! How noble in reason, how infinite in faculty, in form and moving how express and admirable, in action how like an angel, in apprehension how like a god — the beauty of the world, the paragon of animals! And yet to me what is this quintessence of dust?"

WILLIAM SHAKESPEARE

Sylvia Whitman

# Forever Is Composed of Nows

My father passed away on December 14, 2011, two days after his ninety-eighth birthday, in his bedroom above the bookshop. Virginia Woolf said that the death of one of her friends took the substance out of everything. That's how it felt when George died.

Messages came in from across the globe. I read about a customer who had been making his way through the fiction section alphabetically, day after day. George silently gave him a key and told him to move in; this way, the man could continue through the night. I read about the day George announced a "millionaire Communist" had arrived at the bookshop and introduced the Tumbleweeds to Allen Ginsberg. I read about the girl whose autobiography began: "Our lives are made up not only of our actions, but also of the books we read." Upon receiving it, George quoted Emerson greeting Thoreau at "the beginning of a great career" and said she must move in forever and write her masterpiece. I read about a customer who walked into the bookshop for the first time; George looked at him and said, "Can you sit down at the desk? Here's the cash box. I'm going out for ten minutes." He returned a week later.

George didn't believe in boundaries or barriers. He wrote to Gorbachev to propose the creation of a floating university that would sail around the world promoting peace and friendship, and he showed up unannounced on someone's doorstep in Australia: "You stayed in my bookstore, and now I'd like to stay with you." When I first returned to the shop, one of the primary disagreements he and I had — one that always resulted in our laughing hysterically — was our opposing systems of book categorizing. I wanted to alphabetize. George wanted to continue to arrange books as he always had: alongside each other where they made "interesting marriages."

It was through my father that I fell in love with the bookshop. I loved him first. And to love him was also to love the shop.

I remember following him into the front library as a small child, on early mornings, him rattling a huge set of Quasimodo keys, singing to the Tumbleweeds, "Rise and shine, the bells of Notre-Dame are ringing." As we picked our way across the sleeping bodies that covered almost every inch of floor, he would occasionally shout at someone —"Are you a lunatic?!"— then turn around and wink at me. Passing the children's section, he would point out this and that and explain the aesthetics. "You see, there's a reason why I put a mirror here"— then mutter —"Goddamn! Why is this all crooked?" The curtains had to be on either side, not in the middle. This way the children's section looked like a theater. "Books are works of the imagination, so a bookshop should reflect the imagination."

This lesson would continue down the stairs to the main shop. Once, thinking I was helping, I laid a book sideways atop a shelf. "No, no, no, that's all wrong! If you put a book there, people won't be able to see the browsers in the other room. You don't want to take away the mystery and romance." He'd lift me onto the front desk to do a dance welcoming customers and then throw open the front doors excitedly. "I have two favorite parts of the day," he said. "The first is when I open the shop in expectation of welcoming new and old friends to my little palace of books. The second is at midnight, when I close, and I can take six books up to bed with me. They're like jewels, and I'm the miner who's struck it rich."

I'd thought of George and the shop as being inseparable. But the day came, and the bookshop was still the bookshop, while myself and many of George's friends were at Père Lachaise cemetery, one of the most poetic places in Paris. George now rests between Jim Morrison and Héloïse and Abélard… He always did like "interesting marriages."

Entering the shop each morning, I picture him at the third-floor window, his long arms held wide open, his eyes looking out onto Paris and over his bookstore, a crinkle and a smile. *What mischief shall we get up to today?*

## A souvenir of Shakespeare & Co sometimes known as George's bookstore.

When I look back at half a century as a bookseller in Paris it all seems like a never ending play by William Shakespeare where the Romeos and Juliets are forever young while I have become an octogenarian who like King Lear is slowly losing his wits. Now that I am coming into my second childhood I wonder if all along I have just been playing store on one of the back alleys of history, putting obsolete books on dusty shelves while people are riding the information superhighway from one end to another of the global village.

However I can think of a few modest achievements typical of the idiosyncratic way this bookshop is managed. When a French explorer named Michel Peissel visited the book shop I told him I had read his book of travels in Quintana Roo and hoped some day to meet him. He told me we had already met because as a student he frequented the bookstore and the books he read here inspired him to become an explorer. In fact, he said, now that I have published eighteen books I am back where it all started in the little library above the bookstore. I can also remember a little girl 12 years old that I met in the Boston Gardens who dreamed of studying ballet in France and I was able to give her a round-trip to Paris and adopt her for a summer holiday. She was one of many thousands whom I have invited to stay in my house and read my books as a way of repaying the hospitality I received in many countries when I was a vagabond.

I like to think there is a trace of genius in all of us and in my case there might be a vague resemblance to Walt Whitman who also ran a bookstore and printing-press in Brooklyn over a century ago. I feel a kinship with Walt Whitman and believe the bookstore has the faults and virtues it might have if he were the proprietor. It has been said that perhaps no man liked so many things and disliked so few as Walt Whitman and I at least aspire to the same modest attainment.

I once expected to spend seven years walking around the world on foot. I walked from Mexico to Panama where the road ended before an almost uninhabited swamp called the Choco Colombiano. Even today there is no road. Perhaps it is time for me to resume my wanderings where I left off as a tropical tramp in the slums of Panama — the only white man in a black neighborhood. Perhaps like Ambrose Bierce who disappeared in the desert of Sonora I also may disappear. But after being involved in all mankind it is hard to come to terms with oblivion — not to see hundreds of millions of Chinese with college degrees come aboard the locomotive of history — not to know if someone has solved the riddle of the universe that baffled Einstein in his futile efforts to make space, time, gravitation and electromagnetism fall into place in a unified field theory — never to experience democracy replacing plutocracy in the military-industrial complex that rules America — never to witness the day foreseen by Tennyson "when the war-drums throb no longer and the battle-flags are furled, in the parliament of man, the federation of the world."

I may disappear leaving behind me no worldly possessions — just a few old socks and love letters, and my windows overlooking Notre Dame for all of you to enjoy, and my little Rag and Bone Shop of the Heart whose motto is, "Be not inhospitable to strangers lest they be angels in disguise." I may disappear leaving no forwarding address, but for all you know I may still be walking among you on my vagabond journey around the world.

*Amitié Sincère ~ George Whitman*

With my partner, David, and the shop's staff, we hope to continue the spirit and atmosphere George created, while simultaneously embarking on this new era of bookselling. A typical week here includes writing workshops, language exchanges, philosophy lectures, and a children's singing hour — all held in the first-floor library. The bigger weekly events happen on the ground floor, where we've recently been honored to have John Berger, Zadie Smith, David Simon, Lydia Davis, Don DeLillo, Edward St. Aubyn, Jennifer Egan, and Naomi Klein, among other prominent voices. This all occurs amongst the organized chaos of read-all-day customers, impromptu piano concerts, and sometimes an independent film crew, shooing Colette out of the frame.

We still house Tumbleweeds, anywhere from two to six at a time. There have been more than thirty thousand guests since the bookshop first opened. It's a tradition I'm proud of continuing, particularly in this time when societies don't especially encourage us to be hospitable to strangers. George's back bedroom has been converted into a writer's guest room, welcoming published authors — including Ben Lerner, Max Porter, and Eleanor Catton — from a few nights to a few months.

Most weeks, we're out scouting private libraries. Purchasing someone's collection brings that person onto our bookshelves. Once, we took on a collection that had filled the house of elderly twin sisters, each room devoted to a different genre. The cat-interest section was the largest — so, for a week following the purchase, we became a cat-specialist bookshop. We also had the thrill of buying books from the collection of the incomparable Mavis Gallant. Most we kept for our library shelves, though several books were available for sale in the Antiquarian.

Being in the bookshop often feels like being at the Mad Hatter's tea party. In 2010 alone, we hosted our literary festival, revived *The Paris Magazine*, and launched a novella prize. If it ever got too dizzying, I'd go upstairs to lie next to George and read over his shoulder. It was a meditation. These moments brought me back to the essentials: love, humor, and books.

The 2010 festival, Storytelling and Politics, packed writers and readers and volunteers together under a big, white tent in Square René Viviani. I remember →

Opposite: Sylvia, David, and their son, Gabriel, in front of the Antiquarian.
*Photo:* JONATHAN BECKER

Decorating the bookshop for Bloomsday 2012.
*Photo:* MOLLY DEKTAR

NATHAN ENGLANDER
*writer*

Some of my favorite nights have been spent at Shakespeare and Company, evenings when Sylvia and David would serve small dinners on the first floor in the library. There we'd eat and drink and hang out with writerly friends and book-loving folk — and every one of those dinners was special. So when my now-wife and I decided we were going to semi-elope to Paris, we thought that kind of room, with that kind of atmosphere, in that sort of location would be a dream for a super-tiny wedding. When my wife mentioned it to Sylvia and David, they didn't offer up a list of recommended venues that might give us that feel, they didn't even offer up the room itself. What they did, without pause, was tell her that they were giving us the bookstore — the whole thing — closing up shop and turning Shakespeare and Company into a wedding hall. And that's the plan that was put into motion. The doors and walls garlanded with flowers, the main shop floor cleared for tiny tables, the famous wishing well covered up. The front library was used for the ceremony, the piano room the perfect place for signing the marriage contract. And many hours later, after vows and a broken glass, after cheese and champagne (it's Paris after all), after classical guitar played by a friend, and the world's best jazz trio that wouldn't quit, and — again, thanks to Sylvia and David — a surprise appearance by a baritone serenading us with "Toreador"… that is, when it was way late, and way time to go home, our friend Meg just wouldn't have it. She climbed up the low step into the cashier's station at the front of the store, plugged her iPhone into the store's sound system, and she started to DJ. And, like in the ancient stories I grew up with, that postage stamp of a foyer somehow expanded into a dance floor, and that's when everyone went really wild. I'll never forget my tiny mother dancing with Sylvia, and my little niece dancing with the big girls, and a number of people dancing with Colette, the store dog. And then there was my wife, Rachel, dancing with the truest abandon I'd ever seen. Outside, on the edge of the Seine, with Notre-Dame towering over the world's most intimate Jewish wedding, guests would step into the square for some water or a glass of wine, to catch their breath, and breathe the night air. At one of those moments, out there in the dark, I stood alone staring through the lit windows of the shop, watching my own wedding as if from another place — in the way one remembers a dream. I took note of the night, and then the time, and turned to Sylvia, who'd come out as well. I said to her, it's really terribly late, and you've already been so nice and generous — having gifted us with the setting for the best day of our lives. Really, I said to her, we can call it quits and head back across the river. It's been a perfect day. We really don't want to go on too long. And that's when the song changed, and Sylvia looked at me and, once again, without hesitation, she said, "Whitney Houston," as if that explained it all, and disappeared into the store to dance.

poet Jack Hirschman's rich voice floating across the park, inspiring me as we launched the shop into yet another decade: "See the gates opening. Feel your hands going akimbo on your hips, your mouth opening like a womb giving birth to your voice for the first time. Go singing whirling into the glory of being ecstatically simple. Write the poem." →

A poster for the 2010 literary festival.
*Illustration:* JOANNA WALSH

# Path

JACK HIRSCHMAN

Go to your broken heart.
If you think you don't have one, get one.
To get one, be sincere.
Learn sincerity of intent by letting
life enter because you're helpless, really,
to do otherwise.

Even as you try escaping, let it take you
and tear you open
like a letter sent
like a sentence inside
you've waited for all your life
though you've committed nothing.
Let it send you up.
Let it break you, heart.
Broken-heartedness is the beginning

of all real reception.
The ear of humility hears beyond the gates.
See the gates opening.
Feel your hands going akimbo on your hips,
your mouth opening like a womb
giving birth to your voice for the first time.
Go singing whirling into the glory
of being ecstatically simple.
Write the poem.

Clockwise from top left: Nathan Englander and Rachel Silver at their wedding in the bookshop (*Photo:* UNATTRIBUTED); Will Self; Saul Williams; Owen Wilson (*Photo:* LAUREN GOLDENBERG); Jimmy Page; Zadie Smith; Daniel Mendelsohn; A. M. Homes. (*Unless otherwise noted, all photos by* DAVID GROVE)

362

Fatema Ahmed, an editor in London, had approached me after finding a copy of the 1967 *Paris Magazine* in a second-hand bookstore. She was charmed by George's "Poor Man's *Paris Review*" and suggested we produce another. Contributors to our 2010 edition included an exciting blend of familiar friends of the shop (Luc Sante, Lawrence Ferlinghetti), French voices (Michel Houellebecq, Marie NDiaye), and then-emerging writers (Rivka Galchen, Adelaide Docx).

That same year, we launched a novella contest with the de Groot Foundation. On Bloomsday, 2011, a panel of judges announced the winner of the first Paris Literary Prize: *The Last Kings of Sark* by Rosa Rankin-Gee (which was subsequently published by Virago). We were so energized by all the reading and debating, we decided to do it again. The results of →

A fashion photograph inspired by *Alice's Adventures in Wonderland*.
*Photo:* NAHOKO SPIESS and MAXIME GÉ

ROSA RANKIN-GEE
*writer*

I found out the result of the Paris Literary Prize when I was on the Champs-Élysées buying Nespresso capsules for the office where I worked as a receptionist. It was about a week before the prize-giving ceremony and I hadn't heard anything so, before I went out, I steeled myself and finally wrote an email to the faceless God of Small Things; that is, to info@parisliteraryprize.com.

"I'm exceedingly sorry to be a pest, and I know I haven't won, but I happen to live in Paris, so I would love to come to the prize readings, should that possibly, maybe, *potentially* be OK, maybe. Sorry again for bothering you!" Or something like that. I'm English. We speak in the conditional tense.

I pressed send and left the office, my stomach tangled. My mobile phone at the time was pretty much made of wood but, five minutes later, I attempted to see if I had a reply. It was the equivalent of a dial-up connection. You could almost hear the rustling *dee-dar-dee-dar-doeuurrrr* of a behemoth Dell … yet somehow (somehow!) there was a response. Stomach unraveling now, or the knots getting tighter, who knows, I read the first line.

"Well, Rosa, as it happens, I really hope you will come to the reading at the prize-giving because … Congratulations! You are —" and then (then!) the email refused to load further.

Generally, the word *congratulations* is a good word, but I was … what? I sat on a bench, adrenaline doing laps up and down my fingers. Each time I refreshed the email, it paused in the same place. I searched wildly for a signal. I held my phone to the heavens, to Ladurée, to the Arc de Triomphe.

When, finally, the full email appeared, I read it about fifteen times before I almost believed it, and then (even then!) I must have read it a hundred more times in the following days, terrified that I would delete the message, terrified that it would all disappear.

The days that followed were soft-focused, full-hearted, one of those rare moments in one's life when you have a piece of good news waiting in the wings, when you think, *There's something good … wasn't there something good?* And you remember and your soul lifts.

Before the prize ceremony, I met my friend Natalie in a small park between the Maison des Écrivains and the Metro so she could help me change into my dress. We did this in some bushes. A nice elderly man saw. I didn't care. The evening was warm, musically operatic, infinitely generous, golden — but, when I think back to that time, most of all I remember my bath the next morning. I don't know if you can imagine it, but my bathtub was both in my kitchen and directly underneath my bed. I lay in it for an hour that day, listening to "Love Train" by the O'Jays, Phoenix's "1901," and Chet Baker's "Tenderly" in a triptych repeat, my skin enclosing a happiness that was whole, solid to the touch.

Reading in the piano room.
*Photo:* JONATHAN BECKER

the second contest were announced in 2013, once more on June 16. The winning novella, C. E. Smith's *Body Electric*, was released in a beautiful paperback edition, copublished by the bookshop and our friends at *The White Review*.

David and I had been contemplating publishing on a more regular basis. We were inspired by Sylvia Beach, of course, and also by Lawrence Ferlinghetti, who often said to us that there is nothing more natural for a bookshop than to be a publisher, too. Booksellers are in a strategic position to know what people want to read, and our shops are ready-made test labs for new and experimental works. In coming years, we look forward to releasing new writing and illustrated books, along with beautiful editions of classic texts and works in translation. →

Outside Shakespeare and Company Café.
*Photo:* DAVID GROVE

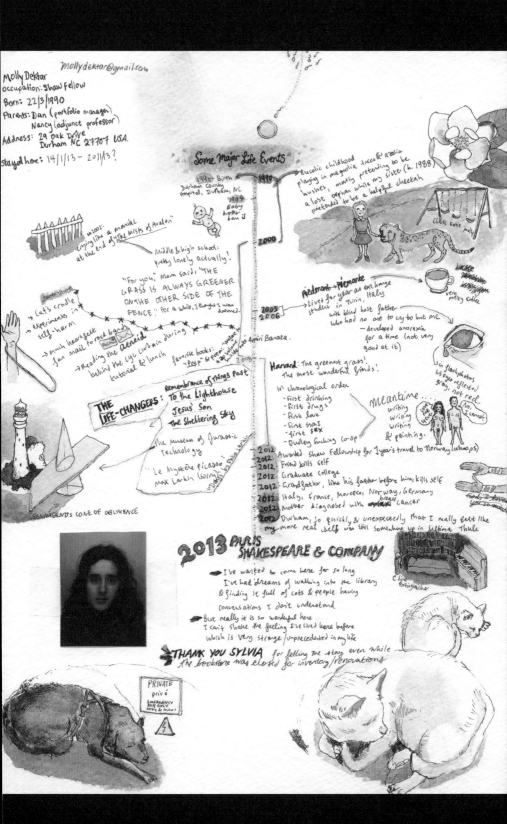

Molly Dektar  
mollydektar@gmail.com  
Occupation: Shaw Fellow  
Born: 22/3/1990  
Parents: Dan (portfolio manager)  
Nancy (adjunct professor)  
Address: 29 Oak Drive  
Durham NC 27707 USA.  
Stayed here: 14/1/13 – 20/1/13?

## Some Major Life Events

1990 Birth — Durham County Hospital, Durham NC

1990

1994 Baby brother born !!

Bucolic childhood tree & aralia playing in magnolia bushes, mostly pretending to be a lost orphan while my sister (b. 1988) pretended to be a helpful cheetah

*Cheetah Katie party*

2000

c. 2002: singing "like the end of the mists of Avalon"

Middle & high school: Pretty lonely actually!

"For you," Mom said, "THE GRASS IS ALWAYS GREENER ON THE OTHER SIDE OF THE FENCE." For a while, I thought I was doomed.

2003-2006  
→ Let's cradle experiments in self-harm  
→ much heartfelt fan mail to rock bands  
→ Reading the Aeneid behind the 7yr curtain during tutorial & lunch

favorite books: "PMP" & poems — ...Amiri Baraka.

2005 2006  
Piedmont → Piemonte  
→ Lived for year as exchange student in Turin, Italy with blind host father who had no one to cry to but me  
— developed anorexia for a time (not very good at it)

very milky coffee

in flashphotos his eyes reflected gray, not red.

2008

THE LIFE-CHANGERS: Remembrance of Things Past, To the Lighthouse, Jesus' Son, The Sheltering Sky

The museum of Jurassic Technology

"Le Mystère Picasso"  
Max Larkin (sorry)

SONNABEND'S CONE OF OBLISCENCE

Harvard: The greenest grass! The most wonderful friends!

In chronological order  
- first drinking  
- first drugs  
- first love  
- first SSRI  
- first sex  
- Dudley fucking Co-op

MEANTIME...  
writing  
writing  
writing  
& painting.

2012 — I worked Shaw Fellowship for 1 year's travel to Norway (whoops)  
2012 — Friend kills self  
2012 — Graduate College  
2012 — Grandfather, like his father before him, kills self  
2012 — Italy, France, Morocco, Norway, Germany  
2012 — Mother diagnosed with breast cancer  
2013 — Durham, so quickly & unexpectedly that I really felt like my more real self was still somewhere up in Ultima Thule

## 2013 PARIS SHAKESPEARE & COMPANY

➤ I've wanted to come here for so long  
I've had dreams of walking into the library & finding it full of cats & people having conversations I don't understand

fire extinguisher

➤ But really it is so wonderful here  
I can't shake the feeling I've lived here before which is very strange / unprecedented in my life

➤ THANK YOU SYLVIA for letting me stay even while the bookstore was closed for inventory/renovations

PRIVATE  
privé  
EMERGENCY EXIT ONLY  
service de secours

Kelsey Ford / 22 yrs / New York, NY / tumbleweed May 31 - June 24, 2011

1. I was born in Fort Worth, TX & lived in Jackson, MS for 3 years, until we moved to Washington. In the South I was blond, but in the Pac NW I became a brunette. My doctor dad took care of druggies in the E.R. My mom worked as a nurse, breaking news to loved ones. At first, they gifted me anatomy books, thinking I'd step into a hospital one day too. Mrs. Claus signed one; I kept it much longer than any of the others.

2. In 2nd grade, I wrote a fairy tale (borrowed liberally from the story of the girl and the pumpkin). When hung, it stretched from floor to ceiling. My teacher said it was the longest she'd ever had & I thought: This is what I'll do now. The next year I wrote a short story titled "Kidnapped Too Young" and illustrated it with gel pens.

3. From ages six to nine, people sang at me: "All I want for Christmas is my two front teeth" because I had none. The teeth grew in crooked. I got headgear the same time I got my first pair of coke-bottle glasses and the boy I had a crush on called me "surgery face." When I told my mom, she laughed.

4. Nancy Drew then Agatha Christie then Lois Duncan & Jane Austen then Ian McEwan & Jose Saramago & Haruki Murakami & Gabriel Garcia Marquez then Kelly Link & Ray Carver then (still) (always) Flannery O'Connor & Herman Melville & Bolaño & Anne Carson & Emily Brontë & Dickinson & Borges & Alice Munro.

5. Four years ago, I moved from my small hometown obsessed with squirrels (we had the Nutty Narrows Bridge) to a New York college equally obsessed with squirrels ("Sarah Lawrence, where even the squirrels wear black.") At first it didn't agree with me. I slept all hours and only ate bagels. But then I moved in and forgot what I wasn't. I fought cockroaches & centipedes, read *Tom Jones* & Dostoyevsky & William Blake, drank awful mixed drinks, walked from W 133rd to E 4th, overshot and ended up on Houston.

6. My favorite story is the story of the lonely whale. If you have a chance, google "lonely whale NYTimes." I have it tattooed, thumb-sized and silhouetted, to my back, over my top rib. There's a watercolor blue whale above my bed, a sperm whale magnet on my fridge, and soon a beautiful drawing by a close friend I made here, while tumbleweeding.

7. Before I officially moved into my apartment in Harlem, I had to chase a squatter away with five cops and their hushed walkie-talkies. He left behind a size 14 pair of black jeans. Now I live there alone, surrounded by no one I know. I painted walls and arranged my shelves and thought maybe I'd teach myself to cook, which I haven't. I own too many but never enough books. One of my most treasured is a used copy of Borges' "Book of Imaginary Beings." On the inside cover, the last owner wrote:

>       I want someone to say
>       nice things to me
> me to
> you do
>       I want you to say nice things
>       to me
> like what
> sweet dreams
>            & I sleep better
> with you here.

1. George Whitman, 2. Kitty the cat, 3. Michael Smith, 4. Ezra Pound,
5. Gregory Corso, 6. Olympia, 7. Lawrence Ferlinghetti, 8. James Joyce,
9. Paul Auster, 10. Frank Sinatra, 11. Colette the dog, 12. Martin Amis,
13. Henry Miller, 14. Aaron Budnick, 15. Richard Wright, 16. Sylvia Whitman,
17. Lawrence Durrell, 18. Allen Ginsberg, 19. Jack Kerouac,
20. Ernest Hemingway, 21. F. Scott Fitzgerald, 22. Gertrude Stein,
23. Alice B. Toklas, 24. James Baldwin, 25. Sylvia Beach,
26. Ray Bradbury, 27. William Burroughs, 28. Dionysus, 29. James Jones,
30. Zadie Smith, 31. Generic spirit of beatnikism, 32. Anaïs Nin

DAVID DELANNET
*comanager*

I first came to the shop one Sunday morning
in 2006, searching for English-language books
on Shakespeare for my degree. Sylvia was sitting
at the desk in the Antiquarian — I ordered
a (very) rare book (which she is still looking for),
and we have been together ever since.

Being with Sylvia meant also being involved
with her world at the bookstore. As a native
Parisian, I soon found myself helping with
the French administrative aspects of the shop.
Once I'd completed my Ph.D. at the Sorbonne,
I started working here officially, and Sylvia
and I began exploring ways to add more rooms
to the bookstore, something George was
always keen to do.

Around the corner from us is the Esmeralda,
Paris's most bohemian and charming one-star
hotel. Serge Gainsbourg and Jane Birkin met
there (if you want to catch the ambiance of the
place, listen to the song "L'Hôtel particulier"),
and the graphic novelist Hugo Pratt used
to stay in one of its rooms. Until recently, it was
owned by an aging French woman, Michelle
Durand-Bruel, who would wander around
the block in her fur coat and beret, an elegant
cigarette holder between her fingers. She had
one eye that never opened — it had been gassed
in May '68 — and she often came to the shop
to borrow books. (From time to time, the hotel
staff would walk over, arms full, to return them.)
As Michelle got older, she had to sell some
of her properties, including the retail space next
to the hotel in 6 rue St.-Julien-le-Pauvre,
a building which touches the back of
Shakespeare and Company. After two years
of discussions and suspense, we managed
to acquire it. Soon we were knocking through

a fifty-centimeter wall and extending the
bookshop floor.

With this new section, we added a beautiful
cellar to our existing ones — it was only later,
when we went to install a support column,
that we discovered a second, hidden basement
level below it. Lydia Davis, at the shop to give
a reading, was intrigued. She had just visited
Bourges, where the ancient infrastructure for
underground life is very elaborate. As she and
I went down with a flashlight, I asked the reason
for her interest. "Global warming," she replied.
"Cellars will take on a new role." I wondered
how these cellars had been used in the past.
Tumbleweeds sometimes ask about an obscure
passageway, located right beneath the entrance
to the building, which looks as if it cuts under
the Seine and leads straight to Notre-Dame.
About seven meters into the tunnel, a wall bars
the way; one can only guess what lies behind
it. What we do know for a fact is that a stream
(maybe a sister of the river Bièvre) runs beneath
the building — it's visible by lifting one of the
cellar's heavy flooring stones. A few months ago,
two geologists came into the shop, their
arms and hands spread out like antennas.
"There is water here," one of them said. "I can
feel it," said the other. They left before I could
confirm their intuition.

While we were dusting the beams and
installing bookshelves in the new ground-floor
St.-Julien section, another neighbor became
the sole owner of the retail space next to the
Antiquarian. It had been empty for more
than twenty years, entangled in some kind of
Balzacian judicial knot. Now, finally, the former
stationery shop was about to become available

for rent. We were not the only ones interested in this prime location, of course. A big chain was bidding against us — when we saw them pull up in front of the bookshop in a Ferrari, we knew that we could be in trouble. The owner graciously ended up renting to us. She did so partly in memory of George. As a young girl in the '60s, she remembered him, already an old man in her eyes, coming to see her parents every few months and trying to convince them to let him open a café in that same space.

Needing more room for the website team and visiting authors, we've also rented a garret apartment on the fifth floor, overlooking the Seine. Jacques Tati was once a frequent visitor to the flat opposite; his manager rented the place, living there and storing the original negatives of all of Tati's films (despite the flat owner's protests about insurance and liability). I like to imagine the very French, long figure of Tati climbing the stairs, bumping into Tumbleweeds and anglophone authors arriving for their readings. The bookshop is a kind of paradox: it is at once utterly Parisian and something of a foreign land to many locals. Contemporary French writers who have described the shop in their work (Patrick Modiano, Yannick Haenel, Amélie Nothomb, among others) have often noted this. Modiano: "Shelves full of books on the sidewalk in front of the shop, with chairs and even a couch. It was like the terrace of a café. You could see Notre-Dame from there. And yet once you crossed the threshold, it felt like Amsterdam or San Francisco."

As we were starting the building works, we were also organizing the bookstore's archives. Sylvia and I were astonished to discover a 1969 interview in *Holiday* magazine in which George predicted two of today's developments. George: "I'm going to open a literary café. Everything will be cooked under my supervision. There's only one way to make a good lemon pie, you know." And on extending the bookshop floor: "I've got to raise enough money to buy the store behind this one, then we can knock out a wall, and the store will reach right back into the garden of St.-Julien-le-Pauvre." We debuted both the St.-Julien bookshop space and the café (serving lemon pie daily) in October 2015, realizing George's vision, half a century later. There's nothing Sylvia and I would want more than to have him here with us, seeing his bookshop grow, welcoming more books and bibliophiles. Reading his words, we have the strange feeling that he is up there in his own atheist's paradise, joyfully laughing at our surprise.

The negative predictions about brick-and-mortar bookshops and paper books have only spurred us to adventure deeper into this Wonderland—that

is, to remain faithful to what the shop is while simultaneously searching for new ways to gather writers and reach readers. Recently, we produced a five-day run of *Macbeth*, directed by Cressida Brown, in the park next to the bookshop, refurbished the Antiquarian, launched a website selling books, and acquired keys to new spaces. The bookstore and its offices now spread over six floors, and we've taken on two small shops around the corner on rue St.-Julien-le-Pauvre. This has allowed us to expand the bookstore laterally by carving a new doorway into an old wall, connecting our ground floor to the adjacent building's, something George had hoped to do since the 1960s. The space houses an enlarged children's section, mirroring the shop in miniature, with books on French history, art, and poetry, all to excite lifelong readers. We also recently opened a literary café next door to the Antiquarian, serving Flapjack Kerouacs and hosting morning coffee talks with authors. →

CRAIG TAYLOR
*writer in residence*

How many people tell stories of this place? How many remember it as they click a car seat into position or cut vegetables in some North American kitchen? How many people are out there right now wandering back in time to Shakespeare and Co.? How many people had their time?

One night, during my own stint at the bookstore, I lay on the couch in the upstairs office and read through autobiographies of previous Tumbleweeds. The binders stretch back to the 1960s, bio after bio, weed after weed. In their entirety they form the most interesting novel on the shelves of Shakespeare and Co. It's a long book, made almost entirely of earnest beginnings. It's the story of impermanence.

I understand I don't get ownership of this place. I won't get to sleep in the soft bed in the upstairs bedroom forever. Even the best Tumbleweeds can't own their patches. They have to go back to their old lives, or press forward into new ones. There's only one way to achieve permanence at Shakespeare and Co. It takes time, but you can begin that process in Paris. Go about your day. Eat the *salade* at La Méthode, eat the croissants at Le Rostand near the park. When you're done, wipe the table with your forearm, send the remaining bits of pastry to the ground, and start to work. Finish that book, your book, the one that might sit on these shelves someday, the one slowly emerging from the endless drafts that rest, one after the next, on the various tables beneath you.

A sleeping Tumbleweed. *Photo:* MOLLY DEKTAR

One of the things my father often said to me was "I hope you'll be happy here." It always seemed such a light and sweet sentence, but now these simple words have taken on a more profound meaning for me. George believed that the books we read form an essential part of our identities, that books signify freedom, and that books connect us. In building his shop, he expressed these convictions in every corner. A bookstore — or, in this case, a "socialist utopia masquerading as a bookstore"— is a place of possibility, where ideas and curiosity permeate the millions of pages lining the walls. As I watch visitors wind through the shop, reaching out with wonder, gathering small towers of books in their arms, I'm reminded of my favorite lines in George's vagabond journals, written when he was twenty-four: "As the circle of knowledge widens, life grows more beautiful and heroic. We are a part of everything — men, women, books, cities, railroads —all made from the same atoms and molecules, all living together and dying together, joined into one imperishable unity that can never be divided."

Pages 378–379: The bookshop's esplanade. *Photo:* DAVID GROVE

Opposite: Friends meeting in the bookshop. *Photo:* MOLLY DEKTAR

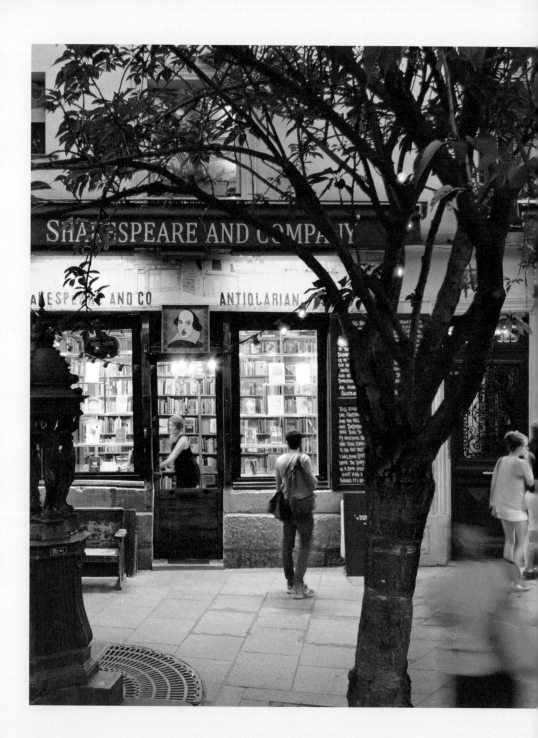

## Notes

### Foreword

Opening bookshop in Paris:
Sylvia Beach, *Shakespeare and Company*
(Lincoln, NE: Bison Books, 1991).
the business of books:
Richard C. Miller, "Roving Yank Settles
Down in Paris Bookshop," *Denver Post*,
December 2, 1951.

### Introduction

drifted into the bookstore: Sylvia
Whitman, interview by Krista Halverson.
more than just a project: George
Whitman to Henry Miller, Paris, undated,
Shakespeare and Company archive.
I must lie down where: William
Butler Yeats, "The Circus Animals'
Desertion," *Last Poems* (Dublin: Cuala
Press, 1939).
is not simply an emporium:
Stuart Sayers, "Writers and
Readers: Shakespeare's Errand Boy,"
*Age*, April 24, 1982.
safekeeping: Bevan Thomas,
email correspondence with Milly Unwin,
January 15, 2014.
I created this bookstore:
Sylvia Whitman, "A Brief History
of a Parisian Bookstore," Shakespeare
and Company history booklet, 2012.
hobo adventures: Sylvia Whitman,
interview by Krista Halverson.
socialist utopia masquerading:
Maggie Lewis, "A Bookstore Poets
Call Home," *Christian Science Monitor*,
September 25, 1980.
I can't write without a reader:
Sylvia Whitman, interview
by Krista Halverson.

### Sylvia Beach Section

bomby: Sylvia Beach, *The Letters of
Sylvia Beach*, ed. Keri Walsh (New York
City: Columbia University Press, 2010).
What a dark age: Ibid.
The situation was quite:
Sylvia Beach, *Shakespeare and Company*.
the largest number: Ibid.

### George Whitman Section

The text in this section was assembled
from letters, journals, and unpublished
non-fiction articles written by
George Whitman between the years 1935
and 1951 — and which are a part of
the Shakespeare and Company archive —
with one exception. The following
passage was adapted from a response
George Whitman gave in a 1990 interview
with Christopher Sawyer-Lauçanno
and which appears in Sawyer-Lauçanno's
book *The Continual Pilgrimage*
(San Francisco: City Lights Books, 1998):
"a tall, well-dressed young man … he just
sits and reads."

### The 1950s Chapter

In the year 1600: Sylvia Whitman,
"A Brief History of a Parisian
Bookstore," Shakespeare and Company
history booklet, 2012.
I'd long wanted a bookstore: Sylvia
Whitman, interview by Krista Halverson.
After the Second World War:
Radio France International Report, [date
unconfirmed], audiocassette recording
in the Shakespeare and Company archive.
I almost didn't take it: Morton
P. Gudebrod, "The Most Parisian
Bookshop in Paris," *Stars and Stripes*,
September 24, 1960.
a slum, with street theater:
George Whitman, "The Rag and Bone
Shop of the Heart," Shakespeare
and Company history pamphlet, 2000.
American books are very popular:
George Whitman, "A Bostonian's First
View of Paris," unpublished, Shakespeare
and Company archive.
We spend our life: Samuel Beckett,
*Stories and Texts for Nothing* (New York:
Grove Press, 1967).
In the morning I wake:
George Whitman to Mary Whitman,
Paris, October 28, 1951, Shakespeare
and Company archive.
When I was in Columbia: Sylvia
Whitman, "A Brief History of a Parisian
Bookstore," Shakespeare and Company
history booklet, 2012.
The philosophy of the bookstore:
Nicholas Bray, "If They Need Beds
or Old Books, They Journey to George's,"
*Wall Street Journal*, February 10, 1983.
I believe we're all homeless:
Rob Lever, "Bookshop Keeps Literature
Alive, Available," *USA Today*,
International Edition, March 11, 1988.

drift in and out with: Sylvia
Whitman, "A Brief History of a Parisian
Bookstore," Shakespeare and Company
history booklet, 2012.
When I'd not sold my: Radio France
International Report, [date unconfirmed],
audiocassette recording in the
Shakespeare and Company archive.
They were a group of hoboes:
George Whitman, event at D.G.Wills
Books, La Jolla, California, February,
1985, audiocassette recording in
the Shakespeare and Company archive.
Jane was getting a little:
Tim Cumming, "Mean Streets,"
*Guardian*, August 8, 2003.
The writers' and artists':
George Whitman to Mary Whitman,
Paris, February 24, 1953,
Shakespeare and Company archive.
With these new premises: George
Whitman to Ann, Paris, February 21,
1957, Shakespeare and Company archive.
There is such an absence:
Michel Fabre, *The World of Richard
Wright* (Jackson, MS: University Press
of Mississippi, 1985).
Sylvia Beach was a very:
George Whitman, event at D.G.Wills
Books, La Jolla, California, February,
1985, audiocassette recording in
the Shakespeare and Company archive.
You are one of the mothers:
George Whitman to Beth, Paris, undated,
Shakespeare and Company archive.
Larry liked to meet his:
Radio France International Report, [date
unconfirmed], audiocassette recording
in the Shakespeare and Company archive.
Who were all these:
Jack Kerouac, *The Dharma Bums*
(New York: Viking Press, 1958).
We're experimenting; we have:
Art Buchwald, "Two Poets in Paris,"
*New York Herald Tribune*, June 26, 1958.
Dame Edith Sitwell: Ibid.
poet was reciting some: Ibid.
I protested it: Ibid.
Nobody was sure what to: Sawyer-
Lauçanno, *The Continual Pilgrimage*.
un menu très Américain: George
Whitman, loose page from diary, undated,
Shakespeare and Company archive.
Jones was the most American:
Sawyer-Lauçanno,
*The Continual Pilgrimage*.
At the party, Sylvia made:
Clive Hart, email correspondence with
Jemma Birrell, November 26, 2011.

SHAKESPEARE AND COMPANY—
WRITERS: Irving Marder, "Left Bank
Shop Tests Buyer's Bookmanship,"
*New York Times*, March 5, 1964.
SPIRITUAL SUCCESSOR: Henry Kamm,
"New Shakespeare and Company
Will Be Doing Business in Paris,"
*New York Times*, April 15, 1964.
SITTING IN THE UPSTAIRS:
Ian Sommerville, inscription
in a Shakespeare and Company
guest book, October 13, 1974,
Shakespeare and Company archive.
IT WAS ABOUT TWO O'CLOCK: George
Whitman, event at D.G.Wills Books,
La Jolla, California, February, 1985,
audiocassette recording in the
Shakespeare and Company archive.
HE AND MILLER CAME TO:
George Whitman, personal notes, 1991,
Shakespeare and Company archive.
A WONDERLAND OF BOOKS: George
Whitman to Cyrus S. Eaton, Paris,
December 8, 1960, Shakespeare and
Company archive.

## The 1960s Chapter

I WANT TO OPEN A TEAROOM: George
Whitman to Ann, Paris, February 21, 1957,
Shakespeare and Company archive.
THE WISHING WELL WAS ORIGINALLY:
Daniel Pierre McClenaghan, email
correspondence with Krista Halverson,
December 20, 2011.
I THINK IT IS A PLEASANT TRADITION:
George Whitman to Nelson Algren,
Paris, May 1, 1960, Shakespeare and
Company archive.
CULTURAL COLD WAR: Frances Stonor
Saunders, *The Cultural Cold War*
(New York: The New Press, 2001).
SINCE ON THE ONE HAND: George
Whitman to Cyrus S. Eaton, Paris,
December 8, 1960, Shakespeare and
Company archive.
NEW SHAKESPEARE AND COMPANY
WILL: Henry Kamm, "New Shakespeare
and Company Will Be Doing Business
in Paris," *New York Times*, April 15, 1974.
BY INFORMAL ARRANGEMENT: Ibid.
APOLOGIES FOR THE DELAY:
Joan and Maureen to George Whitman,
London, undated, Shakespeare and
Company archive.
FREE UNIVERSITY OF PARIS:
Shakespeare and Company flyer, undated,
Shakespeare and Company archive.
HE'S A SAINT, LIVES ON NOTHING:
Piero Sanavîo, "Breakfast with
the Buddha of the Beats," *International
Herald Tribune*, September 6, 1967.

LIKES THE RAIN AND THE NIGHT:
George Whitman, Tumbleweed record,
1966, Shakespeare and Company archive.
SINCE THE DEATHS OF ADRIENNE:
George Whitman, "Lettre à André
Malraux," *Paris Magazine*, 1967,
translated from the French by Milly
Unwin and David Delannet.
YOU THINK YOUR PAIN: James Baldwin,
*New York Times*, June 1, 1964.
THE POOR MAN'S PARIS REVIEW:
George Whitman, "A Window
on the World," *Paris Magazine*, 1967.
IF WE CAN ACHIEVE A LITTLE: Ibid.
WE'VE HAD TO MAKE OUT:
Joan Paulson, "Don Quixote of the Left
Bank," *Holiday*, April 1970.

## The 1970s Chapter

THIS IS MY COMMUNE: Sylvia Whitman,
interview by Krista Halverson.
MANY ANONYMOUS HANDS: George
Whitman, "The Rag and Bone Shop
of the Heart," draft of a Shakespeare
and Company flyer, undated,
Shakespeare and Company archive.
THE STAUNCHEST OF LIBERALS:
Donald Morris, "Bookstore
Salvages Memories of Bygone World,"
*Houston Post*, June 21, 1974.
A MEETING PLACE FOR ANY CAUSE: Ibid.
DEAR GEORGE, I HAVE BEEN:
Dennis Pikes to George Whitman,
Lymington, England, 1974,
Shakespeare and Company archive.
DEAR SIR, I VISITED: R. Emmett Tyrrell
Jr. to George Whitman, Bloomington,
Indiana, United States, August 14, 1975,
Shakespeare and Company archive.
FOR GEORGE WHITMAN, WHOSE:
Jacqueline Kennedy Onassis, inscription
in a Shakespeare and Company
guest book, undated, Shakespeare
and Company archive.
THE MAN WHO BROUGHT ITALIAN:
Giuseppe Recchia, "La favola della libreria
parigina Shakespeare & Company nei
ricordi del protagonista di una stagione
memorabile," *Corriere d'Europa*, undated.
ENTHRONED LAST NIGHT AT GEORGE:
Irving Marder, "Poet/Novelist Sillitoe —
A Talent for Invective," *International
Herald Tribune*, January 15, 1973.
HOW DID GEORGE COME TO: Anaïs
Nin, *The Diary of Anaïs Nin, Volume Five:
1947–1955* (New York City: Houghton
Mifflin Harcourt, 1975).

I MIGHT HAVE LOVED ANAÏS:
Pia Copper-Ind, interview
by Krista Halverson.
[NIN] HAS BEEN CLAIMED:
Irving Marder, "Anaïs Nin: New Times,
New Friends," *International Herald
Tribune*, November 14, 1974.
SO I WOULD LOAN HIM: Alix Sharkey,
"The Beat Goes On," *Observer Magazine*,
March 3, 2002.
HE WAS BANNED FROM CITY LIGHTS:
George Whitman, "Shakespeare and
Company: Ein amerikanischer Buchladen
in Paris," *Sender Freies Berlin*, 1998.
PERSONAL RESOURCES: John Floresco,
"To Be Franc, You Can't Be Poor in Paris,"
*The Globe*, August, [day unknown], 1978.
I USED TO THINK JACK KEROUAC:
Bruce Handy, "In a Bookstore in Paris,"
*Vanity Fair*, November 2014.
UNDER THE INFLUENCE: Hanif
Kureishi, interview by Bruce Handy
for *Vanity Fair*, 2014.
I ARRIVED A YOUNG WOMAN:
Kate Grenville, email correspondence
with Krista Halverson, October 1, 2013.
THERE ARE TOO DAMN MANY:
Judith Valente, "Yank in Paris Finds
Home in Bookshop on Left Bank,"
*Sunday News*, March 28, 1976.
IT SAVES ME WORK: Kathryn Hone,
"Tumbleweed Hotel of a Bookshop,"
*Irish Times*, July 28, 1990.
SWAMPS OF CHOCÓ COLOMBIANO:
George Whitman, "The Rag and Bone
Shop of the Heart," Shakespeare
and Company history pamphlet, 2000.
THERE HAVE BEEN MANY MINOR:
Chapin F. Koch to George Whitman,
Paris, July 28, 1976, Shakespeare
and Company archive.
QUITE CHAOTIC: Diane di Prima, email
correspondence with Krista Halverson,
September 22, 2013.
LIVING IN THE TUMBLEWEED HOTEL:
George Whitman to Lawrence Durrell,
Paris, September 7, 1978,
Shakespeare and Company archive.
I HASTEN TO REPLY:
Lawrence Durrell to George Whitman,
Sommières, France, undated,
Shakespeare and Company archive.
APPRENTICE: Ron Carlson,
"A Wonderland of Books," *Massachusetts
Daily Collegian*, [date unknown], 1979.
MISMANAGED: George Whitman,
"Extracts from a Recent Board
of Directors' Meeting," Shakespeare
and Company flyer, 1980.

By hook or by crook:
Virginia Woolf, *A Room of One's Own*
(London: Hogarth Press, 1929).
Beijing is unfavorable to opening:
George Whitman to Barbara Schreyer,
Singapore, April 13, 1979, Shakespeare
and Company archive.
Aragon is eighty-two: George
Whitman to Carl Whitman, Paris, undated,
Shakespeare and Company archive.
She took every penny: George
Whitman, "A Life in the Day of George
Whitman," *Sunday Times*, January 25, 2004.
Passing stranger! you do
not know: Walt Whitman,
"To a Stranger," *Leaves of Grass* (Boston:
Thayer and Eldridge, 1860).
We're slowly reconstructing:
George Whitman to unidentified
recipient, Paris, March 3, 1980,
Shakespeare and Company archive.

## The 1980s & 1990s Chapter

If the baby was: George Whitman
to Bill and Eliza Whitman, Paris, May 21,
1981, Shakespeare and Company archive.
We met here thirty years:
Anonymous, Mirror of Love
message, undated, Shakespeare
and Company archive.
Dear Stranger, You may: Ibid.
Dear Mr. Whitman, my son:
Patricia Belcaro, Mirror of Love message,
September 27, 2001, Shakespeare
and Company archive.
I got my first taste: Darren
Aronofsky, email correspondence with
Tanya Seghatchian, September 5, 2013.
An absurd place — almost down:
Bruce Handy, "In a Bookstore in Paris,"
*Vanity Fair*, November 2014.
There seemed to be: Ibid.
Today I am catching up: George
Whitman to Bill and Eliza Whitman,
Paris, May 21, 1981, Shakespeare
and Company archive.
The whole idea is: Maggie Lewis,
"A Bookstore Poets Call Home," *Christian
Science Monitor*, September 25, 1980.
Whitman explained the time gap:
John Foy, "Whitman and Co.:
Paris," *International Herald Tribune*,
September 29, 1984.
Mr. Whitman is working:
Clyde H. Farnsworth, "In Paris There
Is a Bookstore That Is a Story in Itself,"
*New York Times*, August 7, 1975.
All the characters: George
Whitman, hand-drawn sign, undated,
Shakespeare and Company archive.

I am on a four-month leave:
George Whitman to Anne, Brisbane,
February 12, 1986, Shakespeare
and Company archive.
I must lie down where: William
Butler Yeats, "The Circus Animals'
Desertion," *Last Poems* (Dublin: Cuala
Press, 1939).
It's such a great line:
Eric R. Alterman, "Feasting on Literary
Intrigue by the Seine," *Boston Globe*,
June 30, 1985.
To me, feeling is everything:
Joan Levine, "Memento of Henry Miller,"
*Paris Magazine*, Summer 1989.
In old age, it is hard: George
Whitman, "The Rag and Bone Shop of
the Heart," *Paris Magazine*, Summer 1989.
Don't mourn. Organize:
Eric Mottram, preface to *Fire Readings*,
ed. David Applefield, Richard Hallward,
and T. Wignesan (Vincennes, France:
Frank Books, 1991).
The burned-out apartment:
George Whitman to Christopher
Sawyer-Lauçanno, Paris, August 15, 1992,
Shakespeare and Company archive.
Walt Whitman said, We hear:
George Whitman, introductory notes
to Allen Ginsberg reading, undated,
Shakespeare and Company archive.
We are torn between nostalgia:
Carson McCullers, "Look Homeward,
Americans," *Vogue*, 1940.
The fact is the future: George
Whitman to Miranda, Paris, April 21, 1996,
Shakespeare and Company archive.
Carpeted with Scandinavian:
Bruce Handy, "In a Bookstore in Paris,"
*Vanity Fair*, November 2014.
Life at the Paris bookshop:
Janet Guttsman, "Paris Bookstore Offers
Travelers a Read, a Bed," *Ottawa Citizen*,
March 21, 1987.
More than just a project: George
Whitman to Henry Miller, Paris, undated,
Shakespeare and Company archive.
If I was to put: George Wallace,
"With George Whitman in Paris, France,"
*Long Islander*, February 26, 1998.
Perhaps ironic for a Marxist:
Emily Lodge, "An American
in Paris: Shakespeare and Company,"
*Book*, March/April 2000.

I'd like to form: George Whitman
to Lawrence Ferlinghetti [quoting
from a letter Ferlinghetti sent to George
years earlier — Ed.], Paris, October 23,
[year not given], Shakespeare and
Company archive.
All [your lawyer's] talk: George
Whitman to Lawrence Ferlinghetti,
Paris, November 26, 1987, Shakespeare
and Company archive.
I won't last much longer: George
Whitman to Lawrence Ferlinghetti, Paris,
October 23, [year not given], Shakespeare
and Company archive.
Truly old and old fashioned:
Don Bell, "City of Books," *Biblio*,
September 1998.
As you say, I am the most: George
Whitman to Lawrence Ferlinghetti,
Paris, November 26, 1987, Shakespeare
and Company archive.
George had a single-minded
vision: Alix Sharkey, "The Beat Goes
On," *Observer Magazine*, March 2002.

## The 2000s Chapter

You and I age now: Desmond
O'Grady to George Whitman, Kinsale,
Ireland, July 1999, Shakespeare and
Company archive.
Make the apartment a sort: George
Whitman, "Rag and Bone Shop of
the Heart," Shakespeare and Company
history pamphlet, 2000.
I am eighty-eight years old: Ibid.
Growing old is such:
Ron Bauer, memento essay for George
Whitman, undated, Shakespeare and
Company archive.
Today the shop is: Devanshi Mody,
"Destinations: Shakespeare and Co.,
Paris," *Serendib*, January/February 2005.
I wish your daily activities:
Carl Whitman to George Whitman,
February 20, 2001, Shakespeare and
Company archive.
I was nineteen, and my father:
Sylvia Whitman, interview
by Krista Halverson.
My father and I had: Ibid.
I'm a writer from New York: Ibid.
The bookshop is magnetic: Ibid.
In the last century:
George Whitman to Sylvia Whitman,
Paris, undated, Shakespeare and
Company archive.
At the time, I didn't: Sylvia
Whitman, interview by Krista Halverson.
George yelled out: Ibid.
When I first arrived: Ibid.

# Permissions

This image of the Beaux-Arts poster "La Beauté est dans la rue" appears thanks to the publisher Four Corners Books, which worked with an original poster for its book *Beauty Is in the Street: a Visual Record of the May '68 Paris Uprising*. Lawrence Ferlinghetti's contribution was adapted, by the author, from his novel *Her*, published by New Directions. This version of the text first appeared in *Zoetrope: All-Story*. Copyright © Lawrence Ferlinghetti. Used by permission of the author.

"The Sidewalkers Moved…" from *The American Night* by Jim Morrison, copyright © 1990 by Wilderness Publications. Used by permission of Villard Books, an imprint of Random House, a division of Penguin Random House LLC. All rights reserved. Any third-party use of this material, outside of this publication, is prohibited. Interested parties must apply directly to Penguin Random House LLC for permission.

Christopher Cook Gilmore's text is adapted from his interview in the documentary *Portrait of a Bookstore as an Old Man*, Sycomore Films, 2003. It appears here by permission of Anita Gilmore and the filmmakers, Benjamin Sutherland and Gonzague Pichelin.

Jean-Jacques Lebel's text was adapted from an interview conducted for this book by David Delannet. It has been translated from French by Alexandre Guégan.

## The 1970s Chapter

Hugo Santiago's text was adapted from an interview conducted for this book by David Delannet. It has been translated from French by David Delannet.

Giuseppe Recchia's contribution was adapted from an interview for this book, conducted in French by David Delannet, along with an essay written by Recchia in Italian and published by *Corriere d'Europa*. The texts were translated into English.

Ted Joans's text was adapted from an archival interview conducted by Mary Duncan in 1991. It appears by permission of Ted Joans's estate and of Mary Duncan.

"Inscribed in George Whitman's Guest Register" by Allen Ginsberg is copyright © 2016 by the Estate of Allen Ginsberg.

## The 1980s–1990s Chapter

David Rakoff's Tumbleweed autobiography is copyright © David Rakoff and is reproduced by arrangement with the Estate of David Rakoff and Irene Skolnick Literary Agency.

The *Paris Passion* article, written by George Whitman, appears by permission of Time Out Group.

Paintings and illustration by Neil Packer are copyright © Shakespeare and Company Paris.

Mary Duncan's text is adapted from her memoir, *Henry Miller Is Under My Bed*, and is copyright © Mary Duncan.

"Darkness, Chez George Whitman" by Lawrence Ferlinghetti is copyright © 1984 by Lawrence Ferlinghetti. The poem first appeared in Ferlinghetti's poetry collection *Over All the Obscene Boundaries: European Poems and Transitions*, published by New Directions. It appears here by permission of the poet.

## The 2000s Chapter

Jonathan McNamara's text was adapted from an interview conducted for this book by Adam Biles.

James Gregor's text is adapted from his essay "A Weed in My Flower Garden," published in *The Millions*.

Tara Mulholland's text was adapted from an interview conducted for this book by Adam Biles.

The film still from *Before Sunset* is licensed by Warner Bros. Entertainment Inc. All rights reserved.

"The Old Dogs Who Fought So Well" by Kate Tempest is copyright © Kate Tempest. The poem first appeared in Tempest's collection *Hold Your Own*, published in 2014 by Picador Poetry.

## Epilogue

"Path" by Jack Hirschman is copyright © Jack Hirschman. It appears by permission of the poet.

The fashion photograph inspired by *Alice's Adventures in Wonderland* features model Alexia Giordano, with art direction by Maxime Gé and photography by Nahoko Spiess.

*Shakespeare and Company*, by the art collective Le Gun, appears courtesy of Le Gun and Cob Gallery, London, which commissioned the painting.